MAP of the TRANS-MISSISSIPPI TERRITORY
Showing the location of Forts · Trading Posts · Trails and Indian Tribes

BLACKFOOT COUNTRY

FORT MCKENZIE

Missouri River

Muscleshell River

Yellowstone River

FORT UNION

Little Missouri

Powder River

MANDANS

FORT CLARK

Grand River

Moreau River

ARICARA VILLAGES

ABSAROKA THE HOME OF THE CROWS CHEYENNES

Big Horn River

Wind River

JACKSON'S HOLE

South Fork

BLACK HILLS

Cheyenne River

FORT KIAWA

FORT RECOVERY

White River

James River

S I O U X

SOUTH PASS

FORT PHIL KEARNY

OREGON TRAIL

FORT BRIDGER

FORT LARAMIE

Niobrara River

PAWNEES

FORT ATKINSON

Platte River

White River

River

South Platte River

Platte River

OTOES AND MISSOURIS

FORT LEAVENWORTH

PIKE'S PEAK

ARAPAHOES

Big Sandy Cr.

Kansas River

INDEPENDENCE KANSAS POST

PUEBLO

OLD FORT BENT

SPANISH PEAK

RATON PASS

San Juan

TAOS

THE SANTA FE' TRAIL

CIMARRON DESERT

Arkansas River

OSAGES

Rio Grande

SANTA FE'

APACHES

KIOWAS

Canadian River

Cimarron River

COMANCHES

FORT GIBSON

D1228855

MOUNTAIN MEN

JAMES BRIDGER, ABOUT 1866
From the only known portrait

MOUNTAIN

MEN

by

WALTER STANLEY CAMPBELL
(STANLEY VESTAL, pseud.)

WITH ILLUSTRATIONS

Essay Index Reprint Series

BOOKS FOR LIBRARIES PRESS
FREEPORT, NEW YORK

STANDARD BOOK NUMBER:
8369-1397-3

LIBRARY OF CONGRESS CATALOG CARD NUMBER:
77-99620

PRINTED IN THE UNITED STATES OF AMERICA

TO
MY DAUGHTERS
WHO LOVE THE MOUNTAINS

PREFACE

THIS book deals with the mountain men of the American Rockies, the Old West, in the days when the Old West was new. Few passages of history can show so bright a pattern of daring deeds, high heroism, and useful service to American civilization. These were the boys who trapped the beaver, fought the Injuns, brought home the bacon, created the wealth in the pockets of the dandies in ruffled shirts. Strong, self-reliant, undisciplined as so many savages, they swaggered into the settlements, St. Louis or Taos, throwing away their 'beaver' with a reckless generosity nothing short of magnificent. And their services to the United States were no less magnificent than their daring deeds and their reckless spending.

The empires of the English-speaking peoples have not, as a rule, been gained through the efforts of officials. Among these peoples, the men who have led the way into strange lands have generally been civilians, private individuals, bent only upon their own concerns, men unhampered —

and unaided — by official responsibilities and powers whether military or civil. And so, when the territory of the United States expanded westward, and the military forces moved into the wilds to conquer and control, they found a hardy race of pioneers already there, already familiar with every range and river, past-masters in dealing with red Indians and wild beasts, able to guide and direct the official so-called 'explorations.'

These were the mountain men, a breed of heroes; yet not heroic by intention or profession, but only in the nature of the circumstances, and as part of their day's work. These mountain men, far more than the soldiers and the statesmen, were the real means of seizing, holding, and settling our vast Far West. They were the men of destiny, whose skill and courage enabled those Americans who followed their trail to conquer a continent within half a hundred years.

Though they sprang, for the most part, from the half-horse, half-alligator pioneers on the old frontiers east of the Mississippi River, and knew the squirrel rifle and the pack-horse from their infancy, it was not until William Henry Ashley organized his bands of trappers at St. Louis in 1822 to invade the rich Northwestern fur country that the mountain men came into their own.

Before that time, the American fur trade had usually been carried on here as it was in Canada, where the Hudson's Bay Company bought furs direct from Indian trappers at well-established permanent trading-posts and factories. But Ashley had other ideas. He preferred to dispense with traders and forts and Indian trappers. He favored a less expensive and more elastic system. He employed white trappers and dealt with them at an annual summer rendezvous — a fur fair held at some convenient center in the mountains. Overnight, these American innovations created a new profession. Ashley's trappers, daring every danger of the wilds alone or with a few companions, fighting the redskins, enduring incredible hardships, harvesting the fur, became masters of the wilderness, monarchs of all they surveyed — independent as so many hogs on ice. They became, in short, the mountain men.

Ashley made the mountain men an institution, and most of those who later became famous in their hard profession were young men who first went West under his orders. James Bridger, Thomas Fitzpatrick, Jedediah Smith, David E. Jackson, James P. Beckwourth, Etienne Provost, William Sublette, Robert Campbell — to name no more — all entered upon their careers under Ashley's auspices, learned their trade in his brigades, and underwent their baptism of fire fighting his Indian enemies. The expeditions of Ashley very properly begin this book on the mountain men. He made them, and they made him.

For a generation their exploits filled the minds of their contemporaries. By the end of that time their task was almost done. By the mid-century, the old-time fur trade was 'rubbed out,' the western half of the continent had been explored, conquered, in great part settled — or was held by the military. That survey and that conquest were largely the work of the mountain men.

And so, in such a book as this, packed as it must be with the daring exploits and hard scrapes of these bold fellows, I should fail if I omitted certain important historical events in which the mountain men played leading parts. To tell all that could be told would require not a single volume, but a whole shelf of books. But I have included outstanding, typical figures and events, both public and private, which make up and represent the record of the mountain men's achievement.

The table of contents will indicate the scope of the book and reveal the dominating figures on the scene. Kit Carson alone, of these paladins, has had his due portion of space scanted, since my biography of Kit is a companion volume to this one, and there is abundant material here, without subjecting the reader to duplication.

Some new matter obtained from the Indians, or from other sources, is offered here — notably as regards the life and boasts of Solomon Silver.

But let these tell their own story. Ashley's keelboats are waiting. Turn the page.

STANLEY VESTAL

CONTENTS

ILLUSTRATIONS

I. RENDEZVOUS

O N MARCH 20, 1822, the *Missouri Republican*, published in St. Louis, carried the following brief advertisement:

TO ENTERPRISING YOUNG MEN. The subscriber wishes to engage one hundred young men to ascend the Missouri River to its source, there to be employed for one, two, or three years. For particulars inquire of Major Andrew Henry, near the lead mines in the county of Washington, who will ascend with, and command, the party; or of the subscriber near St. Louis.

(Signed)   WILLIAM H. ASHLEY

St. Louis was then a small town of less than three thousand inhabitants, but booming with the expanding fur trade, of which it had been the Western headquarters for nearly thirty years. It was the jumping-off place for all who craved travel, exploration, or adventure in the Great American Desert. On the unpaved streets of small stone houses straggling down the hill to the boiling waters of the muddy river — that highway to the unknown wilderness — a motley and polyglot horde of people moved.

Silent, blanketed Indians rubbed shoulders with Kentucky hunters clad in buckskins, debonair French creoles, barefoot negroes, tough, combative keelboatmen, gay, tuneful *voyageurs*, mule-skinners and packers in homespuns and checked woolen shirts, hardy trappers in from the Rockies wearing wolfskin caps or old wool hats, and the rich merchants of the fur trade in their ruffled shirts and tall-crowned beavers. Those men talked and dreamed of furs, of the magnificent profits to be made in a single lucky season, of trapping brigades and Injun fights. That advertisement needed no explanation there.

Enterprising young men did not have to ask who the authors of it were. Both were well known: the Virginian Ashley, General of the Missouri Militia, slated to become Lieutenant-Governor of the State, already enriched by his powder factory at Potosi; Major Henry, the Pennsylvanian, long experienced in the fur trade, then operating his lead mine near-by. The enterprising young men flocked to join their company.

This was no ordinary organization. It was founded upon a new plan — a plan already tested and proved (though on a small scale) by that daring Spaniard, Manuel Lisa. Before that time, American fur traders had imitated the system set up by the far-flung Hudson's Bay Company in the British Possessions. The Hudson's Bay Company maintained permanent forts or factories in the wilderness, and bartered with the Indians for their furs. This required, for its success, a monopoly of the business, governmental powers over the Indians and *engagés*, large capital, a series of expensive establishments, and costly staffs of traders, clerks, hunters, mechanics, and *voyageurs*. In order to maintain these, it had to conserve the fur-bearing animals, and this — though profitable in the long run — materially reduced the yearly dividends. The Hudson's Bay Company was therefore opposed to immigration into its territories, and had authority to exclude settlers. Without such powers, it would have failed.

Henry and Ashley realized that such methods would never work in democratic America, where free competition and ruthless exploitation were the rule, and where — beyond the frontier — no authority of government existed strong enough to exclude citizens, control the redskins, or preserve the animals which provided the fur. They threw the British system overboard, and proposed to take a leaf out of Manuel Lisa's book. They had a plan of their own.

They wanted no traders, no permanent forts, no Indian trappers. Instead, they hired daring young white men, men who knew the long rifle and the steel trap as they knew their own hands, men who could ride, and shoot, self-reliant, lusty fellows who would harvest the fur wherever and whenever it could be found in spite of hell or high water, in spite of rival trappers, hostile Injuns, or the Devil himself. In place of permanent forts, Ashley and Henry held an annual rendezvous — a fur fair — at some convenient, previously appointed valley in the mountains. There, every summer, their trappers brought the furs they had taken, received their year's wages, and obtained a new outfit for the fall hunt. Under this elastic and inexpensive system, most of the men had no occasion to return to the settlements, or sleep under a roof, from one year's end to the other. In winter they trapped, hunted, and maybe traded with the savages; in summer they were kept busy exploring the country, looking for untrapped streams where beaver were plenty. Only the packers and the boatmen would be needed to carry the furs to market.

Thus, overnight, this new system created a new career, a new profession — in truth, a new breed of men — a race of explorers, fighters, hunters, trappers, known then and thereafter (because they lived the year round in the Rockies) as the *mountain men*.

When this challenging news of Ashley's advertisement got around, one hundred enterprising young men were not long in presenting themselves. Within thirty days, all preparations had been completed, Henry and Ashley had been licensed to enter the Indian country, and the expedition embarked in two big keelboats, ready for the start.

These keelboats were unusually large, each over a hundred feet in length. Like all the other craft built to navigate those shallow rivers, they drew only about three feet of water. Their cargoes and crews were carried above decks, in the cargo box, which was eighty feet long, higher than a man's head above deck, and so wide that it left only a narrow runway on either side, on which the polemen worked. Immediately forward of the cargo box was a stout mast, rigged with a square sail, but more often used in towing the boat upstream. This was done by attaching

THE SUMMER RENDEZVOUS

a long tow-rope, or cordelle, to the top of the mast; the towers scrambled alongshore, through water, over rocks, sometimes swimming, sometimes wading, sometimes on solid, dry ground — for of course there was no tow-path.

Forward of the mast was the cook's galley, more generally called a 'caboose.' At the stern, a great rudder or sweep extended to the top of the cargo box, where the steersman had his station. In the cargo box were bunkrooms for the crew and passengers, though they generally slept on deck, or on the flat top of the cargo box. The boat was provided with half a dozen oars on each side, forward of the cargo box, but these were used little, since the Missouri River was too strong for oarsmen to contend with. The boats had to be poled or towed upstream, and the men who did that heavy work were necessarily of iron strength and endurance. Those keelboatmen have not received their due share of glory for their part in civilizing the Old West.

Not that they themselves were at all civilized. Far from it. A more godless crew never navigated fresh waters. Mark Twain, who surely knew rivermen, calls them 'rough and hardy men; rude, uneducated, brave, suffering terrific hardships with sailor-like stoicism; heavy drinkers, coarse frolickers in moral sties . . . heavy fighters, reckless fellows every one, elephantinely jolly, foul-witted, profane, prodigal of their money, bankrupt at the end of the trip, fond of barbaric finery, prodigious braggarts . . .' Such were the boatmen who, in the first stages of Ashley's expeditions, were the heroes of his company.

No doubt, after their carouse of the night before, some of them felt shaky that fine April morning. But they forgot all that as they watched the crowds swarming down to the levee to see them off. The boatmen stood to their poles on the runways alongside the cargo box, ready to set off, pushing the prows out into the boiling, muddy current. The people on the bank cheered and waved. A volley of muskets roared over the water.

Mike Fink, patroon of the leading keelboat, yelled lustily, 'Set poles for the Three Forks of the Missouri!' The steersman blew his horn, the oarsmen plied their oars. The polemen set their poles at the bow, placed their shoulders against the sockets, and moved slowly toward the stern, pushing with all their strength. Slowly the boats began to move against the strong current, as the men forced their way to the stern. Then, at the patroon's shouted command, they turned, ran back to the bow, set their poles again, and once more shoved the boat forward against the current. It was reckoned to be 1760 miles from St. Louis to the mouth of the Yellowstone.

On the way up, one of the boats sank near Fort Osage, causing the partners a loss of about ten thousand dollars. But they pushed and pulled the remaining boat onward, and at last halted at the mouth of the Yellowstone, built a fort — for protection, not for trade — and set about the fall hunt.

It was there that Mike Fink, King of the Keelboatmen, had the adventure which has made his name memorable.

Mike, his close friend Carpenter, Talbot, and several

other men were sent west to trap and winter on the Mussel-shell River. Both Carpenter and Mike Fink were good shots with the long rifle, and when they were carousing, it was the usual thing for them to fill cups with whiskey and shoot them off each other's heads — at a distance of seventy yards! Every time they drilled the cup, and never harmed a hair.

On the Musselshell, however, Mike and his friend quarreled over a squaw. But on returning to the fort on the Yellowstone, Talbot and the other men patched up a treaty of peace between them. Then Mike suggested that, as a mark of sincerity, they revive their old friendly custom of shooting the cup.

They flipped a coin to see which should have the first shot. Mike won. Carpenter was afraid of Mike's treachery, but would not admit it. Mike loaded his gun, and then filled the cup with liquor and placed it on Carpenter's head.

Then, from a distance of sixty paces, he fired. Carpenter fell dead, drilled through the forehead. Mike professed surprise, and declared the killing an accident. But Talbot would not believe him, and with his pistol shot Mike through the heart. There was no law on the Yellowstone in those days, and nobody cared to call Talbot to account. He remained a member of the Ashley-Henry brigade in good standing until he was drowned the following summer.

So much for the boatmen of that Rocky Mountain Fur Company. Most of them returned with Ashley to St. Louis that summer. Ashley went down to recruit one hundred more men, replace the lost property, and launch two new boats — *The Rocky Mountains* and *The Yellowstone Packet*. In these, on March 10, 1823, he set out once more for the Upper Missouri.

The personnel of the Ashley expeditions cannot be known in full. But the roster contained the names of most of the mountain men who later became famous in the annals of the West: such men as Jim (Old Gabe) Bridger, Thomas Fitzpatrick (later dubbed Broken Hand), Milton and William Sublette and their younger brothers, Robert Campbell, Henry Fraeb, Hugh Glass, Edward Rose, Jim Beckwourth the mulatto, Jedediah Smith, David Jackson, Étienne Provost. Most of these worthies have left their names upon some river, peak, or valley in the mountains they explored which will forever serve as monuments to their achievements. But when they went upriver for the first time, they were, for the most part, simply unknown young fellows, fit, lusty, and eager for adventure.

They had adventure in plenty.

II. JOHN COLTER'S RACE
FOR LIFE

JOHN COLTER had been on the Upper Missouri before. Though his name was not recorded as on Ashley's expedition (1822), it seems likely that he went
along. He lived in St. Louis, or close by, and was fond of
life in the mountains. But whether or not he went up
again with Ashley, his story must be included here, because
it is a vital part of the history of the fur trade. Colter
caused the mountain men more trouble than any other one
man living. For hostile Injuns gave the trappers more
trouble than all other things combined, and of all the hostiles on the Missouri, the Blackfeet were the worst. That
is why Colter may be said to have caused the mountain
men so much trouble. He it was who made the Blackfeet
hostile!

It happened in this way: Manuel Lisa, that old fox of
the fur trade, was burning up with eagerness to trade with
the Blackfeet. All traders were, for that matter, because
the Blackfeet had a magnificent range, rich in fur and
game of all kinds, and utterly unspoiled — since they allowed no white trappers in their country. Lisa had talked

with some Blackfeet at his fort at the mouth of the Big
Horn, and had found them friendly. He rubbed his greedy
hands, and made up his mind to send a man to the Three
Forks of the Missouri to fix things up with the chiefs.

John Colter was the best man Lisa had. John Colter was
the man to go. And because old Lisa was so greedy, he sent
Colter also to the camps of the Crow Nation — then on
the Upper Wind River, near Jackson's Hole.

It was five hundred miles to the Crow camp. But Colter,
a veteran of the Lewis and Clark expedition, who had already spent several winters trapping on the Upper Missouri, simply filled his shot-pouch and powder-horn, slung
a thirty-pound pack on his shoulders, picked up his long
rifle, and hit the trail alone. Five hundred miles was nothing to John Colter. Before he was through, he walked
five thousand.

He found the Crows on Wind River, and informed them
that Lisa was coming to trade. Then he asked the chiefs
to send a man to guide him over the mountains to the headwaters of the Missouri. No white man had ever gone that
way before.

That request made the chiefs grunt and stare. They
knew that no Crow living was bold enough to venture
alone into the country of the hostile Blackfeet. For ages
those two tribes had been deadly enemies. Old Lisa's
packs couldn't hold enough vermilion, gunpowder, or
butcher-knives to pay for a risk like that. They didn't
like to admit that, but it was true. And so they merely
stared and grunted.

But Colter insisted, and at last, after conferring among themselves, the chiefs agreed to guide him through.

'Good,' said Colter. 'Who will go with me?'

The oldest chief grinned at the fearless white man. 'We *all* go,' he said grimly.

Then Colter and a heap of Crows headed west through that wild, rugged country, crossed the Wind River Mountains by Two-gwo-tee Pass and the Teton Range by Teton Pass. That brought them to the Teton Basin, known in old times as Pierre's Hole.

That lovely valley was dangerous country — a battleground of warring tribes. The Blackfeet and their allies, the Gros Ventres of the Prairies, claimed the Hole as their hunting grounds. No spot in the mountains held more peril for the mountain men.

One afternoon, as the colorful cavalcade strung down into the broad valley, Colter suddenly halted. Up ahead, behind a clump of sagebrush, he had seen somebody moving. But now that he had halted, he saw nothing. There was not a sound to be heard.

Then, suddenly, a man sprang up and tossed a double-handful of dust into the air, as an angry buffalo bull paws up the earth before he charges. The wind caught the dust and spread it into a broad tawny banner — the Injun call to battle. At the same moment the war-whoop chattered in Colter's ears, raising prickles along his spine: *Wah-ah-ah-ah-ah*!

'Blackfeet!' yelled the Crow chief, pulling the buckskin cover from his fusil.

Blackfeet — or Gros Ventres — they certainly were, and
on the warpath! A hundred of them suddenly rose from
the ground like magic, and came plunging pell-mell out of
the ravine and across the open. On they came at the dead
run on their spotted ponies, with motley ornaments and
arms, splendid war-bonnets of lustrous black-and-white
eagle feathers swinging about their heads, half-naked,
painted, yelling at the top of their lungs, brandishing their
bows and lances.

The Crow chief rode back and forth, yelling at his men.
They were all in confusion, stripping off their buffalo
robes, jerking the covers from their shields, unlimbering
their bows, yelling and singing war-songs to make their
hearts strong. Looking at them, Colter almost wished he
had come alone.

He sat still in his saddle. He had no wish to fight the
Crows' battles. He had come there to smoke with the
Blackfeet.

But already the battle had been joined. The foremost
Blackfeet were upon the Crows, charging them confidently,
with all the advantage of superior numbers, surprise, and
the fierce momentum of attack. They circled along the
Crow front, waging a hit-and-run warfare, pushing the
disorganized Crows back. Every moment the Crows gave
ground. Colter found himself out in front, alone.

The Blackfeet charged past him like swallows or swoop-
ing hawks. The first to pass tapped him smartly over the
head with his bow. The second stung his left leg with an
arrow, which passed through, pinning him to his pony's

ribs. The horse reared and shook his head, fighting the
bit, as the third Injun dashed up and tried to split Colter's
skull with a hatchet.

Then Colter went into action. His rifle lay across the
pommel of his saddle. Without raising it, he yanked back
the hammer, pulled the trigger, and dropped the nearest
of his enemies. Then he swung his rifle in one hand and
knocked the second from his saddle. The third he caught
by his long hair, pulled him backwards across his own
horse, and stabbed him in the ear.

That was enough for the Blackfeet. The others sheered
off from Colter, and gave him time to gain control of his
plunging horse, cut off the shaft of the arrow through his
leg, dismount, and reload.

Then the Crows, seeing their lone ally victorious, rallied.
And as they swarmed back towards him, Colter threw
himself prone, leveled his rifle, and picked off another
painted enemy. His third shot killed the Blackfoot
Chief's horse. At that, the Blackfeet galloped away out of
range, the chief hanging on to the tail of one of the Blackfoot ponies.

From that safe distance, they made insulting gestures
at the Crows, and called to them in the Blackfoot language,
which Colter understood well enough. 'The white man
saved you,' they jeered. 'Wait,' they yelled. 'We have
friends with guns, too. Stay where you are, and tomorrow
we will rub you out to the last man.'

The Crows skirmished with the Blackfeet until sundown. Then the Blackfeet rode away.

Colter dressed his wounded leg as best he could. His leg was sore, but his heart was sorer than his leg, for he knew that this chance fight had made his mission a failure. The Blackfeet had seen him, knew him for a white man, blamed their defeat upon him. Probably they would recognize him if they saw him again. He dared not venture farther into their country after that. His only consolation was that it warn't his fault.

That night the Crows did not make camp in the Hole. They hit the trail for their camp on Wind River.

Colter protested, but the Crows covered their ears. Their chief said blandly: 'You asked us to bring you over the mountains. We have done it. Now we go home.' And away they went.

Colter refused to go with them. He remained in the Hole with his wounded leg. But not for long. He mounted, rode on the trail of the Crows until he found a place where he could diverge from it and cover his trail. Then he struck into the pines and rode for Lisa's fort at the mouth of the Big Horn. That unexplored route took him across what is now Yellowstone Park. It was the summer of 1807.

Thus Colter was the first white man to behold the wonders of the Yellowstone, to see the Three Tetons, Pierre's Hole, and the headwaters of Snake River. At last he got back to the fort, where he passed the winter. His leg healed nicely, and he had little to do but grow a beard.

Old Lisa was deeply disappointed. But he could not give up his dream of trade with the Blackfeet. In the spring he ordered Colter to go and visit them again! This time a man named Potts went along.

The two of them made headquarters on the Jefferson Fork of the Missouri, and set their traps, waiting for Injuns to show up. They had not long to wait.

Neither of these men was very eager to meet the Blackfeet. They set their traps by night, and took them up again before sunrise. One morning very early, the two of them were paddling silently up a small creek on the Jefferson Fork, examining their traps from their canoe. All at once they heard a great noise, as of a herd of horses, or buffalo. The banks of the little stream were too high for them to see what caused the racket.

Colter whispered to his comrade: 'Injuns. Let's cache!'

'You must be scairt, for sartain,' Potts sneered. 'Them's buffaloes.'

Colter might have argued the matter. But before he could say anything, the Indians came in sight, hundreds of them — and on both sides of the creek. They signaled the white men to come ashore.

The trappers had no choice. They paddled to the bank. The moment the canoe touched the bank, the nearest Indian grabbed Potts's rifle. But Colter, who was a big man, and as strong as he was brave, wrested it from the redskin and handed it back to Potts. Colter stepped ashore. But Potts, now thoroughly frightened, stayed in the canoe, and shoved off into the water.

That move ended all pretense of friendship. One of the

Indians shot an arrow at Potts. The man in the canoe called out, 'Colter, I'm wounded!'

'Come on back, you fool!' Colter yelled. 'You cain't get away now.'

But Potts, losing his head again, raised his rifle, took aim at the mass of Indians, and fired. One of the redskins dropped, dead as a nail. Immediately the air was filled with arrows, and Potts collapsed in the canoe, stuck full of feathered shafts. As Colter said, 'He was made a riddle of.'

The folly of Potts had put poor Colter in terrible jeopardy. The Indians grabbed him, tore off his clothing, held him fast. Then they began to talk and gesture, arguing as to the method by which he should be put to death. He waited, helpless, naked as a jaybird, while his executioners coolly discussed the method of his slaying.

Most of them favored setting him up as a target for their arrows. But one of the chiefs, wishing to show his authority, differed from the rest. Going up to Colter, he took hold of him by the shoulder, shook him, and demanded to know how fast he could run.

During his stay with the Crows, Colter had made it a point to learn some Blackfoot words. Their language was commonly understood by their neighbors. Colter knew what the chief was saying. He knew that he had a chance to make 'the Injun run.'

The trapper was a swift runner, and he infinitely preferred a run for his life to being tied up and slowly tortured to death with arrows. Therefore he cunningly replied that he was a very bad runner. 'No good,' he answered. 'Heap no good.'

The chief grinned grimly. Taking Colter from his captors, he led him out on the prairie some three hundred yards from the horde of redskins. Then, turning the white man loose, he said, 'Run, then, and save yourself, if you *can!'*

The chief beckoned to his followers. They yelped the war-whoop. Colter sprang forward, and ran so fast that he surprised himself.

Before him stretched the open prairie. Beyond it, six miles away, lay the Jefferson Fork. He ran for that, and for three miles he did not look back.

No wonder. The plain was thick with prickly pear, and Colter's feet were bare. Soon the soles of his feet were filled with the spines of the cactus. But Colter did not let that slow him down. He preferred cactus spines to arrows in his body. He ran like a deer. And when he did look back over his shoulder, he took courage. Most of the Indians were far behind. Only one — a long-legged fellow armed with a lance — was nearer than a hundred yards.

For the first time, Colter began to hope that he might escape. He put everything he had into the race, and sprinted so hard that a torrent of blood burst from his nostrils and covered his chest and belly. That almost finished him, but he labored on, though he knew that the man with the lance was gaining.

The river was only a mile off now. But suddenly he heard the thud of his enemy's feet coming up behind.

Every moment he expected to feel the spear-head strike his naked back. He looked over his shoulder — the warrior was not twenty paces back! He knew that it would not be long now.

Colter was a fighter; he had no intention of being stabbed from behind without a struggle. And so, unarmed, bleeding, and naked as he was, he suddenly stopped, faced about, and spread out his arms.

The warrior, startled at this sudden move, and at Colter's body all covered with blood, tried to stop, and raised his lance to strike the white man. But he was tired also, and stumbled as he threw the lance. The point struck the earth and lodged there; the shaft broke in his hand. The Blackfoot went down.

Colter snatched up the lance-head, stabbed the redskin before he could get up. Then he ran on. When the foremost Indians reached their dying comrade, they halted, and all at once began to wail and yell.

But Colter, gasping and exhausted as he was, never faltered. He plunged on to the river-bottoms, rushed through the fringe of stately cottonwoods, and plunged into the cool waters of the river. The current swept him down, half-fainting.

Not far below lay an island, and about it a great clutter of drift timber had piled up, making a sort of raft above the island. Colter dived under these interlocked logs, and, coming to the surface, bumped his head several times upon them. Finally, when his lungs were ready to burst, he managed to find a space among the trunks above water, and rested there, drawing deep breaths in the darkness. His hiding-place was covered with small drift, leaves, and sticks — a layer several feet deep.

From that refuge he heard the Blackfeet come running down the bank, screeching like so many devils. All that day they poked about the pile of driftwood. Sometimes he could see them through the chinks of his hiding-place. But whenever he thought they might see him, he pulled himself entirely under water. He began to think he had saved his life, until it came to his mind that they might set the wood on fire!

So he remained, torn with anxiety, until at last night came. Then, hearing nothing of the Blackfeet, he dived out from under the ruck of logs, and floated downriver until he thought all danger of discovery was ended. Then he swam ashore, and hurried overland towards Lisa's fort all night.

He was fully seven days' journey from the fort. He was starving, and had no means of killing meat. He was naked and exposed to the rays of the summer sun. His feet were full of spines, swollen and sore. But it was the season when the tipsin ripens, and Colter fed himself on this root as he went along. Somehow or other he reached the fort at last.

Such was John Colter, who probably went upriver with Ashley on the second trip. His two encounters with the Blackfeet made that tribe and its allies deadly enemies to the whites. Of course, that was hardly Colter's fault, but the fault of Manuel Lisa, who had sent him to the Blackfeet in the company of their enemies the Crows, and of

Potts, whose reckless action, inspired by terror, had compelled Colter to kill a Blackfoot for the second time. Colter would have been a valuable man to Ashley, and if he was still living, it seems certain that Ashley must have asked him to go along.

But, in any case, Ashley took along plenty of young fellows of the same caliber. On the thirtieth of May, 1823, his keelboats anchored just below the Arikara Indian villages, near the mouth of Grand River.

Right there they ran head-on into a man-size war.

III. ARIKARA TREACHERY

THE young men who went up the river with Ashley earned their fame. They learned in a hard school. From the start, they were faced by dangers and hardships unknown to earlier adventurers. That spring of '23 they endured a dreadful baptism of fire at the hands of the Arikara.

These Indians, who then lived in permanent fortified villages near the mouth of Grand River, had been friendly to white men when, in 1805, they were visited by Lewis and Clark. But the booming fur trade, the fierce rivalry of the cut-throat fur companies, gunpowder, whiskey, disease, and inter-tribal warfare had brought many intruders and much trouble to their country. When Ashley's keelboats anchored below their villages, they were ripe for mischief.

Everywhere the Indians were restless and hostile that season.

On Pryor's Fork of the Yellowstone, the Blackfeet had smashed the brigades of the Missouri Fur Company under

Jones and Immel, killing both leaders and many of their
men. Afterward, they attacked a party of eleven of
Henry's men, killing four. The Assiniboines had run off
fifty of Henry's horses. But these affairs were small
potatoes compared with the disaster to Ashley's men at
the hands of the Arikara. They gave him and his men their
bellyful of fight. It was one of the biggest scrapes in the
history of the fur trade, and had much to do with de-
termining the attitude of the mountain men towards the
Indians, the troops, their own partisans, and each other.
It was one of those decisive events which throw their
ominous shadows across the future.

Ashley had plenty of warning.

When he stopped at the post of the Missouri Fur Company below the Arikara towns, the president of that company, Joshua Pilcher, told him how badly the Arikara had
been behaving, and warned him of their treacherous nature. Not long before, a party of Pilcher's men had run
into a band of Arikara. Two or three Sioux were traveling
with the whites, and when the Arikara saw them, they demanded that the whites surrender the Sioux to themselves.
As the two tribes were at war, this would have meant
death for the Sioux — a tribe with whom Pilcher traded.
Naturally, Pilcher's men refused. Then and there the
Arikara swore to be revenged, and, according to Pilcher,
were lying in wait for the first unwary white man who
might come their way.

Ashley, of course, was no greenhorn. But the Arikara
had treated him well the year before, and he was inclined

to give them the benefit of the doubt. In any case, he had to anchor at their villages, for Henry had sent an express bearing urgent word that Indians had stolen his horses, and that he *must* have more. Ashley planned to trade for horses with the Arikara, and send a party overland to join Henry.

Ashley, at first, was cautious. He anchored his two keelboats in deep water a hundred feet offshore, and left them there, while he and his interpreter, Edward Rose, went ashore. The Indians tried to induce him to come and trade with them in their villages, but Ashley insisted that he would trade only on the bank of the river. There was a wide sandy beach there, well suited to his purpose. And after a time the Indians gave in.

When the chiefs had agreed to this, Ashley gave them some powder and ball and muskets, and seeing their grins of pleasure, lost all his caution. He told them he had heard of their trouble with the whites down the river, and warned them not to try such tricks in the future. But they were as pleasant as could be, said they were very sorry about that little difficulty with the Missouri Fur Company, and assured Ashley that they loved him like a father, and would never think of harming him. 'The white men are our brothers,' they said. 'Your coming makes our hearts good.' Ashley went back to his boats, and next morning the trade began.

It was the first day of June. All that morning, and most of the afternoon, the Indians haggled with Ashley, and long before sunset, he had traded for enough horses to

carry for cy of his men and their plunder overland. By that
time, Edward Rose, the interpreter, felt in his bones that
mischief was afoot. Rose was a half-breed Cherokee Indian, with more than a gill of negro blood in his veins, who
had lived in the Arikara villages for three years, knew
those Indians well, and spoke their language fluently.
He could tell from the bearing of the chiefs, the behavior
of the warriors, and the distance kept by the women and
children who looked on, that trouble was surely brewing.
And when a beady-eyed messenger came from Chief
Bear, head man of the lower village, inviting Ashley to a
feast in his lodge, Rose warned Ashley. The trading was
over; there was no longer any reason to humor the chiefs.

'General,' he warned, 'you better swim them horses
acrost the river, and anchor your boats farther off. This
ain't no time to go visitin'.'

There must have been something about Edward Rose
which made men distrust him. Hunt had distrusted him,
in 1811, and now Ashley made the same mistake. Perhaps
Ashley knew that Rose had been a river pirate on the Mississippi, and once in the chain-gang. The man's appearance was against him, for Irving describes him as 'a dogged,
sullen, silent fellow, with a sinister aspect, and more of the
savage than the civilized man in his appearance.' Whatever the cause, Ashley disregarded his wise advice, and
rode up the trail to the Arikara village.

The two villages were nearly the same in size. Each
contained about seventy great earth lodges, every one
fifty or sixty feet in diameter — huge, mound-like struc-

tures, resembling giant mole-hills perched upon the bluffs. As Ashley climbed the path, he saw that the village was fortified with timber palisades made of logs standing on end, twelve to fifteen feet high, and nearly a foot thick. There was a trench outside the pickets, and another inside, with a breastwork of earth thrown up to shelter riflemen lying behind it. Ashley himself had seen that the Arikara were armed with good London fusils — weapons accurate as a rifle at short range. The Arikara were well prepared for a siege — or an attack.

But Ashley rode in through the gateway and alighted before the tunnel-like doorway of Chief Bear's lodge. Raising the leather curtain, he passed down that primitive corridor, and soon found himself in the big round-house, where his host and a number of other chiefs had gathered around the central fire, to talk to the white man, to learn his plans, and to assure themselves that he suspected nothing. They fed him, they smoked with him, they sent him away. And then they made their preparations to wipe him from the face of the earth.

To tell the truth, Ashley did everything he could to aid them in the attempt.

Once more Edward Rose warned him, begging him not to neglect common caution in the defense of his men and horses. But Ashley, his mind full of the smiles and blandishments of the Arikara chiefs, scorned to guard against surprise.

The lay of the land favored a disaster. The lower village, opposite which Ashley was anchored, stood on a curving bluff, cut back into a semicircle by the water, and this curve was extended into almost a complete circle by a long sandbar in the river, opposite the town. The main current ran between this bar and the village, and at the head of this bar, where it came nearest to their village, the Indians had built a little fort of timber which commanded the channel. No one could pass without exposing himself to their fire. Besides, Rose declared that a party of warriors was hidden on shore in the brush above the bar. Perhaps some white man, skilled in fortification, had planned these defenses. However that may be, they formed a perfect trap.

That evening, a shifty Arikara chief, one Little Soldier, sneaked down and told Ashley he had better look out. But Ashley, knowing him to be tricky, paid no heed.

Thus, in spite of repeated warnings, Ashley neglected to take precautions. Maybe he understood Indians so little that he thought any show of caution would make them despise him. If so, he was wrong; the surest way to an Indian's respect was perfect readiness to repel attack; he should have known that. But, at any rate, he did not shift his keelboats across the river, but left them anchored, one below the other, barely a hundred feet offshore. Halfway between the boats, on the open beach, he left his precious horses — an almost irresistible temptation — guarded by forty luckless young men. Among these horse-guards were William Sublette, Jedediah Smith, and David Jackson — after whom Jackson's Hole and Jackson's Lake were later named. Jackson used to say it warn't no wonder the young uns who went with Ashley that trip turned out so well. 'That war because the Gineral set 'em such a bad example. He sure l'arned 'em what *not* to do — and l'arned 'em plenty quick!'

About half-past three next morning, Edward Rose shook Ashley awake. One of his men had been killed by an Arikara; there was every sign of an attack to come at dawn. Then Ashley took action, making preparations for defense. But time was short; there was little he could do. At daylight the Indians opened fire from behind their pickets.

There were between six and eight hundred warriors in the two villages. From the look of things, every one of them had a gun. Their guns flashed along a line fully six hundred yards in length. It was a bitter thought for Ashley, that they were using the powder and muskets he had given them to kill his own men.

Things happened very quickly. The horse-guard, unprotected on the open beach, were hard hit. At the first volley, several of them fell. The others 'forted' behind the horses, and so saved themselves for the time. Ashley, seeing their danger, and no doubt eager to save his horses, too, called to them to swim the animals over to a submerged sandbar in mid-river. But when it was tried, the Indians shot down so many of his men that he had to countermand the order.

Desperate then, Ashley turned on his boatmen, and ordered them to launch the skiffs and go to the rescue of their comrades ashore. Those boatmen were, many of them, fierce and tough as wildcats in a rough-and-tumble fight.

Every keelboat on the river was a perfect cockpit of combat, and the champion of each boat commonly wore a cock's feather in his hat as the insignia of his superior manhood. But it is one thing to kick and gouge and scuffle on the planks of a deck, and quite another to row across a narrow stream in open boats, exposed to the merciless fire of six hundred rifles blazing from cover. These boatmen had no experience of Indian warfare, and wanted none. To them, it seemed that Ashley's order was a command to commit suicide. They refused to obey — flatly. It was open mutiny.

Just why Ashley did not force them to obey at the muzzle of a pistol has never been explained. Perhaps, if he had shot down one of his own men, he might have controlled the others. But Ashley seemed to have lost his head. He let the boatmen have their way. He was frantic with despair.

But the youngsters on the bloody beach were not.

That handful of mountain men, behind the kicking carcasses of their dying horses, went on loading and firing as steadily as so many veterans, determined to avenge their dead and wounded comrades, eager to count a *coup*. And when Ashley finally persuaded a few of his boatmen to row the skiffs to the forlorn hope ashore, not one of the able-bodied would leave their fort. Only a few of the wounded scrambled into the skiffs, to be rowed back to the keelboats offshore. Ashley, determined to bring his men to the boats, sent the larger skiff back again. But as it left the boats, one of the oarsmen was shot down, and the other, cowering in the bottom, lost control; the skiff drifted helplessly away down the swift current. The men ashore were left without means of escape.

By that time, half of them were dead or wounded, and all the horses were down. The Indians, creeping forward under cover along the curving shore, fired into the little fort of the trappers from three sides. The huddled defenders of the beach could not hold out longer, and survive. The boatmen were terrified, the skiffs useless. The one hope lay in swimming for the boats.

'Swim for it, boys! To the boats!'

At the word of command, they jumped up, and ran for the river, plunging into the muddy waters, losing their rifles. As they ran, the Indians gave them a volley. Some fell on the beach. Others were swept away by the fierce current, missed the boats, and were drowned below, or killed and scalped by the Indians there. The wounded soon chilled and sank gasping under the cold water. But most of the others made it. Spent, cold, and bleeding, they clambered upon the runways of the keelboats. The boatmen of one weighed anchor; those on the other cut the cable. The two boats, with their dead and wounded, their frantic commander, and their craven boatmen, drifted swiftly downstream, out of range of the murderous savages.

Thirteen were dead. Reed Gibson was dying of his wounds. And eleven others, some of them later famous in the annals of the mountain men, lay severely wounded in the cargo box: Old Hugh Glass, John Larrison, Joseph

Manso, Joseph Thompson, Bob Tucker, Jim Davis, Aaron Rickette, Jacob Miller, August Dufren, Dan M'Clain, and a negro, Thilless.

Ashley, overcome with horror, would not accept the responsibility for this disaster. 'To describe my feelings at seeing these men destroyed is out of my power,' he says, and adds, 'I feel confident that, if my orders had been obeyed, I should not have lost five men.'

Few persons, then or since, can ever have felt much confidence in the truth of that last statement. The disaster was the fault of Ashley, and of him alone. He lays blame upon those who would not obey orders; yet the commander who cannot get his orders obeyed is unfit for his post. Men will obey any man in whom they have confidence. If they have none, is it their fault? Ashley could have avoided the whole disaster. He could have dropped back downstream and anchored in some secure spot, where Indians could not fire at him from the pickets around their town. Perhaps he could have poled up past the village the afternoon before, instead of wasting time palavering with treacherous chiefs. As it was, he did nothing — and in the face of the plainest warnings. Yet he was so far from realizing how well his men had sized him up that next day he actually proposed to return and try to pass the Arikara villages again.

That was a little too much — even for Smith, Sublette, and Jackson. The men knew that the current was against them. They could not row against it, or sail past the Indian towns. They would have to pole upriver, or cordelle the boats up, passing slowly under the palisades, exposed to the fire of their victorious enemies. Some of them knew that a victorious Indian is twice as deadly as a doubtful one. They stared and muttered at Ashley; the man seemed to have gone out of his head.

The boatmen — almost to a man — flatly refused to obey. Not a few of them openly announced that they intended to desert. Ashley then, to his intense 'surprise and mortification,' saw that he had totally misconceived the temper of his men.

Accordingly, fearing that they would go and take the boats with them, he called for all those who were willing to stay with him until they could hear from Major Henry. He said he would immediately send an express to his partner upriver, asking him to come with all the men he could spare from the fort at the mouth of the Yellowstone. Of the eighty-odd men remaining alive, thirty agreed to stay, among them only five boatmen.

That meant that one boat could be held there. Accordingly, Ashley unloaded the cargo of the *Yellowstone Packet*, and, carrying five of the badly wounded men aboard, ordered the patroon to drop downriver four hundred and fifty miles to Fort Atkinson (near Council Bluffs) with a message begging Colonel Henry Leavenworth to bring troops and artillery to punish the treacherous Arikara. The Indian Agent, Major O'Fallon, also was to be informed of the disaster. Not that Ashley had much hope that the military would move against the Indians without orders from St. Louis.

For Ashley pinned his real hopes upon the courage and speed of his partner, Major Henry, then far upriver beyond the Arikara villages, in his fort at the mouth of the Yellowstone. The problem was — how send word to Henry?

The distance was great, the dangers many. Ashley dared not risk going himself, for the temper of his men made him certain that, once he was gone, many of them would desert. Then the expedition would fail and fall to pieces, the Indians would steal the cargoes of the boats, everything would be lost. Ashley would be utterly ruined, and discredited besides. At the same time, Ashley could not spare any large number of men to carry that appeal for succor. He needed them all to defend the boat and his property from the victorious Arikara, at that very moment dancing over the hair of his men they had slain. One man must go alone. Ashley assembled his men.

He faced his young men with some misgivings. He knew that he was asking a great thing, and of men who had little reason to respect his judgment. But it had to be done, and Ashley made his appeal.

'Boys,' he said, 'the soldiers may not be sent to back us up. Our best hope is to get help from Major Henry and the men of his party. The Major is a long ways off, and the country is dangerous. We can't spare many men to go: one, maybe, or two. Now, you all know how things stand. I call for volunteers!'

So Ashley finished his appeal, and stood waiting.

The silence was absolute. The men listened without moving. The wounded and the boatmen heard him indifferently — they knew his words were not for them. The others stood stolidly, or sullenly, silent. Some of them would be damned before they would risk their skins for Ashley a second time. Some may have hoped that he would fail, so that they could be relieved of their promise to stay with him until word was sent to Major Henry; for, if word was never sent, there was no reason to abide by it. All of them knew how dangerous that long and lonesome trip would be, through strange, wild country swarming with hostile Injuns. They knew how mean an Injun could be — they had come of Injun-fighting stock, most of them — and they knew, too, that the news that the Arikara had licked Ashley would make all the tribesmen ten times more insolent and dangerous than before. And so they listened, but they did not stir. Not Edward Jackson, not even William Sublette.

Ashley's face slowly reddened in the silence as he waited. His eyes moved over the watchful faces before him. He knew then what his men thought of him. If he failed now, his whole expedition was ruined!

Then, suddenly, Ashley heard a clear, youthful voice speak up. Jed Smith had stepped forward. 'I'll go,' he said.

For a moment Ashley was too astonished to reply. He and his men kept silence, in amazement. Jed Smith was the youngest of the party — an apple-cheeked, downy-faced youngster, hardly dry behind the ears. Ashley's keen eyes swept up and down the young un's lank figure, from the new wool hat and steady eyes, over the bulge in his hunting-coat which marked the Bible in his pocket, down the buckskin leggins bagged and worn a little at the knees, where Jedediah had knelt nightly to say his prayers, down to the smoke-tanned moccasins, spattered with the blood of battle of the day before. That boy had courage galore, and brains to match. He was from New York State, of good family, and an educated man.

Still Ashley wondered. For this was Jed's first trip to the mountains. And Ashley knew — none better — that experience was as needful as courage in the life of a mountain man. But Ashley did not venture to refuse. The need was great, and the men who had fought shoulder to shoulder with Jed on the beach were sure that — if anyone could get through — Jed could. Their eyes kindled when they looked at him. Some of them had been soundly mauled on the trip up for sneering at the young un's prayers. They knew him for a fighting Methodist.

Ashley accepted Jed's offer.

Afterward, he persuaded a seasoned mountain man, a French Canadian who knew the country, to go along. The pair set out that night.

IV. THE MISSOURI LEGION

JEDEDIAH SMITH carried the message through.
When he reached the mouth of the Yellowstone
with Ashley's tale of woe, Major Henry acted
promptly. He loaded the furs he had taken into his boats,
and taking all but twenty men, whom he left to guard the
fort, he set out down the Missouri River as fast as he could
go. The party passed the Arikara villages without mishap,
and joined Ashley at the mouth of Cheyenne River about
the first of July.

The partners had little hope of military assistance in
chastising the Arikara. They decided to send the furs on
down to St. Louis in charge of young Smith. Meanwhile,
they themselves moved down to Teton River to buy
horses from the Sioux, so that they could strike out overland, thus avoiding the tricky Arikara. But at Fort
Brasseaux they learned to their great delight that troops
were actually on their way upriver. In fact, the troops
were close at hand.

Colonel Henry Leavenworth was a soldier with a distinguished record. When he learned of the Arikara attack, he did not wait for orders from General Atkinson at St. Louis. To send word and get a reply would have delayed the expedition until late in the fall. The Colonel, therefore, acted on his own discretion, and set out at once for the seat of trouble, with six companies of the Sixth United States Infantry and some small artillery. Most of the men marched; the cannon and supplies were transported up the river in three keelboats.

When Joshua Pilcher, president of the Missouri Fur Company, learned that, he rubbed his hands with satisfaction, and swiftly prepared to join the punitive expedition with all available forces. He was keen to avenge his men Jones and Immel. Major O'Fallon, the Indian Agent, obligingly appointed Pilcher sub-agent for the duration of the campaign. With this commission added to his influence as a fur trader, Pilcher induced five hundred Sioux to join him. These Sioux — mostly Yanktons and Saone (Sans Arc, Two Kettle, Hunkpapa, and Blackfoot Sioux) — were highly pleased to have a hand in rubbing out their old enemies, the Arikara. In those days the Arikara were numerous, for the smallpox had not yet decimated them; they were known as brave men, too — it was said that they would swim out into the river and rope or stab buffalo swimming past their villages.

Colonel Leavenworth set out full of zest and determination. But on the way up, one of his keelboats ran upon a submerged snag, ripped out its bottom, and sank within a few seconds, taking seven men, seventy muskets, and supplies galore to the bottom of the muddy Missouri. This disaster was a heavy blow to the campaign; some believe it was the deciding factor. For Colonel Leavenworth, having taken the field without orders, knew that he would be held responsible, and that knowledge seems to have cooled his ardor. Perhaps he dreamed of courts-martial. His anxiety for the remaining boats was keen, for he did not know when a second one might be sunk. Day after day of this anxiety made him more and more lukewarm.

But the Colonel carried on. At Fort Recovery all parties assembled to organize the Missouri Legion and give the Arikara the whipping of their lives.

Ashley and Pilcher gladly supplied rifles to take the place of the muskets lost in the wreck. And with these new arms, the Colonel equipped and reorganized his forces. They consisted of five companies of Regulars, mountain men under Ashley and Pilcher, and the five hundred Sioux under Chief Fireheart. Many of the mountain men were temporarily commissioned as officers of the United States Army, and bore military rank for the first — and certainly for the last — time in their lives. Edward Rose was ensign, Jed Smith captain, Thomas Fitzpatrick quartermaster, William Sublette sergeant-major. Henry Vanderburgh and Angus MacDonald were named captains, while Moses B. Carson was first lieutenant, and William Gordon shave-tail. All present and accounted for, the Missouri Legion, including the Indians, numbered nearly eight hundred well-armed men. Things looked bad for Chief Bear and his Arikara.

By the time the force reached the Indian villages, on August 9, several hundred more Sioux had joined, making the total force more than eleven hundred men. They were eager to attack, and outnumbered the Arikara almost two to one.

Leavenworth left his boats twenty-five miles below the villages, with orders to bring on the artillery. He and his troops marched on the enemy towns.

Pilcher went first, to station his men beyond the villages so as to prevent escape. Meanwhile, the Sioux, thirsting for the blood of their ancient enemies, charged on up the valley horseback, passing Pilcher, yelling like devils out of hell. The Arikara raced to meet them, and for a little while there was a lively mixup on the open prairie half a mile below the villages. There, in a great cloud of dust and powder smoke, the Sioux charged back and forth, counting *coups*, shooting, and yelling, trying to kill and put their enemies to flight. In this charge the Sioux lost two killed and had seven wounded.

For the Arikara would not give ground. Outnumbered though they were, they had tasted the blood of their enemies too recently to be readily tamed. And though the Sioux shot down thirteen of their warriors, the Arikara stood firm. Pilcher began to think that the Sioux would get the worst of it. If *they* ran, he and his men would be in a pretty fix. Pilcher raced back, calling for reinforcements.

At his call, the whole Legion rapidly advanced up the west bank of the river. Ashley was nearest the water; in the center the Regulars marched; Riley's riflemen moved on the left flank. As the Sioux were between them and their enemies, they could not fire until they had passed the Sioux. But as soon as they began to shoot, the Arikara took to their heels and ran back to the protection of the palisades around the town.

The Colonel, not thinking it wise to charge such fortifications, ordered a halt until the boats could bring up the six-pounders. Nothing more was done that day.

Next morning, the Arikara were still within their defenses, ready to fight. The Colonel divided his force, and attacked the two villages at the same time. At the start, the artillery wrought havoc, killing Chief Gray Eyes with the first shot, and knocking the big medicine-pole down with the second. But those small cannon could not demolish the palisades, nor do any real harm to the thick walls of the earth lodges. It was clear that the Legion must storm the villages if the Colonel wanted a victory. But, meanwhile, the bombardment continued, and a hail of bullets from the rifles was poured into the towns. However, the Arikara soon learned to lie low and keep their heads down, with the result that nobody was hit.

By this time the Sioux were becoming impatient. They took no part in these tactics, which they thought useless and silly. They said they would wait until the whites drove their enemies into the open. But as hour after hour dragged by without any results, the Sioux told Pilcher that they were thinking of going home. 'White man's war is just shooting,' they said. 'Why don't you rush in and strike somebody, take his gun, or his horse? That's the way for a *man* to fight. That is the warrior's way.' They wanted an open, running fight, where a man had a chance to distinguish himself, display his bravery, and count a *coup*. Pilcher took their complaints to Colonel Leavenworth. Still nothing was done.

By mid-afternoon, most of the ammunition for the artillery was used up, the Arikara were as safe as ever, and the Sioux were utterly disgusted. Colonel Leavenworth ordered the Legion to retire downstream. The hungry soldiers raided the Arikara cornfields, and sat down to the first square meal they had had in two days. While they munched the corn, the Sioux openly jeered at the white men. So far the Sioux had done all the real fighting, had suffered the only casualties. They did not conceal their contempt. 'These Americans,' they sneered, 'they are just a lot of old women.'

The mountain men resented such talk. They felt that the campaign had just begun. No Injun was going to have the laugh on them. They would show these cussed redskins how Americans could fight. Just wait until morning!

Imagine their indignation when they learned that Colonel Leavenworth now proposed to make peace! When he induced the Arikara to come down and smoke with him, they would not join the council. Pilcher was so angry he could not sit down, but walked up and down, up and down, like an Indian about to start a fight. This behavior alarmed the Arikara and annoyed Colonel Leaven-

worth. And it did not soothe him any to learn that the
Arikara would not make peace unless the mountain men
agreed to it! That demand seemed a reflection upon the
Regular Army.

While the Colonel was digesting these indignities, he
saw the Sioux moving away. They took station on a near-
by hilltop, and Fireheart sent word that he would wait and
see which side came out on top. Everybody, both friends
and enemies, seemed to take a malicious delight in showing contempt for the Colonel. It enraged him. He told
the mountain men not to forget that they were under
military orders. 'You will do as *I* say,' he told them.

The mountain men were restive. They were not used to
unreasoning obedience. Knowing Indians as Pilcher did,
he was sure that peace without victory would be fatal to
the prestige of the Americans. He and the other mountain men demanded a charge, some decisive action, that
would definitely show their mettle and intimidate the
Arikara. They knew that their reputation, their future
safety, depended upon that. Indians, they explained,
respected brave men, honored victory; how could the
Colonel hope to settle anything if he made peace with
the Arikara without whipping them first? 'You cain't
pacify Injuns, Colonel, lessen you lick 'em first.'

But the Colonel, whether from fear of more losses on
this unauthorized expedition, or from anger at the behavior of the mountain men, declared that *he* represented
the authority of the United States, and that the interests
of the United States demanded a truce.

If the Colonel had conquered the Arikara then and there, it would have been long remembered by the Plains tribes. All those later battles and campaigns might have been rendered unnecessary; Custer might never have had to ride to his death on the Little Bighorn. But some soldiers appear to think of their enemies as hunters do of game animals — as something which ought to be preserved for future sport. Sport has been called the image of war; it would be fair enough to call Colonel Leavenworth's war the image of sport. He weakened, and when that shifty Arikara, Little Soldier, begged him to postpone the attack until next day, the Colonel agreed. Leavenworth gave, as his excuse, that, if the attack were made so late in the day, the wounded would have to be cared for after dark!

Pilcher, Edward Rose, all the men who knew Injuns, pleaded with the Colonel not to listen to Little Soldier. They knew that the shifty Arikara was begging for time to get himself and his relatives out of the villages during the night. And they urged that, if the Colonel did postpone the attack, he ought to guard the villages well to prevent the escape of the besieged.

But the Colonel turned a deaf ear to their pleas. No precautions were taken. When the sun rose, the villages were deserted.

The whites entered the towns. There they found only one old woman, blind and helpless — the mother of the dead chief, Gray Eyes. After all that shooting and two days' warfare, not thirty Arikara had been killed, and most of these had died at the hands of the Sioux. And when, after two more days of fruitless attempts to find the vanished Arikara and induce them to return, the Legion retired downriver again, they left plenty of food and supplies for the old woman. She was the only one to profit by all that martial display, all those months of hard labor, all that expense of thousands of dollars of public money. However, the troops had gained some experience of camping out!

The mountain men, helpless under the orders of the military organization to which they then belonged, were very bitter and scornful about the whole affair. Leavenworth had made a laughing-stock of the white men. Far from avenging their blood, he had made the redskins despise them. After the troops marched away, some of them slipped back and set fire to the villages. It was all they could do.

Leavenworth blamed Pilcher for that, and so called down upon himself a storm of abuse and reproach such as few officers of our Army have ever endured. The Colonel had exonerated Moses Carson and Vanderburgh from all blame, and these two men were so ashamed to be praised by Colonel Leavenworth that they shed angry tears, explaining to their comrades that they had done *nothing* to deserve the commendation of such a man!

Pilcher wrote what he thought of Leavenworth in no uncertain terms, and sent his letter to that officer. Since it has been previously published,[1]* and well expresses the

*See Notes, at end of this volume.

feelings of the mountain men concerned, it may be quoted here.

Pilcher wrote to the Colonel:

> Humanity and philanthropy are mighty shields for you against those who are entirely ignorant of the disposition and character of Indians, but with those who have experienced the fatal and ruinous consequences of their treachery and barbarity these considerations will avail nothing. You came to restore peace and tranquillity to the country, and to leave an impression which would insure its continuance. Your operations have been such as to produce the contrary effect, and to impress the different Indian tribes with the greatest possible contempt for the American character. You came (to use your own words) to 'open and make good this great road'; instead of which you have, by the imbecility of your conduct and operations, created and left impassable barriers.

It was true that the Colonel had succeeded in recovering some of the arms and other property stolen from General Ashley. But in the more important mission — that of intimidating the Indians, impressing them with the power of the United States, and clearing the river for future commerce — Leavenworth had utterly failed. He had not avenged the blood of the men engaged in the fur trade. So far as the mountain men were concerned, the Colonel might better have remained at home.

This blundering failure on the part of the Army convinced the mountain men of certain truths, and established certain traits in them, certain beliefs and customs, which thereafter set them off from other men in the Old West. In the first place, they learned (from Ashley) that the best bourgeois in the world was capable of fatal mistakes. Secondly, they learned (from Leavenworth) that neither the Army nor the fur companies could be relied upon to protect or avenge them against the redskins. Thirdly, they learned (from the Indians themselves — both hostile and friendly) that force and courage and success were the only things on earth an Indian would respect, and that weakness, hesitation, or failure would only invite scorn, hatred, and attack.

The mountain man saw that henceforth he would have to walk alone, relying solely upon himself and his fellows, working and fighting on his own hook. Traders, Indian agents, soldiers, explorers, settlers — all were thereafter regarded with distrust, suspicion, and contempt by the true-bred mountain man.

And before it was all over, all these types came to admit that the mountain man had learned his lesson well — that he could take care of himself.

That was demonstrated almost immediately by one of the most heroic exploits ever performed by a mountain man. His name was Hugh Glass.

V. HUGH GLASS AND
THE GRIZZLY

AFTER Colonel Leavenworth's wretched failure to chastise the treacherous Arikara, General Ashley and Major Henry abandoned all hope of going up-river again past the Arikara villages. The Indians, finding their villages burned, had left that neighborhood: some of them had gone up the Missouri to the Mandan villages near Fort Clark; others, under Chief Elk Tongue, had set out towards the Platte, intending to join their relatives, the Skidi Pawnee, on Loup River. The partners could not know that; but they did know that their men were in no mood to cordelle keelboats through redskin ambuscades. And so Ashley, as usual, went down to St. Louis to attend to the sale of the furs; Henry led a party of eighty picked men overland, heading for the mouth of the Big Horn, on the Yellowstone River, where he intended to fort and make his winter hunt. It was already the middle of August. Henry was in a hurry.

Henry's party contained the best of his men from up-river and many of the courageous fellows who had stuck to Ashley after the first disaster at the Arikara villages.

The muster-roll was packed with names afterward famous in the exploration and conquest of the West. In fact, it would be hard to match that expedition; probably no other in American history has included so many great pathfinders: Jim Bridger, Jedediah Smith, Thomas Fitzpatrick, William Sublette, Dave Jackson, Louis Vasquez, Edward Rose, Seth Grant. Among them, too, was an old, gray-bearded hunter from Pennsylvania, Hugh Glass.

Although wounded in Ashley's first fight with the Arikara, Glass went along with Henry. Glass was a tough, sinewy old fellow, all hair, bone, and hard muscle, with the dauntless heart of a bear. And because he was such a good shot, Henry often sent him ahead of the party to hunt. As usual, the mountain men lived on the country as they went along.

They struck out to the west and northwest, following Grand River. In those days grizzly bears were common along the Missouri, and boats passing up and down often sighted those great brutes, dangerous as tigers, prowling alone or by twos and threes alongshore, or basking on the sandy beaches. All the early travelers mention the numbers and ferocity of the grizzlies in that region. One of their favorite haunts was the sheltered valley of Grand River, where an abundance of brush and thickets of wild plum, cherry, and buffalo-berry bushes afforded them ample food and cover. It was on Grand River that young Sitting Bull, in later years, had the adventure with a grizzly bear which made a warrior of him.

Many white men and Indians had been torn to pieces by these ferocious beasts, for in those days the bears had not been much hunted, and feared no man. Often they ran in groups of two or three, and would instantly attack or chase any man they saw. Since they were not very keen-sighted animals, the man who was seen by them was generally too near, when seen, to get away. He had to kill or be killed on the spot. Such bears were terrific adversaries, hard to kill. Lances and arrows made little impression upon their thick coats, their tough hides, their iron muscles covered with layers of fat. Bullets were sometimes not much better, and Prince Maximilian[1] tells of a bear which ran away from his party, carrying the lead of fifteen rifles in his carcass. The trappers dignified the grizzly with a title all his own; they called him 'Old Ephraim.' The Indians counted *coup* upon grizzlies as they did on human enemies, and the man lucky enough to kill one proudly wore the claws as a necklace.

On the fifth day out, old Hugh Glass and a companion were hunting in advance of the party. Glass was in the lead, following the stream, and was forcing his way through a dense thicket of plum bushes. The wild plums grow in sandy places, in thick clumps. When Glass came out of the thicket into a small clearing by the water, he found himself within a few paces of a huge she-bear and two sizeable cubs lying on the warm sand.

Old Glass knew that there was no chance to run. He was hemmed in by the dense brush, through which he could only move slowly, while the bear could plow through

BEAR HUNT ON THE MISSOURI

it as if it were only grass. Everything depended on the single shot in his long rifle. He threw the muzzle forward, crooking his gnarled thumbs to set his triggers.

The bear launched herself upon him with a ferocious grunting growl — that dreadful sound imitated by Indian warriors when bent on instant murder. Before Glass could level his rifle, the she-bear had him by the throat, jerked him from the ground, and flung him down, gasping, with a sickening thud. Crouching upon the helpless old man, she caught his thigh in her teeth, tore off a mouthful of his flesh, and turned to offer it to her waiting cubs.

Breathless and bleeding, Glass took advantage of her move to escape that yellow-red terror. He scrambled to his knees. But the moment he moved she was back again, pouncing upon him. Her strong teeth met in his shoulder; she shook her head and rolled him over. Glass threw up his arms to shield his face and throat. She caught them between her teeth, bit him severely again and again through the wrists and arms. He heard, as well as felt, her cruel teeth rasping on his bones.

Hearing the growls of the bear and old Hugh's yells, the other hunter plunged through the hampering brush, tried to help. But the nearest cub, catching the spirit of its enraged mother, rushed on him. He had to jump into the river to save himself. There, standing in water waist-deep, he raised his rifle, shot the foremost cub. Then he yelled for help.

By that time, the main party had heard the cries and shots of the hunters. They charged to the rescue. Man after man burst through the thicket. There they saw the bear, growling horribly through bloody fangs, standing over the torn body of their comrade. Seeing them, she rose and stood facing the intruders — a shaggy fury, six feet tall, waving her great paws set with those sharp hooks, ready to attack. From all sides rifles cracked. At the first shots, the she-bear tumbled, rolled over, growling and squealing, clawing at her wounds, until at last she dropped dead across the mangled body of her groaning victim.

The trappers dragged the heavy carcass from their comrade's body. Of course there was no surgeon in the party, but it needed no doctor to tell those pitying men that old Glass had only one chance in a hundred to live. He had been frightfully torn and mauled. They tried to help him up, but he could not stand. He fell back upon the sand, rolling and screaming in agony, covered with blood.

Major Henry and his men made the poor fellow a bed of robes and blankets under the shade of a tree. They pitied him, but there was little they could do. That night they camped on the spot, and all night long old Hugh's groans and writhings disturbed their sleep. Next morning the Major called a council. What to do?

Little was said. Every man knew that the party must go ahead at once. August was already half gone, and, if the beaver fur was to be taken before the animals retired behind their ramparts of ice and frozen mud for the winter, the men would have to hurry. In that region, it was

said, there were only three months — July, August, and
Winter. The whole success of their year's venture depended upon getting to work promptly. Yet they knew
that old Glass was in no condition to travel.

Had he been only slightly injured, they might have
tied him in his saddle. Had he had a broken leg or a gunshot wound, they might have put him into an Injun drag,
or travois, and carted him across the prairie, jouncing
along under the old nag's tail. Even a very sick man
might have been carried in a litter slung between two
mules. But everyone could see that Glass was unfit for
travel, even in a litter. He could not be moved.

One reason for the success of the mountain men was, of
course, that they had the habit of adapting themselves
completely to the circumstances in which they found
themselves. They, like their forbears in Kentucky and
Pennsylvania, habitually acted on the old principle: when
in Injun country, do as the Injuns do. And so, this time,
they stepped right in the tracks of the redskins.

When a Sioux warrior was badly wounded on the warpath and could not travel, his comrades would generally
leave him (often at his own request) in some comfortable
spot — a cave, a sheltered thicket — with arms, dried
meat, a buffalo robe, and such healing medicines as they
might have along, and then go on home, on the chance
that he would recover in his own good time and turn up at
camp as soon as he could. Many true stories of such exploits are known, and Wounded Knee Creek, in South
Dakota, takes its name from such a happening. The moun-

tain men, faced by the same conditions as the Sioux braves, adopted their well-tried methods. It was voted that Hugh Glass would have to stay behind and take his chance.

But Major Henry and his men were not hard-boiled enough to ride away and leave that helpless old man to die alone. Mountain men were, as a rule, as generous as they were brave. And so the Major decided that two men must remain behind and care for Glass until he died — or was able to travel. That meant, to everyone present, *until he died*. Nobody really expected him to recover.

Major Henry called for volunteers.

Naturally, nobody was eager to remain with Glass in that dangerous region. They were still in the heart of Arikara country, and nothing would please the Arikara more than to catch three white men in such a fix. Moreover, that country was a battleground of all the warring tribes, swarming with hostiles, Injuns to whom any stranger was an enemy. And now, after Leavenworth's failure to lick the Arikara, the rating of an American was so low that even the friendly Sioux could hardly be counted as allies.

None of the men hankered for that chore. They knowed well enough that, to the Injuns, a scalp's a scalp, anyways you fix it. Major Henry proposed that every man contribute to a purse to be given to the men who volunteered to stay.

That seemed fair, and every man pledged a dollar. Some writers talk of passing the hat, but it is not likely that many of those trappers had coins in their possession.

The year's work was just beginning, and mountain men were accustomed to living on credit until they met at rendezvous and were paid their year's wages. Probably Major Henry received their pledges and promised to advance the money, deducting it from the pay of his men. At any rate, eighty dollars was contributed.

Then a man named Fitzgerald agreed to stay, and with him a youngster named Jim. Some would have it that this Jim was Jim Bridger, and certainly Jim Bridger was plenty brave enough to volunteer for such a perilous duty. But judging from what happened afterward, it is hard to believe that Jim Bridger was the man. Though only a youngster at the time, not old enough to vote, Jim Bridger was as honest as he was brave. That story sounds like one made up later by some fellow who was envious of Jim Bridger's fame. It does not fit the man.

Henry and his men went on, and Fitzgerald and young Jim began their lonely vigil by the deathbed of the moaning, mangled graybeard.

Day after day dragged by, and old Glass refused to die. They fed him on soup, dressed his fearful wounds with cold water — their only remedy — and kept the flies away. They hardly dared to build a fire, for fear the smoke or flame should be seen by roaming Injuns. They hardly dared to shoot, for fear the reports of their rifles should tell some savage of their hideout. There was nothing to do but sit and worry. Forty dollars a head seemed a small price for a life now that the pressure of their comrades' presence was removed.

On the fifth day, so far as they could tell, Glass was no better — and no worse — than ever. That morning Fitzgerald saw Injun sign. He was frightened. The younger man caught the contagion of his fear. Fitzgerald declared he would stay no longer. 'We cain't do no good here,' he insisted. 'The old man's shore to die, anyhow. If we stick around much longer, we'll lose our hair.'

The younger man gave in at last. Both agreed to abandon old Glass and strike out after their comrades. Glass was hardly conscious; it would be easy to slip away.

But Fitzgerald knew that, if he turned up at Fort Henry with word that Glass had not died, the consequences would be unpleasant. On the other hand, if Glass were declared dead, it would be necessary to produce his plunder in proof of it; the Major would naturally expect to have the old man's effects brought in. Probably Glass owed him for them. And so Fitzgerald and the boy stole the old man's rifle, his powder-horn, bullet-pouch, knife, and flint, and sneaked away that night. They left him utterly defenseless.

When these two frightened rascals turned up at the fort on the Big Horn, and reported that Glass was dead, nobody doubted their story. It was just what everyone had expected to hear. And the rifle and other things bore mute testimony to the same effect. Fitzgerald and young Jim were praised for their manly deed.

Perhaps, if they had stayed on with Glass, the old man would have died. But when he roused from his coma and found himself deserted by his two comrades, found that

all his possessions but his clothes and the buffalo robe he
lay on had been stolen, his old heart burned with fresh
determination. He formed a bitter resolve to live — to
live and have revenge upon those treacherous murderers.
'The lousy skunks,' he muttered. 'I'll git 'em yit!'

Helpless, starving, sick and feverish, without food,
arms, or protection, Hugh Glass showed himself a true-
bred mountain man. He had the heart of a bear. And
so he set about helping himself.

The camp had been made near a spring. Glass dragged
himself to it, so that he could drink. Around the spring,
naturally enough, buffalo-berries and wild cherries grew,
now ripe to blackness. Glass swallowed the cool water,
sucked the juice from the ripe fruit within his reach.
Probably that diet was better for a man in his condition
than anything his comrades could have served him.
At any rate, Glass survived, nursing his strength and his
wrath, until he felt able to stir from that miserable spot.
He knew he must find food and shelter before winter set
in.

The nearest place where he could expect to find white
men was Fort Kiowa, a trading-post on the Missouri
above the mouth of the White. That was away downriver, fully a hundred miles away. Glass set out to *crawl*
to that fort!

He dared not go back down Grand River, for the Arikara villages lay at its mouth. Besides, the most direct
route lay to the southeast. And so poor old Glass, still
sore and sick, thin as a rail and pale as a ghost, painfully

left Grand River, crept up the bluffs, and dragged himself
wearily out upon the high prairie, heading towards
Moreau River. He was quite unable to stand, and managed to make only a few hundred yards a day.

Where can one match such fortitude?

He had no arms, no way of making a fire, no food, and
no way to catch or kill any. The country was open, full
of hostile redskins, any one of whom would think it a good
joke to scalp a helpless man alive, and let him lie in the
sun. But if, at times, his helplessness racked him with despair, he never quit. Steadily he crawled along, bent on
revenge, hoping against hope that Providence would take
pity upon his sufferings and avenge his wrongs.

Sometimes fortune favors the brave.

After Glass got upon the high prairie, he saw, far off, a
commotion — a lone, lost buffalo calf surrounded by
wolves. The pack was trying to drag the frantic, dodging
little square-head down. One after another, the wolves
would rush in and snap at throat or hamstring, until at
last the bawling calf fell a victim to their cruel teeth.
Glass dragged himself forward, his jaws working and drool-
ing with famine. By the time he came near enough for the
wolves to scent him, they had satisfied their first hunger.
Glass felt that he had to risk their attack. He kept going,
and the wolves ran off and let him alone. He crept up and
rested, gasping, beside the mangled calf.

He had no knife, no flint to make a fire. But his old
teeth were still sound. He crouched above the dead calf,
and little by little was able to satisfy his gnawing hunger.

Then, tearing off as much flesh as he could carry, he thrust it inside his shirt and crawled away, still heading for Fort Kiowa.

After many hardships, he crossed Moreau River, and passed slowly over the wide plains towards Cheyenne River.

Following that stream down to the mouth, he saw familiar country at last. There wound the broad Missouri, flashing in the morning sun. There was still a third of his journey before him, but he was stronger now, and no longer cursed by fits of despair. His thirst for revenge was sharp as ever. Those Missouri bottoms were dangerous ground, but at last the cottonwood pickets of little Fort Kiowa showed in sight. Glass scrambled to the gate, pounded and yelled for help.

The men of the American Fur Company took him in and made him comfortable. The story of his fearful adventures would have seemed incredible but for the terrible scars he bore, and the tatters which hung about his skeleton frame.

After such hardships, any other mortal would have remained at Fort Kiowa all winter, resting and regaining strength. But Hugh Glass had only one passion — revenge. And as soon as a boatload of trappers heading upriver appeared at the fort, Glass joined them. They pushed steadily upstream, and reached the bend in the river below Tilton's Fort, a post belonging to the Columbia Fur Company, standing opposite the Mandan villages. Glass, who was too weak to be of any service in cordelling the boat around the bend, decided to walk across it and thus lighten the boat. He did not know that the hostile Arikara had moved up to the Mandan towns, and were making life miserable for James Kipp and other whites thereabouts.

Glass had walked painfully almost to the fort when he saw two squaws. From their dress he knew at once what they were. *'Rikaras!* He flung himself down. But they had seen him, and ran screaming for the warriors. The Arikara men came running out to kill him. Glass was too feeble to fight; he turned and tried to run away. On came the hostile Arikara, yelling in triumph, running over the prairie, shaking their London fusils in the air. Glass thought he was gone beaver, sure enough. They were almost within gunshot.

Two mounted Mandans, seeing the white man's danger, raced out to meet him. Catching him by the arms, they swung him up behind one of them. Then, quirting their ponies, they dashed away to the fort, leaving the Arikara disappointed in the dust. Glass was grateful. He had good reason to be, for next day the Arikara killed every man of the party which had brought him up the river. Glass felt that Providence was with him. 'I'll git them two skunks yit,' he assured Kipps. That very night he slipped out of the fort and started alone for Henry's fort on the Big Horn.

Relentlessly, he marched on alone through that wild country, then overrun with savages. For thirty-eight days he walked, up the Missouri to the Yellowstone, up the

Yellowstone to the Big Horn. There he found Major Henry and his men. They took Glass for a ghost.

Probably he looked like one, unkempt and disfigured as he was. But he was not long in convincing everyone of his reality. He found young Jim, and soon had him cornered. The young un trembled in his moccasins, and laid all the blame on Fitzgerald. After scaring him good and plenty, old Glass decided to let the boy go. 'After all, maybe 'twarn't his fault. I reckon Fitz is the ornery skunk I'm after,' he declared. 'Whar's Fitz?'

Fitzgerald, they told him, was at Fort Atkinson, away down the Missouri, at the mouth of the Platte, far below Fort Kiowa. They watched old Glass as he digested this news. But if they expected him to weaken or relent, they were disappointed. Glass announced his intention of going down there forthwith. Learning that Major Henry wished to send a message down river, Glass volunteered to carry it. Four others went along. They left Henry's fort on the twenty-eighth of February, 1824.

Heading down the Yellowstone to the mouth of Powder River, they followed it up to the headwaters, and crossed over to the Platte. There they stopped and made bull-boats of willow sticks and raw buffalo hides. In these leather tubs they floated down the gray waters of the river, taking it easy. But wherever Glass went, the Arikara seemed to be waiting for him. He and his party soon found themselves in the hands of a band of these redskins. Their chief, Elk Tongue, knew Glass, who had spent a winter with him in earlier years. The wily redskin enticed

Glass and his men ashore, and hugged him like a long-lost brother. This welcome put Glass off his guard, and he and his friends went with the chief to a feast in the Arikara camp.

While he was putting the buffalo beef away, Glass heard a child cry. Looking up, he saw that the Indian women were removing all their things from the lodge, dragging the children out in haste. Glass knew that they were clearing the lodge for action — that the massacre was about to begin. He and his friends jumped up and ran for their lives. The Arikara warriors, though taken by surprise, soon overtook and killed two of the whites. But Glass was lucky enough to cover his trail and hide among some rocks. The cussed Injuns could not find him, and finally he got clean away.

In his own words, printed in the *Missouri Intelligencer*, Glass declares: 'Although I had lost my rifle and all my plunder, I felt quite rich when I found my knife and steel in my shot-pouch. These little fixins make a man feel right peart when he is three or four hundred miles away from anybody or anywhere — all alone among the painters and the wild varmints.'

Once more Glass headed for Fort Kiowa. This time he was able to feed himself without much trouble, as the buffalo were calving, and he had his knife. Within fifteen days he was at the fort. As soon as he had a chance to go down-river, he went, and reached Fort Atkinson sometime in June. He had been the better part of a year on his relentless trail of vengeance. At last he had reached his goal.

Fitzgerald was at Fort Atkinson! Glass had the biggest kind of heart to kill the skunk.

But now Fitzgerald was in the Army! It was a serious thing, killing one of Uncle Samuel's soldiers. People would call it murder, like as not. And Hugh Glass had too correct a conception of revenge to imagine that it was worth a prison sentence or a hangin'. 'He'll hang anyhow,' Glass said. 'I reckon the skunk ain't wuth it.' He went to the commanding officer.

That officer, learning the facts, compelled Fitzgerald to restore the old man's property and gave Glass a new outfit. And then, the fust thing Glass knew, the officers war settin' in a ring around him, listenin' to his stories.

Just how anyone with a story like that to tell could drop out of sight for nearly ten years is hard to understand. But little is recorded of Glass after that time. He went back up the river, and was employed at Fort Union and other posts as a hunter. But at last, as Prince Maximilian tells us in his *Travels*, the Arikara killed him — in the winter of 1832–33.

Old Glass died as he had lived. When his enemies killed him, he was out hunting — hunting *bear!*

VI. JEDEDIAH SMITH'S
EXPLORATIONS

O F ALL Ashley's young men, Jedediah Smith was
the greatest pathfinder. Not all who went up the
Missouri with rifle and beaver trap went solely
for riches or adventure. Some loved the wild country,
and though they could not express their feelings, and
would have been ashamed to admit it, had a genuine admiration for the beauties of mountain and plain. Jed
Smith was educated, a man of energetic mind and a devout
Christian, and early formed the determination to become
an explorer. He ranks with Lewis and Clark: in fact, he
surpassed them. They merely passed over from the Upper
Missouri Basin to the Columbia Valley. Smith crossed
from the Middle Missouri country to the Great Salt Lake,
the Colorado, and the Pacific Coast. They traced a single
route to the Western Ocean; Smith found three. No man
living in his time was his equal in first-hand knowledge of
the Far West. In gaining this knowledge, so necessary to
the expansion of the United States, Smith had adventures
galore.

After the end of the campaign against the Arikara,

Smith went to the Crow country, and wintered in the mountains near the mouth of the Big Horn. In the spring, he was with Fitzpatrick, probably, when he crossed the South Pass to Green River. Later that year, Smith led Ashley's men through South Pass to the Columbia, and wintered on the Great Salt Lake. From there he went to rendezvous on Green River, and thence by the Big Horn and Yellowstone to St. Louis. Not a bad showing for so young a mountain man.

But it was in the spring of 1826 that Smith, setting out with Ashley from St. Louis, started on his first independent exploration. Ashley halted at the Great Salt Lake, but Smith pushed on to California by a new southwestern route, returning the next year through Nevada by the central route. Ashley had sold out to Smith, Dave Jackson, and Billy Sublette, and the new partners entered upon the business with keen enthusiasm. But they were not satisfied to harvest the fur in the regions already opened up by Ashley; they looked to the future, and sent Smith westward looking for new worlds to conquer. They knew that, at the rate things were going, the fur would not last forever. Smith had already informed himself as to the extent of the operations of the Hudson's Bay Company. Now he was to find out what lay to the west and southwest.

Smith found more geography than beaver in the deserts and sierras, and was held up by the Spaniards on the Coast for a time. But his fine character convinced them that he came in peace, and they let him go northward towards Oregon in the spring of '28. In July, Smith and his men found themselves within a few miles of the Hudson's Bay Company's post at the mouth of the Willamette River, Fort Vancouver. The trip was almost ended, the weather fine, the Indians friendly.

Only one or two little rifts in these friendly relations had occurred: one of the men had shot an Indian, and an Indian had stolen an axe. Smith had made every effort to prove that the killing had been accidental, that the whites were not the aggressors. The Umpqua Indians brought things to trade, and made light of the casualty.

Next morning, Smith left camp to find the best trail out of the valley. Heavy rains had made travel difficult. Having found a passable route, Smith turned back towards camp. Suddenly, he saw a man running towards him. It was John Turner, who breathlessly told how the Umpquas had without warning rushed on the camp. Turner was a man of giant stature and great strength, and had been busy over the cook-fire when the attack began. He had grabbed a burning stick from the fire, and with this had managed to beat off the savages. Then, seeing that his comrades were all killed, he had run for his life.

There was no chance to recover the property. Smith and Turner had to save their skins, though Smith bitterly regretted the loss of his journals — the record of his explorations. It was long before they reached Fort Vancouver. There they found, to their delight, one of their men, Arthur Black, who had also escaped the massacre.

John McLaughlin was in charge of the fort. Though the

company he served looked with no favor upon the rivalry of the American fur companies, he was a humane and generous man, and could not tolerate robbery and murder among the Indians in his field of operations. He liberally rewarded the friendly tribesmen who had brought Arthur Black into the fort. McLaughlin was even ready to send out a strong force to punish the savages. Thomas McKay commanded it. Probably Smith went along.

McKay did not attack the Indians. He traded for their furs, and whenever any of Smith's furs turned up, he refused to pay for them, telling the Indians they were stolen, and that they must collect from the Indians who had sold the furs to them. In this way McKay fomented a war among the tribes, and the result was the destruction of the murderers by their own people. Not only the furs were recovered, but the precious record of the explorations. More than that, John McLaughlin bought Smith's furs on the spot, giving him a draft on London in the amount of thirty-two thousand dollars. Such were the big men of the fur trade.

In return for these favors, Jedediah Smith promised McLaughlin that he and his partners would leave the Snake River country to the Hudson's Bay Company. Sublette and Jackson lived up to this promise, though it meant a considerable loss to them.

While Smith was at Fort Vancouver, some of his men had been exploring what is now Yellowstone Park, and soon after ran into a big camp of Blackfeet, who gave battle, killing a Snake Indian and his squaw. The six

white men in camp rushed out to attack the raiders, ably
backed up by Snakes and Utes. Each of the whites, armed
with pistols, fired a shot, and six Blackfeet dropped dead!
The Utes and Snakes fought bravely, and after killing
more Blackfeet, and suffering some losses of their own,
put the raiders to flight.   Later a small party of Blackfeet rushed Tullock's men on the march, killed three, and
swept away forty-four pack-horses laden with nearly forty
thousand dollars' worth of furs.   Smith, Jackson, and
Sublette had no luck at all that year of '28. Every one of
their oufits met with disaster.

That autumn, as usual, Sublette took the furs to St.
Louis. Next spring he was back, and with the other partner set out to find Smith. They finally found him in
Pierre's Hole. There Smith told his friends of his promise
to McLaughlin. As the Snake River country was now
closed to them, they had to go back into the dangerous
Blackfoot country, and after some trouble there, managed
to get out and cache their furs and establish their winter
camp in the Wind River Valley. But they could not find
forage there, and soon moved over to Powder River.
Once more Smith tried the Blackfoot range. But he and
his men were driven out, and at rendezvous the next summer, the three partners sold out their business to Thomas
Fitzpatrick, Jim Bridger, Milton Sublette, Henry Fraeb,
and Baptiste Gervais. They kept the name of the Rocky
Mountain Fur Company. Smith and his partners returned
to St. Louis with the biggest lot of furs ever brought in by
one party — nearly two hundred pack.

Smith declared he had had enough of the mountains. The end of the beaver trade was already in sight. The animals were becoming rare and wary, the competition grew keener and more ruthless every season, and the silk hat, newly invented, promised the end of the fashion which had made beaver fur a profitable product. Smith decided to enter the Santa Fe trade.

Every year the Santa Fe trade had increased, since William Becknell, in 1821, sold the first wagonload of goods from the States in Santa Fe for seven hundred dollars. Yankee merchandise brought high prices in Taos and Santa Fe, and was paid for in gold and silver bullion. True, there were dangers of Indians on the Santa Fe Trail, streams to ford, deserts to cross, requiring iron constitutions and alert minds in those who conquered them. But Jedediah Smith had the qualities demanded.

That spring of 1831, he set out from Independence with wagons of his own and eighty-odd men. With him went his two brothers, Dave Jackson, Billy Sublette, and Thomas Fitzpatrick. They carted along a fieldpiece to frighten the Injuns. But for all that one of their men was rubbed out on the Arkansas by the Pawnees.

That summer of '31 was a scorcher. How the mountain men longed for the thin air and cool climate of the Rockies as they crossed the blistering plains, crawling at the snail's pace of laden wagons along the endless Arkansas River through the dancing haze of heat!

So they plodded on: from Independence to Council Grove, 150 miles; from Council Grove to the Grand Arkansas, 270 miles; then on past Walnut Creek, Pawnee Rock, Ash Creek, Pawnee Fork, Coon Creek, the Caches, to the Ford of the Arkansas, the Cimarron Crossing, 392 miles. There they were little more than halfway to Santa Fe. And there the real hardships and dangers of the Trail began.

Below that point stretched the so-called Cimarron Desert, a high, dry, barren plain, without water, without landmarks, with a hard, parched soil on which nothing could grow but scattered cacti and patches of withered buffalo grass. The endless plain dazzled the travelers with continual mirages, and the meanest Injuns in the Southwest, Kiowas and Comanches, ranged there in numbers, hostile to the last man. Even the Blackfoot record for killing white men was beaten by that of these red desperadoes of the Southern Plains.

The Cimarron Desert stretched away thirty-six miles or more, and that was three days' hard travel for the laden wagons. And by the time the oxen had snaked the wheels through the heavy quicksands of the Arkansas River, they were in no case to travel fast.

To add to the drouth and heat, one of those scorching hot winds blew into the faces of Smith's party — a wind that made a gun-barrel hot to the fingers, a wind that seared the skin and withered vegetation like a frost. If there had been any water-holes, none of the party knew where to look for them, and their fevered eyes were continually deceived by the mirages which played over the burning surface of the desert.

For two days they plodded ahead. Everywhere buffalo trails criss-crossed the grass and barren soil, tempting the men to follow in the hope of finding a watering-place. But nobody found water, and on the third day the men began to be light-headed. The party could not agree, and divided. Some went east, some went west. Broken Hand and Jedediah headed south, horseback, breaking trail for their wagons. At last they came upon the burned-out socket of a water-hole. But there was no water for them there. Fitzpatrick, discouraged, dismounted and sat down on the hot sand, waiting until the wagons could come up with him. But Smith, dauntless as always, rode on south, heading for some broken ground which promised the bank of a stream.

Fitzpatrick watched him go on his staggering horse until he disappeared over a swell. That was the last ever seen of Smith. He vanished from the face of the earth. Afterward men learned how.... Smith rode on down the slope, and thought he saw water. Pushing on, he was delighted to see that he had reached the Cimarron River. He urged his tired horse down the grassy slope to the water. There was no current in that ditch, but a series of isolated pools offered all the refreshment he required. He forgot to be vigilant, he thought only of his need. He and the horse drank, and drank, and rested. When he looked up, he found himself surrounded by a band of mounted Comanches. Smith tried to parley with them. But he did not understand the Spanish in which they addressed him. They knew they had him at their mercy. One of them waved his robe in the air to frighten Smith's horse. The animal, now revived by the water it had drunk, whirled round. The minute Smith's back was turned, the Comanches shot him, wounding him in the shoulder.

Smith got his horse under control, fired, and killed the chief, also hitting another warrior just behind him. He dropped his rifle then. But before he could use his pistols, the Comanches were all over him, stabbing him from the saddle with their lances. Then they dragged his body away and threw it into some hole. It was never found.

When the wagons reached the Cimarron, the men made a search for Smith, but gave him up for lost at last, and pushed on into Santa Fe. There they found some Mexican merchants who had just arrived, and had with them Smith's rifle and pistols, obtained from some Comanches, who told how Smith had died.

Smith left a large family of brothers and sisters well provided for. In a letter preserved by the Kansas Historical Society, he addresses his brother in these words, which well express his devout and courageous character:

> It is that I may be able to help those who stand in need, that I face every danger. It is for this that I traverse the mountains covered with eternal snow. It is for this that I pass over the sandy plains, thirsting for water where I may cool my overheated body. It is for this that I go for days without eating, and am pretty well satisfied if I can gather a few roots, a few snails, or better satisfied if we can afford ourselves a piece of horseflesh, or a fine roasted dog, and, most of all, it is for this that I deprive myself of the privilege of society and the satisfaction of the converse of my friends!...

After Smith's death his journals and notes were prepared for the press. But like so many valuable records of the mountain men — Old Bill Williams's autobiography, the Bonneville journals, Catlin's collections, Prince Maximilian's specimens — they were destroyed (by fire) before they could be printed.

During his life, Jedediah Smith was loved, feared, and admired. And after his death he was not forgotten. The mountain men had long memories.

VII. OLD BILL WILLIAMS BESTS
THE BLACKFEET

IT WAS time for the spring hunt. Old Bill Williams rode into a camp of trappers, then working the headwaters of the Yellowstone, and announced that he intended to make his trap with them. La Bonte, a seasoned mountain man, had organized the party, and with him were such picked men as Killbuck, Joe Meek, Markhead, and Marcellin — not to mention one Batiste and two other *vide-poche* Frenchmen from St. Louis. But when Old Bill rode in and unsaddled, La Bonte gladly abdicated in favor of that Nestor of the mountains. It was not often that Bill Williams condescended to join a party. He was by habit and preference a 'solitary.' That name was then commonly given to the old buffalo bulls, surly and ferocious, with scarred flanks and blunted horns, which had been driven from the herds by younger and lustier rivals, and so ranged the plains and parks without companions.

The name fitted Old Bill well enough, too, for he had abandoned the settlements in the beginning because the girl he courted refused him, adding insult to injury by calling him 'lout!' Yet, although unlucky in love, Old

Bill was inferior to nobody in the mountains when it came to hunting, trapping, or fighting Injuns. They knew him as Lone Elk, and described him as 'a great trapper — took many beaver, and a great warrior — his belt was full of scalps'; but having in those days 'no friend; no squaw; always by himself, like the eagle in the sky, or the panther on the mountain.' ¹ And when discretion was the better part of valor, Old Bill knew better how to fort, or cache, or cover his tracks, than any man in Injun country.

The fact is, he preferred solitude because he was fearless, and could do as he pleased when alone. La Bonte and his men were flattered when Old Bill joined them. They made no objection when he announced that they would leave the familiar streams they were working and follow him into strange country. They packed their peltry and put out for the distant peak to which Old Bill pointed.

For two days they followed a mountain stream, riding along the valley, keeping to level ground, and so sparing their animals.

'Williams always rode ahead, his body bent over his saddle-horn, across which rested a long, heavy rifle, his keen gray eyes peering from under the slouched brim of a flexible felt hat, black and shining with grease. His buckskin hunting shirt, bedaubed until it had the appearance of polished leather, hung in folds over his bony carcass; his nether extremities being clothed in pantaloons of the same material (with scattered fringes down the outside of the leg — which ornaments, however, had been pretty well thinned to supply "whangs" for mending moccasins or

pack-saddles), which, shrunk with wet, clung tightly to
his long, spare, sinewy legs. His feet were thrust into a
pair of Mexican stirrups made of wood and as big as coal-
scuttles; and iron spurs of incredible proportions, with
tinkling drops attached to the rowels, were fastened to his
heel — a bead-worked strap, four inches broad, securing
them over the instep. In the shoulder-belt which sus-
tained his powder-horn and bullet-pouch were fastened
the various instruments essential to one pursuing his mode
of life. An awl, with deerhorn handle, and a point defended
by a case of cherry-wood carved by his own hand, hung at
the back of his belt, side by side with a worm for cleaning
the rifle; and under this was a squat and quaint-looking
bullet-mold, the handles guarded by strips of buckskin to
save his fingers from burning when running balls, having
for its companion a little bottle made from the point of an
antelope's horn, scraped transparent, which contained the
"medicine" used in baiting traps. The old coon's face was
sharp and thin, a long nose and chin hobnobbing each
other; and his head was always bent forward, giving him
the appearance of being humpbacked. He appeared to
look neither to the right nor left, but in fact his little
twinkling eye was everywhere.' [2]

Old Bill rode an old, crop-eared, rawboned Nez Percé
pony, with galled back and dogged temper, with his pack-
animals tied to its scrawny tail. And in this way he led the
party up the valley.

They were satisfied. For they knew that Old Bill, however queer he might look, riding along with jingling spurs,

thumping the ribs of his horse at every step, was bound to find the best trail, sure to bring them to some spot where water, firewood, and grass were plenty, when it was time to make camp. And when, at evening, Old Bill reined up, slid from his saddle, unpacked and hobbled his animals, and then — having struck fire for his pipe with flint and steel — coolly sat down to smoke while they made camp, they did not complain. They gladly rustled wood and water, and staked out the horses where the grass was good. They knew that Old Bill, used to camping alone, would be a better guard at night than a whole company of dragoons.

Old Bill was not so well satisfied, and there were times when he had misgivings about the party. One or two of the men, he discovered, were greenhorns, who were ignorant of the customs of the mountains, would cut meat across the grain, and had more rashness than real courage. But Old Bill was stubborn, too, and until he had some cause to change his mind, he stuck to the trail he had taken.

That trail led on into the mountains. It grew rocky and rough, and as they pushed on towards the geysers and boiling springs of what is now Yellowstone Park, and whiffed the smell of brimstone, some of the men began to show real fear. That region was avoided — even by game animals. It was 'too close to hell for comfort.' But Old Bill guided them through, and unsaddled on a creek where there was plentiful sign of beaver.

Scouting round their camp, Old Bill soon returned with a lost moccasin, sure proof that other varmints, too, were in the neighborhood. 'Do you hear now, boys?' he whined.

'Thar's Injuns knockin' around — Blackfoot at that! But thar's plenty beaver hyar too, and this child means to trap, anyhow.'

The greenhorns were all for making tracks out of such dangerous country. But Old Bill was plumb disgusted, and sharply overruled them. 'Hell,' he whined, in his high, cracked voice, 'thar's Injuns everwhar, if it comes to that. Injuns and beaver goes together!'

That night they feasted on mountain mutton, and next morning paired off to go and set their traps. La Bonte went with Killbuck; Markhead with Batiste; Joe Meek with Marcellin; the two Canadians together. Old Bill remained in camp with the other man. But as this fellow wished to hunt, Old Bill was soon alone — as he liked to be — and put in the time keeping a bright lookout and mending his moccasins.

'Markhead and his companion followed a creek, which entered that on which they had encamped, about ten miles distant. Beaver sign was abundant, and they had set eight traps when Markhead came suddenly upon fresh Indian sign, where squaws had passed through the shrubbery on the banks of the stream to procure water, as he knew from observing a large stone placed by them in the stream, on which to stand to enable them to dip their kettles in the deepest water. Beckoning to his companion to follow, and cocking his rifle he carefully pushed aside the bushes, and was noiselessly proceeding up the bank, when, creeping on hands and knees, he gained the top, and, looking from his hiding-place, descried three Indian tents standing on a little bench near the creek. Smoke curled from the roofs of branches, but the skin doors were carefully closed, so that he was unable to distinguish the number of the inmates. At a little distance, however, he observed two or three squaws gathering wood, with the usual attendance of curs, whose acuteness in detecting the scent of strangers was much to be dreaded.

'Markhead was a rash and daring young fellow, caring no more for Indians than he did for prairie dogs, and acting ever on the spur of the moment and as his inclination dictated, regardless of consequences. He at once determined to enter the lodges and attack the enemy, should any be there; and the other trapper was fain to join him in the enterprise. The lodges proved empty, but the fires were still burning and meat cooking upon them, to which the hungry hunters did ample justice, besides helping themselves to whatever goods and chattels, in the shape of leather and moccasins, took their fancy.

'Gathering their spoil into a bundle, they sought their horses, which they had left tied under cover of the timber on the banks of the creek; and mounting, took the back trail, to pick up their traps and remove from so dangerous a neighborhood. They were approaching the spot where the first trap was set, a thick growth of ash and quaking aspen concealing the stream, when Markhead, who was riding ahead, observed the bushes agitated, as if some animal was making its way through them. He instantly stopped his horse, and his companion rode to his side to inquire the cause of this abrupt halt. They were within a few yards of the belt of shrubs which skirted the stream, and before Markhead had time to reply, a dozen swarthy heads and shoulders suddenly protruded from the leafy screen, and as many rifle-barrels and arrows were pointing at their breasts. Before the trappers had time to turn their horses and fly, a cloud of smoke burst from the thicket almost in their faces. Batiste, pierced with several balls, fell dead, and Markhead felt himself severely wounded. However, he struck the spurs into his horse; and as some half-score Blackfeet jumped with loud cries from their cover, he discharged his rifle among them, and galloped off, a volley of balls and arrows whistling after him. He drew no bit until he reined up at the campfire, where he found Bill quietly dressing a deerskin. That worthy looked up from his work; and seeing Markhead's face streaming with blood, and the very unequivocal evidence of an Indian encounter in the shape of an arrow sticking in his back, he asked: "Do'ee feel bad now, boy? Whar away you see them darned Blackfoot?"

'"Well, pull this arrow out of my back and maybe I'll feel like telling," answered Markhead.

'"Do'ee hyar now! Hold on till I've grained this cussed skin, will 'ee! Did 'ee ever see sich a darned pelt, now? It won't take the smoke any how I fix it." And Markhead was fain to wait the leisure of the imperturbable old trapper, before he was eased of his annoying companion.

'Old Bill expressed no surprise or grief when informed of the fate of poor Batiste. He said it was "just like greenhorns, runnin' into them cussed Blackfoot," and observed that the defunct trapper, being only a *vide-poche*, was "no account anyhow."

'Presently Killbuck and La Bonte galloped into camp with another alarm of Indians. They had also been attacked suddenly by a band of Blackfeet, but, being in a more open country, had got clear off, after killing two of their assailants, whose scalps hung at the horns of their saddles. They had been in a different direction to that in which Markhead and his companion had proceeded, and, from the signs they had observed, expressed the belief that the country was alive with Indians. Neither of these men had been wounded.

'Presently the two Canadians made their appearance on the bluff, galloping with might and main to camp, and shouting "Indians! Indians!" as they came. All being assembled, and a council held, it was determined to abandon the camp and neighborhood immediately.

'Bill grumbled: "Do'ee hyar now, boys, thar's sign about? this hoss feels like caching"; and, without more words, and stoically deaf to all remonstrances, he forthwith proceeded to pack his animals, talking the while to the old, crop-eared, raw-boned Nez Percé pony, his own particular saddle-horse, who in dogged temper and iron hardiness was a worthy companion of his self-willed master. This beast, as Bill seized his apishamore to lay upon its galled back, expressed displeasure by humping its back and shaking its withers with a wincing motion that excited the ire of the old trapper; and no sooner had he laid the apishamore smoothly on the chafed skin than a wriggle of the animal shook it off.

'"Do'ee hyar now, you darned critter?" he whined out.
"Can't 'ee keep quiet your old fleece now? Isn't this old
coon putting out to save 'ee from the darned Injuns now,
do'ee hyar?" And then, continuing his work and taking
no notice of his comrades, who stood by bantering the
eccentric old trapper, he soliloquized: "Do 'ee hyar, now?
This niggur sees sign ahead — he does; he'll be afoot afore
long if he don't keep his eye skinned — he will. Injuns is
all about, they are: Blackfoot at that. Can't come round
this child — they can't, wagh!" And at last, his pack-
animals securely tied to the tail of his horse, he mounted,
and throwing the rifle across the horn of his saddle, and
without noticing his companions, drove the jingling spurs
into his horse's gaunt sides, muttering, "Can't come round
this child — they can't!" So, mounting his horse, and
leading his pack-mule by a lariat, he bent over his saddle-
horn, dug his ponderous rowels into the lank sides of his
beast, and without a word, struck up the bluff and disappeared.' ª

Old Bill was determined to part company with such
reckless and unlucky companions. They could not take
care of themselves — that was sartain; all he could expect was endless trouble so long as he rode with them.
He had been a fool to throw in with them, he told himself; he was always better off alone. 'I never seen sich a
passel of feckless greenhorns,' he grumbled, prodding the
spotted pony on its way.

'The others hastily gathering up their packs, and most
of them having lost their traps, quickly followed his ex-

ample and "put out." On cresting the high ground which
rose from the creek, they observed thin columns of smoke
mounting into the air from many different points, the
meaning of which they were at no loss to guess. However,
they were careful not to show themselves on elevated
ground, keeping as much as possible under the banks of the
creek, when such a course was practicable; but, the bluffs
sometimes rising precipitously from the water, they were
more than once compelled to ascend the banks, and con-
tinue their course along the uplands, whence they might
easily be discovered by the Indians. It was nearly sundown when they left their camp, but they proceeded during
the greater part of the night at as rapid a rate as possible;
their progress, however, being greatly retarded as they
advanced into the mountain, their route lying upstream.
Towards morning they halted for a brief space, but
started again as soon as daylight permitted them to see
their way over the broken ground.

'The creek now forced its way through a narrow cañon,
the banks being thickly clothed with shrubbery of cottonwood and quaking aspen. The mountain rose on each side,
but not abruptly, being here and there broken into pla-
teaus and shelving prairies. In a very thick bottom,
sprinkled with coarse grass, they halted about noon, and
removed the saddles and packs from their wearied animals,
picketing them in the best spots of grass.

'La Bonte and Killbuck, after securing their animals,
left the camp to hunt, for they had no provisions of any
kind; and a short distance beyond it, the former came

suddenly upon a recent moccasin track in the timber.
After examining it for a moment, he raised his head with a
broad grin, and, turning to his companion, pointed into
the cover, where, in its thickest part, they discovered the
well-known figure of Old Bill's horse browsing upon the
cherry bushes. Pushing through the thicket in search of
the brute's master, La Bonte suddenly stopped short as
the muzzle of a rifle-barrel gaped before his eyes at the distance of a few inches, while the thin voice of Bill muttered:

'"Do 'ee hyar now, I was nigh giving 'ee hell, I was now.
If I didn't think 'ee was Blackfoot, I'm dogged now."
And not a little indignant was the old fellow that his
cache had been so easily, though accidentally, discovered.
However, he presently made his appearance in camp,
leading his animals, and once more joined his late companions, not deigning to give any explanation as to why or
wherefore he had deserted them the day before, merely
muttering, "Do 'ee hyar now, thar's trouble comin'."' 4
Old Bill was hung up with the same bunch again. But
it was late, anyhow. Time for vittels and hoss-guard.
And so Old Bill, making the best of bad company, remained and made camp with the others.

'The two hunters returned after sundown with a black-
tailed deer: and after eating the better part of the meat,
and setting a guard, the party were glad to roll in their
blankets and enjoy the rest they so much needed. They
were undisturbed during the night; but at the dawn of day
the sleepers were aroused by a hundred fierce yells from
the mountains enclosing the creek on which they had en-

camped. The yells were instantly followed by a ringing volley, the bullets thudding into the trees and cutting the branches near them, but without causing any mischief. Old Bill rose from his blanket and shook himself, and exclaimed, 'Wagh!' as at that moment a ball plumped into the fire over which he was standing, and knocked the ashes about in a cloud. All the mountaineers seized their rifles and sprang to cover; but as yet it was not sufficiently light to show them their enemy, the bright flashes of the guns alone indicating their position. As morning dawned, however, they saw that both sides of the cañon were occupied by the Indians, and, from the firing, judged there must be at least a hundred warriors engaged in the attack. Not a shot had yet been fired by the trappers, but as the light increased, they eagerly watched for an Indian to expose himself and offer a mark to their trusty rifles. La Bonte, Killbuck, and Old Bill lay a few yards distant from each other, flat on their faces, near the edge of the thicket, their rifles raised before them and the barrels resting in the forks of convenient bushes. From their place of concealment to the position of the Indians — who, however, were scattered here and there, wherever a rock afforded them cover — was a distance of about a hundred and fifty yards, or within fair rifle shot. The trappers were obliged to divide their force, since both sides of the creek were occupied; but such was the nature of the ground, and the excellent cover afforded by the rocks and boulders and clumps of dwarf pine and hemlock, that not a hand's breadth of an Indian's body had yet been seen. Nearly opposite La Bonte, a shelving glade in the mountain-side ended in an abrupt precipice, and at the very edge, and almost toppling over it, were several boulders just of sufficient size to cover a man's body. As this bluff overlooked the trappers' position, it was occupied by the Indians, and every rock covered an assailant. At one point, just over where La Bonte and Killbuck were lying, two boulders lay together, with just sufficient interval to admit a rifle-barrel between them, and from this breastwork an Indian kept up a most annoying fire. All his shots fell in dangerous propinquity to one or other of the trappers, and already Killbuck had been grazed by one better directed than the others. La Bonte watched for some time in vain for a chance to answer this persevering marksman, and at length an opportunity offered, by which he was not long in profiting.

'The Indian, as the light increased, was better able to discern his mark, and fired, and yelled every time he did so, with redoubled vigor. In his eagerness, and probably while in the act of taking aim, he leaned too heavily against the rock which covered him, and, detaching it from its position, down it rolled into the cañon, exposing his body by its fall. At the same instant a wreath of smoke puffed from the bushes which concealed the trappers, and the crack of La Bonte's rifle spoke the first word of reply to the Indian challenge. A few feet behind the rock fell the dead body of the Indian, rolling down the steep sides of the cañon, and only stopped by a bush at the very bottom, within a few yards of the spot where Markhead lay concealed in some high grass.

'That daring fellow instantly jumped from his cover, and, drawing his knife, rushed to the body, and in another moment held aloft the Indian's scalp, giving, at the same time, a triumphant whoop. A score of rifles were leveled and discharged at the intrepid mountaineer; but in the act many Indians incautiously exposed themselves, every rifle in the timber cracked simultaneously, and for each report an Indian bit the dust.

'Now, however, they changed their tactics. Finding they were unable to drive the trappers from their position, they retired from the mountain and the firing suddenly ceased. In their retreat they were forced to expose themselves, and again the whites dealt destruction among them. As the Indians retired, yelling loudly, the hunters thought they had given up the contest; but presently a cloud of smoke rising from the bottom immediately below them at once discovered the nature of their plans. A brisk wind was blowing up the cañon, and, favored by it, they fired the brush on the banks of the stream, knowing that before this the hunters must speedily retreat.

'Against such a result, but for the gale of wind which drove the fire roaring before it, they could have provided — for your mountaineer never fails to find resources in a pinch. They would have fired the brush to leeward of their position, and also carefully ignited that to windward, or between them and the advancing flame, extinguishing it immediately when a sufficient space had thus been cleared, over which the flames could not leap, and thus cutting themselves off from it both above and below their position.

In the present instance they could not profit by such a course, as the wind was so strong that, if once the bottom caught fire, they would not be able to extinguish it; besides which, in the attempt, they would so expose themselves that they would be picked off by the Indians without difficulty. As it was, the fire came roaring before the wind with the speed of a race-horse, and, spreading from the bottom, licked the mountain-sides, the dry grass burning like tinder. Huge columns of stifling smoke rolled before it, and in a very few minutes the trappers were hastily mounting their animals, driving the packed ones before them. The dense clouds of smoke concealed everything from their view, and, to avoid this, they broke from the creek and galloped up the sides of the cañon on to the more level plateau. As they attained this, a band of mounted Indians charged them. One, waving a red blanket, dashed through the *cavallada*, and was instantly followed by all the loose animals of the trappers, the rest of the Indians pursuing with loud shouts. So sudden was the charge that the whites had not the power to prevent the stampede. Old Bill, as usual, led his pack-mules by the lariat; but the animals, mad with terror at the shouts of the Indians, broke from him, nearly pulling him out of his seat at the same time.

'To cover the retreat of the others with their prey, a band of mounted Indians now appeared, threatening an attack in front, while their first assailants, rushing from the bottom, at least a hundred strong, assaulted in rear. "Do 'ee hyar, boys!" shouted Old Bill. "Break, or you'll go under. This child's going to cache!" And saying the word, off he went. *Sauve-qui peut* was the order of the day, and not a moment too soon, for overwhelming numbers were charging upon them, and the mountain resounded with savage yells.'

Old Bill, eager to be rid of his troublesome companions, bent forward over his saddle-horn, plunged his spurs into the ribs of his horse, and dived into the smoke, heading for the creek bottom. The other men scattered, each on his own hook, and that was the last of them Bill saw for many a moon.

Old Bill was not running away — not far. He was not the man to let the cussed Injuns steal his animals and packs and scare him out of their country. Bill needed pack-animals, and he intended to have them. That day he skulked in the cañons and gorges, covering his trail. But when darkness fell, he hit the trail of the redskins, and followed it warily until he found them dancing in triumph around their sparkling campfire.

Bill wrapped himself in a buffalo robe, and, scouting around the hostile camp, soon spied out his pack-animals, staked beside a tent near the stream. Boldly he stalked into the camp, stood for a while watching the dancing, and then quietly cut the ropes and led his horses away at a walk, as though taking them to water. Nobody molested him. And as soon as he reached the creek, he twisted a rope bridle around the nose of the gentler nag, jumped upon its back, and was gone into the darkness.

Dawn found him far off, cached on the far side of a

shallow mountain lake, and busy making pack-saddles for his horses. That done, he struck out towards Jackson's Hole, fell in with a pack-train of traders, obtained new traps, and vanished into the mountains.

Twice that spring he appeared at rendezvous with full packs of beaver, and, as summer came on, headed for Bent's Fort on the Arkansas, his old whistle parched for a gourd or two of Taos Lightning. The cussed redskins couldn't come round that old-timer. He knew how to bring 'em, and done it, too!

VIII. "BROKEN HAND"
BECOMES "WHITE HEAD"

OLD BILL WILLIAMS was the dean and Nestor of the free trappers, and they were the salt of the earth, the aristocrats of the Rockies. They had to be, to survive. Only a man of iron nerve, unflinching courage, fortitude, and skill could win out on his own hook against all the hazards of that lonely life — against hostile Blackfeet, savage grizzlies, famine, exposure, endless hardship and vigilance. The free trapper had to be a man of infinite resource, able to do everything for himself — break or doctor a horse, plait a lariat and use it, make a saddle, throw a diamond hitch on a pack, trap, hunt, butcher his game, cook, tan hides and dress furs, handle his single-shot muzzle-loading long rifle with deadly accuracy in hunting or in battle, make his moccasins and clothing, stand guard, wrangle mules, make trails through unexplored country, and anticipate the wiles of tricky Injuns. He was dependent upon himself; he had no employer to hand him wages. He traded his furs for the necessary arms, ammunition, and traps, and made his hunts wherever he liked. He stood on his own feet, even though the toes might be frozen off. He was independent as a hog on ice.

Priding himself upon his endurance, courage, and skill, the free trapper always asserted himself at rendezvous with unflinching self-assurance. He was always ready to accept a challenge to a contest in riding, horse-racing, wrestling, shooting, gambling at 'old sledge' with horse-hide cards on a blanket, or swilling raw alcohol from the camp kettle. He could not endure to have any man get the best of him. He would fight anyone — Britisher, Frenchman, Spaniard, Injun, 'breed, or human — at the drop of the hat.

Like any Blackfoot, the free trapper adored his horse. On his saddle-horse he depended for meat in the mad scramble of the buffalo hunt. It was his safety in flight, and his victory in battle. On its speed he wagered all his hard-won peltries at the rendezvous, matching his horse against those of trapper and redskin. When he had to make tracks through the mountains, the horse carried him through, or — if that was impossible — provided the steaks which saved him from starvation.

Next to his horse and his rifle, the free trapper cherished his squaw. When he womaned, he generally chose the handsomest girl in the Injun camp, or the daughter of a chief. He had his pick of the gals, for a free trapper's wife was not only spared much of the drudgery of her sisters, but occupied a far more exalted social position. The lordly manners of the free trapper extended to his wife; he treated her with a lavish generosity unknown to the squaws of ordinary men. He mounted her upon a handsome spotted pony, high-pommeled Crow saddle studded with brass tacks, or a silver-plated Mexican tree with a horn as big as a dinner-plate, with long-fringed, gaily beaded saddle-bags and a Spanish bridle dripping silver pendants, hair tassels, and hawks'-bells. He dressed her in expensive blue broadcloth (buckskins were too cheap and common for him), covered with elk teeth, with scarlet leggins and blanket, bright-beaded moccasins, and a silk handkerchief tied over her head. Her arms jangled with bracelets, her neck was hung with beads, and her ears were heavy with earrings galore. Her very face was bright with costly imported Chinese vermilion. And around her waist she wore a belt studded with silver bosses the size of teacups, ending in a 'tail' reaching to the ground and covered with silver plates, like the girdle of some medieval queen. The free trapper was as proud of his woman as he was of his horse.

He was the knight-errant of the Rockies, the lone rider, the solitary hero, the gentleman poacher on Injun preserves — man himself. The proudest title in the mountains was that of Free Trapper.

Yet the free trappers could not carry on the big business of the fur trade. The volume of that business was too great, and the free trapper was anything but a businessman. The industry was carried on by the fur companies, which could operate on a larger scale, finance exploration, exploitation, and transport, and supply even the free trapper with the credit and outfit necessary in his lonely enterprises.

Of these, the Rocky Mountain Fur Company founded by Ashley and Henry was long first in the field, reaping a rich profit year after year, though the company itself changed hands. That company soon paid the penalty for its success. Wheresoever the carrion is, there will the eagles be gathered together. The American Fur Company was formed, established posts on the Upper Missouri, and set out to wrench the business from the hands of Ashley's pioneers.

While Old Bill Williams was besting the Blackfeet, and Jedediah Smith's bones bleached on the Cimarron Desert, Thomas Fitzpatrick, striking north along the Rockies from Santa Fe, was struggling to bring the season's supplies to rendezvous on Green River. But he found he had gone the long way round through Santa Fe, and the season was late as he pushed along through the foothills towards the North Platte. Fitzpatrick was a man born to bad luck. His Injun name, at that time, was given him because of it. His gun had exploded, shattering his hand, so that he was known as Broken Hand, or Bad Hand. Wherever he went, bad luck pursued him.

While Broken Hand plodded northward, his partners — Sublette, Bridger, Gervais, and Fraeb — were anxiously waiting for him to appear. They had their own furs, and were eager to barter goods for the furs of free trappers and Injuns, too. But Broken Hand did not show up. Day after day they waited, but still no pack-train hove in sight. Their trappers were starving for coffee, sugar, salt, tobacco, and whiskey. And at last, fearing the competition of their rivals of the American Fur Company — Drips, Vanderburgh, and Fontenelle — they sent Fraeb, with Nelson, Evarts, Reese, and Joe Meek, to look for the lost partisan. It was late summer, 1831.

This little party headed south, and lost themselves in the Laramie Mountains and the Black Hills. Finally they encountered Fitzpatrick on the North Platte. From there they all pushed on to the rich game country along Powder River. There they made the winter camp, set up their lodges, erected their stretching frames and prepared the graining blocks for dressing furs, cut cottonwood boughs for their animals' forage, and settled down for a pleasant season of trading, hunting, and trapping. No hostile Injuns were there to trouble them.

But here came the partisans of the American Fur Company, cutting into their hunting grounds, bribing their trappers to secure information as to good beaver country, winning over their Injun customers by cutting prices, stealing their trade. Drips and Vanderburgh were about as welcome there as wolverines that winter. In fact that was what their rivals dubbed them, using the Injun term for that pestiferous varmint — 'weasel-bears.'

As everyone knows, the wolverine is past-master of wanton and malignant destruction. It will set off traps, steal food, tear open caches, and rend to shreds anything it can get its claws into. What it cannot destroy it commonly defiles. Fitzpatrick and Sublette, Fraeb and Gervais, felt that there was a certain aptness in the term as applied to the men of the American Fur Company. Weasel-bears!

They decided to hit the trail, slip away, and leave the varmints to their own devices. One night they slapped the packs upon their animals, quietly left Powder River, and lit out for Snake River, some four hundred miles to the west across the ranges. There they spent the winter with the friendly Nez Percé and Flathead Indians, trading, trapping, unmolested by weasel-bears.

They made the spring hunt along the Snake, up Salt River, and on the John Day (then called Gray) River. They had agreed to make the summer rendezvous at Pierre's Hole, famous for its scenery, its abundant grass and water — and its rattlesnakes! That would be in 1832.

Crossing the divide to Bear River, Fitzpatrick and his friends ran head on into Drips and Vanderburgh again! Trapper vocabularies were strained to the utmost to express what they felt then. They voted to put out and make tracks to some other region immediately. By that time the hostility of the men of the two companies was such that no man dared venture alone into the camp of the other company. A trapper who had changed sides would have met a bad end.

Before Broken Hand and his friends could start, Milton Sublette met with misfortune. He had admired the daughter of Chief Gray, and the Indian father, believing the white man meant no good, became enraged and stabbed Milton. He was so severely wounded that he could not be moved.

But great stakes were being wagered on that year's trade, and Captain Billy Sublette could not linger, even

JOSEPH L. MEEK

to nurse his own brother back to health. The outfit went on, leaving young Joe Meek to care for Milton. He lay in the lodge for forty days. But Joe Meek, witty, good-natured, kindly, and bold, made an ideal nurse. At the end of forty days he had Milton Sublette on horseback and headed for Pierre's Hole.

Meanwhile, Captain Sublette had set out for St. Louis to buy and bring out the goods for trade at rendezvous. No time was to be lost, what with Vanderburgh and Drips already in the neighborhood, and Fontenelle on the trail to bring goods from Fort Union. It was a race between pack-trains — and what a race it was!

One who has never traveled with a pack-train, or has only watched a string of mules, each plodding along under a hundred and fifty pounds of baggage, would think such a race could not be very exciting. True, the train was not built for speed, and the trails were anything but broad highways. Yet a fortune awaited the man who first arrived at rendezvous and pre-empted the trade of the Injuns, free trappers, and *engagés*. And it proved quite as exacting to make the best time with a pack-train as with any other form of transport — maybe more. As the crow flies, it was all of twelve hundred miles from St. Louis to Pierre's Hole. By the trail, it was easily half again as far!

Sublette organized his train upon an almost military basis. The outfit consisted of sixty mounted men and one hundred and eighty pack-animals, laden with everything used in the mountains — rifles, pistols, knives, lead, powder, flints and bullet-molds, camp kettles, tin cups, frying-pans, blankets, red strouding, broadcloth, beads, rings, paints, mirrors, awls, gewgaws of all kinds, tobacco, and fiery undiluted alcohol in small flat kegs to fit the pack-saddle of a plodding mule. Every one of those animals carried a load worth a hundred dollars; every one would return to St. Louis, if Sublette beat Fontenelle to the Hole, with close upon a thousand dollars' worth of beaver on its back. The prize was worth the trouble.

Sublette rode first, picking the trail. He was the 'booshway' (bourgeois), or boss. Following him came a lively mule toting three small trunks filled with the papers and contracts, the books and articles of agreement belonging to the Rocky Mountain Fur Company. After them trailed the pack-animals, with a camp-keeper to look after each group of three or four. Far ahead the hunters ranged, looking sharp for fresh meat on the hoof. At the end of the column rode a few squaws and children, and at the tail of all the second in command, the 'little booshway.' It was his job to keep the column closed up, to pick up lost articles, and to prevent straggling. So they pushed on up the Platte, day after day.

Well before sunset, the booshway halted, dismounted, and sat down to smoke his pipe. The camp-keepers led their mules into a circle round him, removed the packs, and unsaddled. Meanwhile the little booshway had scoured the country all round on a fleet horse, looking for Injun sign. Satisfied that all was safe, he returned, and the pack-animals and horses were turned loose to graze, under the eyes of a horse-guard. The meat brought in by the hunters was divided, the separate messes built their cooking-fires, and the men ate supper. Before the night closed down, the horse-guard brought in the animals, and the men staked them out within the circle of packs. If they feared attack, the animals might be hobbled as well as staked.

At every halt the booshway, or his lieutenant, made it a practice to inspect the backs of the horses, especially the pack-animals, to make sure they had not become sore or galled. This was most important, for a horse or mule with a sore back was always likely to be ruined, and in any case lost much of its spirit and go. Sublette took pains to treat every gall-sore he found, even altering the saddles or making new ones if necessary. The man whose animals were found ill-cared-for was likely to be docked a week's wages.

Sublette also inspected the arms of the men with strict regularity. A dirty rifle, an empty shot-pouch, were enough to bring severe penalties upon the man who had neglected his duty. Sublette knew that, before they reached Pierre's Hole, they were bound to run into Blackfeet.

Steadily Sublette advanced, making good time.

To his comrades in the mountains, the pace seemed slow enough. They were in contact with Drips and Vanderburgh, watching their every move. They knew that Fontenelle was making all the time he could. They sent Fitzpatrick to meet Sublette and hurry him forward.

Broken Hand rode hard, leading a fast saddler with a light pack, so that he always had a fresh horse. He met

Sublette on the Platte, below the mouth of Laramie River. Sublette and he hastened on. On the way they met some stranded trappers belonging to Captain Gant's bankrupt company, bought their furs for a song, and took them along. Sublette urged Broken Hand to hurry back to the Hole and let the partners know that he was coming. Sublette and Fontenelle were getting into the home stretch now, though neither had any way of knowing which was nearer the goal.

One night, when encamped on Wind River, Sublette and his men were roused from sleep by a cloud of yelling, shooting, robe-waving Injuns, who swept by them, trying to run off their horses. For a moment the air seemed full of flying lead and deadly arrows. Then the savage mob was gone, as if it had never been. Not a man was wounded, owing to Sublette's unremitting vigilance. A few horses had broken away and leaped over the barrier, frantic with the racket made by the redskins, but most of the stock was unhurt. The raid had proved a failure.

Sublette knew from the moccasin tracks that the marauders were Blackfeet, though Wind River was south of their usual range. He took the trouble to explain all this to Wyeth, a New England greenhorn, who had set out for the West, and gladly took advantage of Sublette's offer of protection on the way.

After this attack, everything went off as usual next morning. At dawn, the little booshway, Campbell, roused the men, calling to them to turn out. Then he mounted and scouted the country round for Injun sign. By the time he came back, the men were up and ready to turn out the horses and mules to graze — this time under a strong guard. While the animals nipped off the prairie grass, the men had breakfast and prepared for the trail. Then the animals were driven in, saddled, packed, and the train set out once more. That day the little booshway had no trouble in keeping the men from straggling!

Fitzpatrick now decided to start back and reassure the partners at Pierre's Hole. With two fast horses he set out alone, confident that he could outrun any cussed Blackfeet who might cross his path. On the prairie, where a fast horse can show his speed and a clean pair of heels to enemies, he might have done that — even in daylight. But Fitzpatrick was now in the mountains, where speed counted less for safety than on the plains. An Indian, under such circumstances, would lay low by day, and make tracks in the darkness. But Broken Hand neglected to follow the mountain man's rule — *when in Injun country, do as the Injuns do.* He rode by day, and as a result he had the adventure of his life!

Filled with his good news, eager to reassure his friends in Pierre's Hole, he hurried up what afterward became the Oregon Trail. From the Sweetwater he rode through the South Pass, and reached the valley of the Big Sandy. There he saw a party of mounted men. Broken Hand knew all that region was filling up with trappers gathering for the rendezvous; the horsemen rode like trappers. He wondered who they were: free trappers, men of his own company, or hirelings of those pests, the weasel-bears?

Before he could decide, the query was answered for him. The horsemen halted, were staring at him. Then they came rushing towards him on the dead run, and the war-whoop beat upon his eardrums. Hostile Injuns! Black-feet, like as not! Broken Hand did not linger to find out.

Like an Indian, Broken Hand had been riding his pack-horse, leading his fast saddler. Swiftly he slid from the saddle, let the pack-horse go, and jumped upon the fresh horse. Then he struck his spurs into the ribs of the animal and was away. By hard riding and unusual luck, he threw the Injuns off his trail. They had stopped to catch the horse left behind, the animal had been alarmed by their charge, and dodged about the valley, avoiding capture. This little diversion delayed them, and Broken Hand made good use of that brief respite. Before they could find him, he had covered his trail and was hidden securely in a small cañon.

Waiting there seemed trying business, when he might be making trail for safety and camp. After a few hours he could stand it no longer. He mounted and carefully picked his way out of the cañon, heading back into the main trail towards rendezvous. That was his second mistake.

The Blackfeet, knowing the country, were on the alert. Within an hour they caught sight of him again. This time he had no pack-horse to delay them; his pursuers laid the quirt on their fleet ponies, and the race was on. On the plains, Broken Hand might have won. But in the moun-tains he had to race up hill and down, and his horse, already tired from the earlier race that day, could not maintain its speed. The Blackfeet gained and gained, risking their necks and the lives of their ponies in a mad chase through the rocks. At last the white man's horse began to gasp and heave. Fitzpatrick saw that the animal was done for, stumbling up the slope. He jumped from the saddle as the horse slowed down, and scrambled off among the rocks on his own feet, clutching his rifle.

Once more the Blackfeet, coming up, delayed to catch the abandoned animal. Once more the sacrifice of his horse saved Fitzpatrick's life. He blundered into a hole among the boulders, where some varmint had made its den in former years. A litter of sticks, bones, and earth lay heaped before the opening. Fitzpatrick crawled into the hole and drew the sticks in after him.

None too soon. The Blackfeet, scrambling up the slope, scurried past his hiding-place, never suspecting how nearly they had missed taking the white man's hair. Fitzpatrick remained crouching, cramped in his evil-smelling den, aching and wondering, torn with hope and fear, hour after hour, not daring to stick his nose out. The endless day ended at last. Darkness swept suddenly down over the mountains, and Broken Hand warily pushed aside the filth and sticks which covered him.

Outside, he breathed deeply, and scanned the dark hills, wishing he could remember the way back to the trail. After some consideration, he decided to follow down the creek in the valley below him. He did so, walking as noiselessly as a ghost. . . . But once more luck was against him.

As he crept downstream through the brush, suddenly the gray lodges of the Blackfoot camp loomed against the dark trunks of the trees. He had stumbled into the very camp of his enemies!

The man's heart must have choked him then. He froze, stood silent and motionless as one of the trees themselves. No dog barked, no horse nickered; there was no hint of a guard prowling through the brush. Warily, Broken Hand sneaked back the way he had come, with silent steps, putting his moccasined feet down like a cat, like an Injun, like a mountain man unused to slogging the earth with brutal hard-leather boots. He slipped away, undiscovered, and hastened back to find refuge once more in that dank, stinking hole between the rocks, among the bones and bear-lice of his cramping den. He stayed there all the morning.

Once more he heard the Blackfeet scouring the hillsides for him, and trembled to think that in the darkness he might have left traces of his coming. But at length the noise left him. No sound of voices reached his ears. He crept out and peered down into the valley.

There he saw a group of Blackfeet. They were yelling and singing and enjoying themselves hugely. A horse-race was about to come off. They had matched their best pony against the white man's captured saddler. The Injun jockeys, stripped to their gee-strings, with their braids tied up out of the way, laid their quirts to the flanks of the horses. *Go!* They swept down the straight course neck and neck, in a cloud of dust. At the finish, Broken

Hand's horse came in first. That was cold comfort to him now.

Having studied the lay of the land, he crept back into the hole. He was starving, having had nothing to eat for two days. Fitzpatrick tightened his belt, and when darkness fell slipped out of the hole again. This time he kept along the hillside above the Blackfoot camp until he had left it far behind. Then he descended to the creek again, lay down and drank, then hurried on through the valley. He knew it was all of two hundred miles to his camp in Pierre's Hole.

All that night he plodded on, and at dawn hid himself deep in some brush. There, worn out, he passed the third day, hungry as a bear but afraid to move out of his thicket to look for food. He dared not fire his rifle: the sound would bring his enemies upon him.

That night he set out again. When the sun rose, he was desperate. He could not go on forever without food. Surely, he thought, the Blackfeet had given him up by this time; he must have passed far beyond the range of their scouts. Daring, or too reckless to care, Broken Hand kept on through the daylight, on the lookout for anything he could find to eat. He found some berries and roots to fill his stomach, but did not dare to risk firing his rifle.

Then he reached Green River. The water was cold and deep, he was weak, and besides he had to keep his powder dry. Laboriously he went to work, and managed to make a raft of driftwood. On this he put his rifle and shot-pouch, and set out across the river, poling and paddling as best he might. But when the swift water in mid-stream caught the frail, haphazard raft, it promptly went to pieces. Fitzpatrick found himself struggling in the water, saw his rifle and shot-pouch slide into the stream, and with difficulty saved himself. When he came out, cold and dripping, chilled to the bone, he had no weapon but the butcher-knife in his belt.

Not daring to build a fire to dry his clothing, he pushed on, staggering along, his teeth chattering with the chill of a mountain night. He kept moving, being too wretched to sleep. As the hours passed, the fear of the Blackfeet faded from his thoughts and the fear of starvation dominated them.

'One night, while digging for an edible root in a swamp, a pack of wolves came down upon him, and he escaped only by climbing a tree, where he remained till daylight. Then they moved off, intent upon some other quest, and he descended and went on. He came upon the carcass of a buffalo that had been killed and partly eaten by wolves. Scraping from the bones what meat remained, he cooked it in a hollow of the earth by a fire made by rubbing two sticks together. . . . But as the days passed he found food scarcer; there were no berries and no roots.'[1]

Finally, Fitzpatrick was so weak he could not get up, he could only creep along. This, he thought, was the end of everything. He was helpless. He was doomed. He was so thin he could count the knobs on his backbone from the front. His own mother would not have known him.

Still, he could at least die in peace, he thought. But luck, as usual, was against him, even then.

Two horsemen swam into his blurred vision. They saw him, wheeled their horses round, let out a whoop of joy, and rushed towards him. He could see from their faces that they were Injuns!

IX. THE BATTLE OF PIERRE'S HOLE

THE year 1832 was much the most eventful in the history of the fur trade. In midsummer the Rocky Mountain Fur Company held its annual rendezvous in Pierre's Hole. That beautiful open valley, spreading its grassy prairies for almost thirty miles along the headwaters of Snake River, laced by rushing mountain streams, and overhung by the far-off majestic, snowcapped peaks of the Tetons, was an ideal place for the fur fair of the trappers. Teton Pass near-by gave easy access from Jackson's Hole across the range. There was an abundance of grass for the horses, good water, and thick timber and brush along the streams, especially where these had been widened by the dams of the industrious beaver. Pierre's Hole was, besides, not distant from the richest fur country in all the Rockies — the richest, but also the most dangerous — the hunting grounds of the implacable Blackfeet.

That summer the valley was the scene of one of the bloodiest battles in which mountain men ever engaged.

When Captain William Sublette arrived, early in July, bringing with him a party of sixty men and the year's supply of goods, he found hundreds of friendly Flathead and Nez Percé Indians encamped in the valley, and also — to his intense disgust — those inescapable interlopers, Drips and Vanderburgh, of the rival American Fur Company, already on the ground. Fortunately, their colleague Fontenelle, who was bringing their trade goods from Fort Union, had not yet pulled in. The valley also contained the camps of Sublette's trappers, employees of the Rocky Mountain Fur Company, to the number of nearly two hundred men, besides scattered lodges of free trappers.

Sublette's first words were a question: 'Whar's Broken Hand?'

The mountain men shook their beards. They could not tell. Fitzpatrick had not come in. 'Gone under, maybe,' was all they could say.

William Sublette, who had had a sharp brush with the cussed Injuns himself only a few nights before, and whose brother Milton had been severely wounded earlier that season, was mightily discontented with that news. He was secretly afraid that the Blackfeet, among whom he included the even more hostile Gros Ventres of the Prairie, had taken the scalp of his missing friend and partner in the fur business. But that business could not be postponed; the trappers were ready and eager for trade, and half starving for a swig of the likker in Sublette's flat kegs. Besides, Fontenelle might come along now any time, and throw his goods upon the market. And so Sublette opened his packs.

'Maybeso the old coon will turn up agin after all,' he

declared, comforting himself. 'He knows a thing or two, I reckon.'

The trade began. Then Sublette, having first seen to it that every one of his own men was outfitted for the coming season, opened his kegs. He soon had all the beaver in sight — one hundred and sixty-eight pack. The camps were full of carousing trappers, who spent their days gambling, pony-racing, quarreling, chasing Indian women, and so made the most of their annual holiday, their one release from the strict vigilance and hardship of their dangerous lives.

In the middle of this wild revelry, Antoine Godin and another Iroquois hunter rode into camp. Behind one of them, clinging to the cantle of the Spanish saddle, rode a white man, thin as a rail, red-eyed and ragged, and — what was simply amazing in those days — unarmed! This emaciated scarecrow claimed to be Fitzpatrick, and told a harrowing tale of how he had been stripped of everything by the cussed Blackfeet, how he had barely survived on a meager diet of roots and rosebuds, until his luck turned and he ran into those Iroquois. For a while his partners could hardly recognize him, for his long hair had turned as white as snow. From that day Fitzpatrick was commonly known as White Head.

Within a week's time the trappers' 'beaver' was all gone, they were sober again, and the rendezvous began to break up. On July 17 Milton Sublette led a party out, heading towards Snake River and the country north of the Great Salt Lake. This small brigade consisted of fifteen trappers belonging to the Rocky Mountain Fur Company, Sinclair and his fifteen free trappers, and Nathaniel Wyeth's dwindled band of eleven Yankee greenhorns, who — unable to handle a long rifle or pack a horse, and mightily alarmed by the dangers of Indian warfare — trailed along with the mountain men to save their scalps.

Sublette's little party started late, and moved only eight miles that day. They were sluggish after their week's debauch, and their leader ordered a halt before they were out of the Hole. That night a few Flatheads, led by a minor chief, joined the party. The Flatheads wished to travel with the mountain men in such dangerous country; their tribe had been decimated by the Blackfeet.

But if the men in that camp had dreamed how dangerous the spot was, they would have pushed on all night. A horde of hostile Indians were heading straight for Milton Sublette's camp, a party of the same redskins who had attacked William Sublette on his way to the Hole and had run off some of his horses.

These Indians were not, strictly speaking, Blackfeet, but Atsena, or Gros Ventres of the Prairie, close allies of the Blackfeet. Since their own language was difficult and little known, they generally talked to strangers in the tongue of the Blackfeet, with whom they fought and hunted. Therefore the mountain men lumped both tribes under the one name, Blackfeet.

The Atsena got their name Big Bellies from their habit of stuffing themselves, uninvited, in every tipi where they could find anything to eat. They filled the seats at every feast, and were inveterate beggars. Even the Arapahos, their blood brothers, dubbed them Spongers. And this thieving trait was the first cause of their continual fighting with the mountain men. No other tribe ever gave the trappers so much trouble.

The remnant of the tribe now at Fort Belknap, Montana, seems not to have any tradition of this fight. They are notoriously bad historians, and never kept a tribal winter count or calendar. Moreover, only two years after the Battle of Pierre's Hole, smallpox wiped out most of these people, including the bands immediately concerned. However, their kinsmen, the Arapahos, have better tribal memories. And as the Gros Ventres on this occasion were returning home from a friendly visit to the Arapahos, then on the Arkansas River in Colorado, and had a few Arapaho families traveling with them, I am able to add something from Arapaho lore to the white men's account of this fight.

The Arapahos say that the Gros Ventres were formerly poor in horses, as many northern tribes were, since the best animals were only to be had by raiding the vast herds in the Spanish settlements. About 1825, the Gros Ventres had made their first visit to their kinsmen in the South, and, in fighting their way north again through the territory of hostile tribes, were stripped of the horses the Arapahos had given them, and reached home as poor as ever. This bitter experience made them very savage, and they became desperate warriors. It also made them eager to revisit the Arapahos in order to beg more horses, and they did this every two or three years, as a regular thing. In 1832, they had made such a visit, and, in order to defend themselves along the way had got up a large party of several hundred lodges.

On their way back they attacked William Sublette's party one night on Green River, and ran off some of his horses. Those who had distinguished themselves in this raid, or had captured horses, were naturally eager to get home to dance and show off. As they neared their own hunting grounds, these people became impatient and pushed on ahead of the main camp. They left their heavy baggage and slow horses behind with their relatives, and, taking only a few of the best animals, struck out along the range to the north. Besides the horses, they had some scarlet blankets, abalone shells, and other plunder obtained from the Arapahos who traded at Bent's Old Fort. Parts of two bands made up this party, led by a chief, Baihoh.

In their haste these Indians, all by now well seasoned to the trail, were up and moving much earlier than Sublette's trappers, who were sluggish and soft after their week's debauch. And so, when the Indians came pouring down out of the hills on the morning of July 18, they saw the white men still in camp below them.

Chief Baihoh had been told by Kenneth 'Red Coat' McKenzie, bourgeois of the American Fur Company at Fort Union, to be on the lookout for his clerk, Fontenelle, who would be in Pierre's Hole about this time. When Baihoh saw the white men encamped there he naturally thought they were Fontenelle's men, and rode down to meet them. For of course the Blackfeet and all their sponging allies were hand in glove with McKenzie.

That morning Milton Sublette, still sore from his wound, with a pipe stuck into his long, scarred face, stalked about keeping a lookout, while his men made ready to move out. Suddenly he caught sight of some far-off moving objects streaming down from the hills. Sublette guessed they must be the men of Fontenelle's party, which he was expecting, and grinned to think that he had completed the trade before his rivals could reach the rendezvous. Other men thought them buffalo. But Wyeth, true to his training on the Yankee seaboard, pulled out his long brass spy-glass, squinted through it for a long moment, and uttered one ominous word: 'Indians.'

The men dropped their work then. All eyes were fixed upon that savage cavalcade.

The Indians, most of them afoot, were in two parties. Eagerly the trappers counted heads. Wyeth, staring through his glass, estimated one hundred and fifty. Nobody saw any reason to dispute his calculation.

Concealment was now out of the question. The Indians had already seen them — that was clear. They came down the slopes, yelling and whooping, moved out into the open, and halted just out of range.

At first the trappers could not tell whether they were Crows or Blackfeet. Their women wore the short skirts of the Crows, but their men affected coarse fringes at sleeve-end and shoulder-seam like the Blackfeet. Moreover, they had no uniform way of dressing their hair. Some wore pompadours or bangs, like the Crows; others had long braids and scalplocks like the Sioux and Arapahos. But when their chief rode forward carrying the long pipe, and yelled aloud across the grass, all doubt was ended.

A dozen mountain men muttered the same word together: 'Blackfeet!'

Wyeth's Yankee greenhorns quizzed the mountain men as to what that meant: 'Blackfeet?'

'Injuns — and the meanest kind at that,' was the gruff answer. The trappers knew there was bound to be a hard fight.

The Arapahos do not believe that Baihoh was meditating treachery that morning. They say that if the chief had suspected he was confronting McKenzie's hated competitors, he would never have risked his life by advancing alone with only a pipe in his hand, especially as the Indians outnumbered the whites so much. Nor would he have brought his women and children down out of the hills into danger. They say, too, that the noisy approach of the Indians is proof of their friendly intentions, since Indian enemies always try to sneak up on their foes, making as little noise as possible. That is the Arapaho belief.

What Sublette and Wyeth thought has not been recorded. There had been so much bloodshed between mountain men and Blackfeet that they could hardly have any faith in truces. To them, the noisy approach of the tribesmen may have seemed the sheer arrogance of overwhelming numbers about to annihilate a few helpless victims, and the offer of the pipe a trick to enable the chief to learn all he could before the battle was joined. They must have known that the mere presence of the Flatheads in their camp would be enough to make enemies of the Blackfeet. Sublette was convalescent, and Wyeth a greenhorn. But, whatever they thought, matters were immediately taken out of their hands.

Among the mountain men stood Antoine Godin, the Iroquois hunter, whose own father had been murdered by these very Indians on a little stream, thereafter known as Godin Creek. He stared grimly at the lone chieftain.

'Looks like the cussed Injun wants to talk,' someone suggested. Nobody offered to go forward for the parley.

Godin spoke up, grimly: '*I'll* talk to him.'

Turning to the Flathead who stood at his elbow, rifle in hand, Godin snapped out a brief question: 'Is your piece charged?'

The Flathead glanced quickly at his Iroquois friend. 'It is,' he answered.

'Then cock it and follow me,' Godin replied.

The two of them mounted and rode out abreast to meet the chief halfway: Godin, lithe and swarthy in his fancy buckskins and wool hat, the stocky Flathead with two eagle feathers in the long black hair which flowed down over the shoulders of his fringed scalp-shirt.

Baihoh must have had misgivings as he saw the Flathead coming forward. But if he did, he scorned to show them. He sat his pony, swathed to the waist in a scarlet blanket, with the broad band of bright quillwork across it. On his left arm rested the long stem of the peace-pipe.

Godin rode up on the chief's right hand, the Flathead rode up on his left. Baihoh extended his right hand in friendship. Godin's eyes never left the chief's face. He reached out, grasped the Indian's hand, held it tight. Without looking round he shouted, 'Fire!'

Instantly the Flathead threw up his barrel, gloated for a split second over the shock in Baihoh's face, then fired. Baihoh tumbled from his saddle in a cloud of white smoke. The Flathead whirled his pony round and galloped away. A great howl of grief and rage burst from the throats of the Gros Ventres. Their bullets whistled angrily around the Iroquois.

But Godin, in bravado, whooped in triumph, and, leaning from his saddle, snatched the corner of the dead man's scarlet blanket up, dragged it from under him, and loped away, trailing the blood-red trophy. He and the Flathead both regained their own party unhurt.

By that time the mountain men were returning the fire of the enraged Indians. And as soon as the redskins had recovered from the surprise of seeing their chief shot down, they scuttled for the nearest cover. This was a wide swamp, caused by beavers' damming the stream. The swamp was overgrown with brush, willows and cotton-woods, vines and weeds, all thickly entangled and matted together. Within this thicket the Indians found cover: the men covering the retreat of the women and children; the women hastily raising a 'fort' of logs and branches, and digging trenches with their knives behind that rude breastwork. The mountain men, finding the Indians all armed with McKenzie's Mackinaw guns, and good shots, took shelter in a ravine which ran across the front of the Indian position, and kept firing into the brush.

The Downeasters with Wyeth were wholly unused to such warfare, and exposed themselves recklessly, without being of the least use. Wyeth promptly got them out of the way. He caught up all his horses, tied them up at a safe distance, under cover and out of sight. Then he made a breastwork of his packs, made his men lie down behind it, and ordered them not to leave their post under any circumstances. He himself took his rifle and went off to join the fray.

Meanwhile, the Flathead chief and Milton Sublette had sent off a number of horsemen, hard as they could ride, to carry the news to rendezvous and bring back reinforcements. They covered the eight miles at top speed, and dashed through the scattered camps, yelling at the top of their voices, 'Blackfeet! Blackfeet! Up the valley! Git your guns and come a-runnin'!'

Unhappily, many of William Sublette's men were as green to Indian warfare as Wyeth's Yankees — *vide-poche* Frenchmen from Carondelet, St. Louis. He knew they would only be in the way, and ordered them to stay and watch the camp. He and Robert Campbell peeled off their coats, rolled up their sleeves, forked their horses, and sped away to the fight, with a pistol in one hand and a rifle in the other. On the way each made a verbal will, each naming the other his executor.

When the Gros Ventres saw these hundreds of enemies swarming across the prairies, they fell back into their fort, which was completely hidden in the brush. By that time many of their women and children had already taken to their heels, and were hitting the trail back to the main camp of their people, or hiding in the timber on the mountain-sides. Meanwhile, the mountain men had been repulsed. A half-breed had been severely wounded, and the others hung back. They could not see the Gros Ventres, while the Indians had a clear field of fire. Even the cream of the friendly tribes, eager as they were to strike their hated enemies, were reluctant to run across the open and charge blindly into the brush.

When Captain William Sublette rode up, he called for an attack. He, at any rate, would not hang back. He told his brothers of the will he had just made, and rushed into the thickets. Robert Campbell went in after him, and also Sinclair, the partisan of the free trappers. Only those three, of all the men present, dared to attack. Godin and the Flathead chief proved to be as cowardly as they had been treacherous. Campbell, Sublette, and Sinclair kept going forward, yelling to their men to follow. After a time, others advanced.

Struggling through the brush, the three leaders found themselves facing the open space beyond which the Indians had entrenched themselves. Their improvised 'fort' was simply a breastwork of logs and branches, and its low shelter was extended upward by a curtain of buffalo robes, scarlet blankets, and lodge-covers, which concealed, though it could not protect, the warriors behind it. The brush was so thick that every movement of the white men disturbed it, and so the Indians could see them coming.

Sinclair by this time was in the lead, gently parting the branches as he crept forward. A puff of smoke bloomed from a crevice in the Indian fort. Sinclair jerked back, shot through the body. Campbell lay nearest, and Sinclair, turning to face him, begged, 'Take me to my brother.' Then he fainted.

Campbell crept forward, caught hold of Sinclair's leg, and dragged him back. When he reached the men behind, he let them take the wounded man. They carried him out of the swamp. Then Campbell rejoined his friend Sublette.

All this time Sublette had been snaking his way to the front. Made cautious by Sinclair's disaster, the Captain lay still and studied the Indian defenses, trying to find the loopholes through which the warriors were firing. Suddenly he saw an Indian eye peeping through one of these. Quickly he raised his rifle, fired, and struck the Indian square in the eye. With a grin he turned to Campbell, pointing to the opening. 'Watch that hole,' he whispered, hastily reloading, 'and you'll soon have a fair chance for a shot.' He stood behind a cottonwood to ram home the charge.

Before he could reload, an Indian fired. Sublette was hit in the shoulder. He moved his arm up and down, making sure that the bone was not broken. Then he grew faint, and sagged to the ground. Campbell caught him up in his arms and boldly carried him out of the swamp.

Strangely enough, the ball that passed through Sublette's shoulder also wounded a man behind him in the head.

Warmed to their work by the courage and by the wounding of their leaders, the mountain men began to pour a steady fire upon the Indian fort. They surrounded it, firing from every side. Wyeth, who was leading a group of Nez Percés, found himself endangered by the cross-fire of his own comrades. One of his Indian allies was shot down at his elbow — and the bullet had come from the rifle of a trapper beyond the fort. The hostile Indians did not fire often; they were running short of powder: but when they did fire, somebody was hit. They kept doggedly inside their fort; they gave no quarter, and they expected none. All that day the siege went on.

The Flatheads and Nez Percés, seeing their enemies in the fort were doomed, now took courage, and dared each other to count a *coup*. Now and then one of them, to show off his bravery, ran swiftly up to the Blackfoot fort, snatched down a red blanket or a buffalo robe, and ran back, yelling in triumph. In this way the friendly Indians encouraged each other, and gradually reduced the cover of their enemies. But that sort of thing killed nobody; the Blackfeet lay low, protected by their logs and earthworks. And there was so little cohesion among the besiegers that no organized charge was ever made.

Sublette was tired of that. He proposed to set fire to the brush, which was dry. He sent the squaws of the friendly Indians to gather grass and brush to start the conflagration. The wind was brisk, and once started, the fire would drive their enemies out into the open. 'Burn 'em out, boys,' he said. 'That will fix 'em.'

The Flatheads and Nez Percés, however, objected earnestly to that scheme.

'No, no,' they said. 'Those Blackfeet are rich. They have been visiting, and are bringing back presents. If we burn them out, all those fine red blankets and things will be burned up too. We've got them licked; that loot is as good as ours right now. It would be foolish to burn up our own property.'

While the friendlies and the whites argued and wrangled about the matter, the Blackfeet in the fort had seen the squaws gathering grass and brush. They knew what was doing. They were desperate, and being desperate, began to taunt and threaten their enemies. Their chief began to yell.

'While we had plenty of powder and lead,' the chief shouted, 'we fought you on the open prairie. It was only when our powder ran low that we hid in the brush. We came here to die with our women and children. We are only a handful, and you are many. We know you can kill us all. You can burn us out and shoot us. What do we care? We have thrown away our bodies. But if you are hungry for fighting, just stay beside our ashes here, and you will soon get your belly full. There are four hundred lodges of our brothers headed this way. We have sent for them. They are brave, their arms are strong, and their hearts are big. They will avenge us!'

'What are they yelling?' the mountain men demanded. Then everyone with a smattering of the Blackfoot tongue tried to interpret. The translating went on for some time. It was never very clear, passing as it did through so many Flathead, Nez Percé, and Creole mouths before it was turned into broken English. But out of all that confusion of tongues one statement rang clear: 'Blackfeet! Blackfeet comin'! Heap Blackfeet! Heap big fight!'

That news was bad enough. But suddenly someone called out: 'The cussed Injuns are thar a'ready. At rendezvous! They're raidin' our camps!'

That struck alarm to the besiegers. Back there at rendezvous were their wives and children, their horses and mules, their outfits for the coming season, their clothes, their tents, their priceless 'beaver.' If the Blackfeet captured those, all would be lost!

It was late in the day. Everyone was tired, sore from the kick of the guns, powder-marked, hungry, and dry. Casualties had been heavy: Sinclair and four other mountain men had been killed, along with a half-breed and seven friendly Indians. There were at least a dozen seriously wounded; it had been a hard fight. But when the mountain men heard that danger threatened their camps at rendezvous they did not falter. They threw themselves into their saddles, and rode hell-for-leather to meet those eight hundred savage warriors thirsting for their blood.

X. VANDERBURGH'S DEATH
TRAIL

CAMPBELL and Fitzpatrick led the mountain men back to rendezvous on the dead run. There they found everything just as they had left it. No Blackfeet had been sighted thereabouts. The mountain men scoured the country around their camps, looking for fresh Injun sign. They found none, and, as darkness fell, jogged in and unsaddled where their women were at work about the dancing little cook-fires. That night the battle-weary men remained on guard at rendezvous. There was no attack. Come sunup, they knew that the Injuns in the fort had been lying, had lured them away from the fight with an empty threat, a false alarm. Angry at the deceit, they dashed back to rub out the tricky Blackfeet in the fort. Some of their men had been left there to watch it.

They all surrounded it once more, yelling defiance, and shooting into the logs and earthworks. The Blackfeet did not return their fire, and when one of the whites, bolder than the rest, went up and looked inside, he saw that the fort was empty. The Blackfeet had slipped away in the night, leaving nine dead warriors and twenty-four dead horses behind them.

The mountain men and Flatheads rushed in, ripped off the scalps, looked for the packs. But they found no scarlet blankets, no abalone shells, nor any other plunder. The Blackfeet had got away with all their valuables.

Enraged, the disappointed Flatheads, tireless and relentless as so many wolves, set out on the trail of their enemies, determined to let none escape. Many of the mountain men went with them. Here and there they came upon an abandoned, broken-down horse, a dropped pack, or the body of a warrior who had died of his wounds. The Flatheads counted *coup* on these poor relics, while they or the mountain men lifted the topknots to tie in their belts.

Suddenly they came upon a striking figure. A dead warrior lay at the foot of a great pine. Beside him, leaning against the tree, waited his woman. She was wounded, could not escape, and apparently had no wish to. She beckoned the mountain men. 'Come on, kill me!' she called. The trappers hung back, astonished at this pitiful picture.

But the Flatheads and Nez Percés never dreamed of sparing a woman, who might become the mother of an enemy. They rushed in, screeching, and struck her dead before the whites could interfere. Farther on they killed a second Blackfoot woman, overtaken while running for her life. It was not often that the Flatheads had a chance to shed Blackfoot blood with such impunity.

This pursuit brought the known loss of the Blackfeet up to sixteen dead, all told. But seeing that the fugitives were heading towards the main Blackfoot camp, the trappers and friendlies turned back. That night they rested once more in their camps at rendezvous, in Pierre's Hole.

The Arapahos say that when the fleeing Blackfeet reached their main camp on Snake River, and told their story, their relatives there were much excited. All the chiefs were called to council, and long and heated debates were held. Those whose relatives had been killed in Pierre's Hole were savagely eager to attack the white men there — or anywhere. As it happened, two large parties of mountain men were then encamped close by (Fontenelle's and Bonneville's), and the hostile party were in favor of jumping them, though they had had no part in the battle in Pierre's Hole. Some of these Indians did start off at once, and meeting a small party in Jackson's Hole killed More and Foy, wounded Stephens, and drove the others back to rendezvous.

Those Blackfeet whose relatives had not suffered in the battle were anxious to keep peace with the whites, fearing the displeasure of Kenneth 'Red Coat' McKenzie, the big boss of the American Fur Company, whose headquarters were at Fort Union. They traded with his men, and wanted no trouble with him. Taunts and reproaches flew back and forth in council, but no agreement could be reached. Finally, the chiefs compromised. They decided to leave the whites alone and go to war against the Crows. They said they would slake their thirst for vengeance in the blood of their hereditary Indian enemies. And so they let the whites alone for the time being. Sublette passed

Snake River unmolested; Bonneville and Fontenelle were not attacked. The Blackfeet moved up Wind River.

But the Crows saw them coming, ambushed them, killed forty, and scattered the rest of them like quail. After that, all the Blackfeet were in a very ugly mood.

Back in Pierre's Hole, the white men turned once more to their keen rivalries. The moment the danger from Injuns was past, the competing fur companies began to do dirt to each other. Even in the States, in those days, business was entirely unregulated. On the frontier, where there was no law but that of force or guile, the competition of the fur companies was utterly cut-throat.

Captain Sublette, having recovered from his wound, hit the trail to St. Louis with the year's harvest of furs. The other partisans of the Rocky Mountain Fur Company, Jim Bridger and Thomas Fitzpatrick, now fully equipped, were all ready to pack up, put out, and lead their brigades of trappers out of the Hole for the fall hunt. But they both knew that if they did, the less experienced leaders of the American Fur Company would follow them, hoping to be led into a land of countless beaver. And so Old Gabe Bridger and White Head Fitzpatrick had a talk with their rivals, Drips and Vanderburgh, and offered to divide the country with them. That way, neither company would get in the other's way.

But Vanderburgh and Drips were new to that region. They knew Old Gabe and White Head were old-timers, both slick as a buffalo's nose at tradin' robes, hosses, or beaver. They feared them, even bearing gifts. Maybe they figured they would have better luck following the trail of Bridger and Fitzpatrick, or maybe McKenzie had told them to have no truck with their rivals. Anyhow, they turned the offer down. Bridger and White Head were plumb disgusted. Next morning they hit the trail early, aiming to get the start of their cantankerous competitors.

Drips and Vanderburgh made tracks as fast as they could travel for Fontenelle's camp. There, after four days of busy preparation, they all parted. Fontenelle started back to Fort Union; Ferris went to the Flatheads; Drips and Vanderburgh lit out after Bridger and Fitzpatrick. That trail led down the Missouri River, from its head-waters. Once Drips found it, he clung to it. In fact, he followed so fast that one of his men, who had been wounded in Pierre's Hole, died as a result. Bridger and Fitzpatrick led Drips a stern chase.

In order to make better time, Vanderburgh let Drips go on alone with only the best men and horses, while he cached the heavy plunder and waited for word from Drips. On Drips went, gaining on his rivals, down the Jefferson Fork, clear to the Three Forks of the Missouri. There it dawned upon him that White Head and Bridger had tricked him; they had led him into a region where cactus, and not fur, was the principal crop! Discouraged, Drips turned back.

Bridger and Fitzpatrick, having got rid of Drips, now turned around and went back to trap the Madison River. They had not been there long when — to their intense exasperation — they ran into Drips and Vanderburgh again! Seemed like them cussed varmints war everywhar.

This time, Fitzpatrick did not hold in. He spoke straight from the shoulder, and told his rivals what he thought of them. Then he and Jim Bridger turned up the Madison.

Vanderburgh did not follow. He had what he wanted now. For with Fitzpatrick and Bridger there, he knew he was in good beaver country. Sensibly, he turned down the Madison, and soon after established his winter headquarters above the mouth of the Stinking Water. It was already the middle of October.

In that dangerous region the trappers, who had to work in pairs, never set traps until they had made sure that no hostile Injuns were hangin' around. The morning after making camp, Vanderburgh sent out Ferris and three others to scout over the adjacent country. Ferris had not gone far until he smelled smoke. Following the faint scent, he soon came upon the coals of a small fire — still glowing. Close beside the fire lay a freshly killed buffalo cow, with an arrow sticking in it. Not far off lay two others. All three had been cut into, but the hunters had not had time to butcher. Ferris immediately turned back to warn Vanderburgh.

Drips had already taken his own men off to trap another stream, and Vanderburgh had only fifty men in camp. He knew they would never set a trap until the menace of Injuns was removed. They were scared; many of them had had their first taste of war in the Battle of Pierre's Hole, and had never passed a winter in the mountains. So Vanderburgh made light of the alarm, and in order to show how little it troubled him he rode away with only nine men, heading fearlessly towards the deserted fire of the buffalo-hunters.

Vanderburgh found everything just as Ferris had left it. The Injuns warn't far off — that was certain. He looked over the country, which was open. But about three miles away Vanderburgh saw a clump of trees tucked in the mouth of a small cañon. There, if anywhere, was the Injun hideout. Vanderburgh led his men forward. He had to find out who those hunters were, and whether they were friends or enemies.

In that clump of trees and brush was a party of some eighty Blackfeet — that is to say, Gros Ventres of the Prairie — under the leadership of a minor chief called Bull Calf. They had all been in that unlucky mixup with the Crows, and were sore and ugly. With them was a visiting Arapaho, named Hanake-baah, Bull Thunder.

Bull Thunder had been in the Battle of Pierre's Hole, and after that had witnessed the defeat of his relatives at the hands of the Crows. He was a warrior of some standing in his own tribe, and being an Arapaho considered himself superior to the Gros Ventres. Bull Calf was his brother-in-law, and so he had the right to tease him, joke him, and make fun of him; that was the tribal custom.

Down on the Arkansas River, where he lived, Bull Thunder had learned to drink the diluted alcohol sold by the traders there. And whenever he was too far from the traders to get that, he had found that he could get a con-

siderable degree of intoxication simply by eating the gall
— that is to say, drinking the bile — of freshly killed
buffalo.

That morning, the Arapahos say, the young men had
killed several cows, and Bull Thunder had immediately
opened every carcass and swallowed the bile while it was
still warm and spicy. The others had been hungry, and
had built a fire to cook some of the meat before beginning
to butcher. While they were eating they heard a gun
fired. At once Bull Calf led them back, and they all took
cover in the clump of trees at the mouth of the cañon.
From there, Bull Calf could watch the back trail.

By that time Bull Thunder was feeling the full effect
of his bilious potations. He began to make fun of his
brother-in-law. The conversation, it seems, went about
like this:

BULL THUNDER: Well, brother-in-law, they say you are
a chief. At first I was surprised, but now I know why they
made a chief out of you. You are a regular Big Belly, a
true Sponger. Your people are always running away. I
think that is why they made you chief — you can run so
fast. When I first came up here with you from the South,
you ran away from the white men — but only after an
all-day fight. Next you ran away from the Crows — after
fighting just a little while. And now, this morning, you
run away as soon as you hear a gun go off. Brother-in-law,
if you go on like this, you will soon be head chief of all the
Big Bellies! We Arapahos use our arms sometimes; we
fight. But you people just use your legs; you are always

running. I am getting tired of that. I like to sit down once in a while. I don't like to be on the run *all* the time.

Bull Calf: Brother-in-law, you were in both those fights. I did not see you stand still. You used your legs. When we ran, you ran too. (*Bull Calf had to take saucy talk from his brother-in-law; by tribal custom he could not lose his temper. So now he grinned — a little.*)

Bull Thunder: What else could I do, all alone? But if I had been with three or four Arapahos, I should not have run. We Arapahos stand and fight, or chase the enemy. But see how you behave. Chief Baihoh was a fool, he got killed like one. An Arapaho chief would not have acted like that; he would have sent the women back, and then jumped the white men all at once. He would have killed them first, and talked to them afterward.

Bull Calf: But Baihoh thought those bad white men were our friends from the big trade-house.

Bull Thunder: Yes. And the next time some bad white men come along, *you* will think they are your friends from the big trade-house, and they will fool you, and shoot you down, and run you the same way they did Baihoh. You Spongers are all like him. First you play the fool, and then you run away. You fight like old women, and run like deer.

Bull Calf (*losing his temper*): Brother-in-law, you talk faster than I can run. You talk fire, but your words are only smoke. But what of it? You will see. And the next white men who come on my trail will see, too. I will not run. No, I will shoot. I will show you. I will use my arms. I will kill them, or make them run. They will not fool me this time. You watch!

BULL THUNDER (*looking out of the brush at the back trail*): Well, my dear brother-in-law, yonder they come. Now is your chance. (*Vanderburgh and his men had come in sight.*)

BULL CALF (*startled, but determined*): Good. Now you'll see. Friends, we will let these white men come close; then we will rush them. I want you all to see what a good fighter my brother-in-law from the South is.

BULL THUNDER: Good. When they come close, we'll all shoot together. Then we can charge. You go first, dear brother-in-law. I will be right on your heels. (*This, according to Arapaho tradition, is what was being said in the clump of trees while Vanderburgh and his nine companions were riding up.*)

At the foot of the slope crowned by the trees, a narrow, deep ravine crossed the cañon mouth. The Gros Ventres, crouching in the brush just beyond it, waited for the white men to cross that ditch.

Vanderburgh jumped his hunter across the gully. His men followed. Then all hell broke loose.

All the hidden Indians fired together, then leaped from cover, screeching and yelling, waving buffalo robes and blankets to frighten the horses, rushing forward to the attack.

At the first shot Vanderburgh's horse went down, stone-dead, pinning his right leg to the ground. Three of his men whirled away, over the ditch, and raced to safety. The Indians swarmed forward, drawing their knives, eager to count the *coup*.

Trapped as he was, Vanderburgh did not lose courage. He coolly tried to work his leg free of the dead horse, calling out, 'Boys, don't run!' At the same time he leveled his rifle at the foremost Indian. Bull Calf was coming for him, knife in hand.

Ferris already had a slug in his shoulder. He jumped the ditch and fled. Nelson leaped the gully after him. Pillon, the *voyageur*, was no horseman; his frantic mount bucked him off; before he could recover his feet two Gros Ventres had him by the hair. They stabbed and scalped him in no time.

Then Nelson looked back, saw the terrible danger of his leader, and turned his horse to recross the ravine and rescue him. Just then two slugs struck his own horse. The animal became unmanageable and plunged away, carrying Nelson to safety. Vanderburgh was left to face his enemies alone.

Even then he did not lose heart. He let Bull Calf have the ball from his rifle square in the chest. Bull Calf was dead before he hit the ground. Vanderburgh threw down his empty rifle, yanked out his pistol. But before he could fire, Bull Thunder was on him. At the same instant somebody shot him from behind, and the Arapaho stabbed him. Vanderburgh died fighting.

His death brought panic to the men in his camp. Most of them were ready to abandon everything and ride for their lives. But Ferris cowed them, made them halt and fort in a grove on the bank of the river. There they remained under arms all night, expecting an attack. Next morning, Ferris wanted to go back and bury their dead. But nobody would undertake that job, and his wound made Ferris helpless to do it single-handed. They all packed their animals and started for Horse Prairie, where they had cached their supplies.

Near the Beaver Head on Jefferson River, they saw plenty smoke rising. Again panic paralyzed them. They swerved aside to the nearest cottonwood grove, forted, and passed another anxious night. Next day they learned that the smoke came from the camps of their friends, the Flatheads and Pend d'Oreilles. Hastily the scared trappers moved into the Injun camp.

There some measure of courage and good sense returned to them. Ferris was able to organize a burial party to go back and inter the bodies of Vanderburgh and Pillon.

Meanwhile, the Gros Ventres who had killed these two men were also frightened. For when they examined the bodies they at once recognized the 'White Chief' Vanderburgh and the pork-eater Pillon. They had killed two of Red Coat McKenzie's men — two friends, with whom they traded! They were very uneasy, and began to blame the Arapaho. 'Well,' they said, 'now you've done it. You have got your brother-in-law killed and made some powerful enemies for us. This is what comes of listening to an Arapaho.'

At first they proposed to hide the bodies and tell nobody

about the affair. But the Arapaho laughed at them. He said: 'I killed this man in fair fight. Do you think I am going to keep still about that? This was a hard thing to do, and it is a good thing to tell. I can brag about this as long as I live. Besides, this white man killed my brother-in-law. I struck him, and say what you like, I am going to take his hair. After all, *I* killed him.'

So the Arapaho, Bull Thunder, went to work and scalped Vanderburgh, while the others stood around and wondered what to do. He took off, not merely the scalp, but the skin of the whole head — ears, beard, and all.

Then the Gros Ventres decided to pack the body to the trading-fort, and also the guns, and the saddle, and the clothing. They said they would return these things to Red Coat's men, and make some big presents to 'cover' the body of the man they had killed. In that way they hoped to smooth matters over.

They loaded the body across a pony and set out — actually. They were that scared. But it was a good two hundred miles to Fort McKenzie, the nearest post of the American Fur Company. After a few miles' travel they gave up that notion. They decided to leave the body, and take in only the arms and saddle. Some of them said the body ought to be hidden instead, and in order to keep it from being identified, they skinned it completely. Then they threw it into the river.

Bull Thunder, the Arapaho, having entirely lost the gall which had inspired him to outdo the Gros Ventres, now began to worry about his own danger. He refused to go to

FORT McKENZIE, WITH THE COMBAT OF 28TH AUGUST, 1833

the fort with the rest, but went off and joined another band of the same tribe, under Chief Iron-that-Moves. That chief was known to be fearless, and not too friendly to the whites. But, as it happened, by the time the other warriors reached the fort they had got over their alarm. Their fears had melted away, and they openly displayed the arms of Vanderburgh in triumph there.

When the burial party reached the scene of the fight, Vanderburgh's body could not be found. Somewhat later, the Flatheads found the bones in the water, and buried them on the bank of the river.

The death of Vanderburgh was a heavy blow to the American Fur Company: it broke up their fall hunt entirely for that year. Bridger and Fitzpatrick had the whole country to themselves. But they, too, paid a heavy penalty for trapping in Blackfoot country.

When Chief Sun heard how some of the young men of his people had killed Vanderburgh, his heart was on the ground. He called a council, and made a speech. 'This thing was not our fault,' he declared. 'We have fought with white men several times, but those we fought were always different white men, and not our friends of Red Coat's trade-house. This is a bad thing. So now, whenever we meet white men, we ought to make peace with them, and smoke, and talk, and find out who they are before anybody goes to shooting. Then we can look Red Coat in the eyes, we can shake his hand, we can smoke with him with a glad heart.'

The next time Chief Sun heard that white men were

approaching, he told his people to be friendly, and they all moved out to meet the strangers. The white men were Jim Bridger and Thomas Fitzpatrick. They halted on the prairie: the Gros Ventres moved out to meet them, but halted near some rocks, where the women and children could hide in case of a fight. Then the chief signaled that he came in peace, called to them to send a few men forward to meet him on the prairie, halfway between the two parties, to shake hands and smoke.

Bridger and Fitzpatrick were willing enough to have peace — if only the peace could be made to stick. But they were doubtful whether to smoke with the Blackfeet, after what had happened. The Blackfeet had killed their own trader, Vanderburgh; it warn't likely they would stop at tricking his rivals. The two trappers hesitated.

Then a young Mexican, Loretto, a free trapper who was traveling with them, spoke up. Loretto had an Injun wife, a handsome Blackfoot girl. She had been captured by the Crows. Loretto had ransomed her and made her his wife; their baby boy was perched on his mother's back. Loretto told Bridger and Fitzpatrick not to be afraid. 'I know those Injuns,' he declared. 'They are my wife's relatives.'

White Head Fitzpatrick nodded, and turned to Bridger. 'Well, Jim, you heard what the Spaniard said. Reckon I'll go and talk to 'em. You stay here with the packs and the men. Keep your eyes skinned. Maybeso the cussed Injuns will try to play tricks. Happen you see anything queer, holler.'

Bridger agreed. Loretto grinned. Fitzpatrick went

forward, trailed by seven lank, brown trappers, their buckskin fringes whipping through the grass. Chief Sun came forward with seven braves to meet them. He had everybody sit down first, and *then* shake hands, so that the peace would be *firm*. That done, the long pipe was lighted, passed, smoked. The palaver began; it went on and on.

Meanwhile, Loretto's wife, staring at the Indians across the way, suddenly uttered a cry of joy: 'There's my brother!' Putting her small son into her husband's arms, she ran across to her own people. They welcomed her with open arms and many caresses, as one returned from the grave.[1] It was their first reunion since she had been taken by the Crows. And when they learned that one of the trappers had rescued her, their hearts warmed and softened towards the white men. All the Blackfeet came swarming to greet her, making a commotion.

One of the braves in council saw the movement among his people, and signaled to learn what had happened. One of the young warriors rode quickly out to the council to explain it.

Seeing this move, Jim Bridger became suspicious. The young warrior on the horse had a bow in his hand. Therefore Jim mounted his own horse, and taking his rifle rode out to make the numbers at the council even. His rifle rested across the pommel of his saddle. When Bridger rode up, Chief Sun got to his feet to shake the white man's hand.

Bridger, whose eyes were on the young warrior on the

horse, saw that he had four arrows in his bow hand. Knowing how rapidly an Injun could shoot, Jim thumbed back the hammer of his rifle, in order to be ready for trouble.

The chief reached for Bridger's hand. But when his ears caught the click of Jim's rifle, the memory of how Chief Baihoh had been murdered flashed through his mind. With lightning quickness the chief grabbed the barrel of Jim's rifle, pushed the muzzle down. In that tense moment, Jim's finger automatically pressed the trigger; the charge exploded into the ground between the chief's feet.

Before the men on the ground could gain their feet, the young warrior on the horse had loosed two arrows into Bridger's back. Reeling from the pain and force of those sharp points, Jim found himself helpless against the strength of the outraged chief. Sun wrenched the rifle from his hands, swung it high, and brought the stock hard against Bridger's ear with crushing force. A sheet of flame soared up before Jim's eyes, and he went down into darkness.

The chief jumped into Jim's saddle and galloped away to rally his people. There followed a time of wild excitement. Each side rushed to cover among the rocks. Women ran, dragging screaming children after them. Men jumped back and forth like dancers, dodging the bullets of their enemies. War-whoops and the crack of rifles answered each other. The battle had begun.

Poor Loretto was thunderstruck. His Indian wife was with his enemies — he was with hers. He could see her struggling with her brother's people, trying to get away and run back to him. But they held her, they stopped her, they dragged her screaming away. He 'saw her struggles and her agony and heard her piercing cries. With a generous impulse he caught up the child in his arms, rushed forward, regardless of Indian shaft or rifle, and placed it in safety upon her bosom. Even the heart of the Blackfeet chief was reached by this noble deed. He pronounced Loretto a madman for his temerity, but bade him depart in peace. The young Mexican hesitated: he urged to have his wife restored to him, but her brother interfered, and the countenance of the chief grew dark. The girl, he said, belonged to his tribe — she must remain with her people. Loretto would still have lingered, but his wife implored him to depart, lest his life should be endangered. It was with the greatest reluctance that he returned to his companions.' [2]

Come night, the shooting ended, as each party pulled out under cover of the darkness. There was no victory, as there had been no reason for the fight. But from then on the Blackfeet and their allies the Gros Ventres saw little reason to hope for peace with the whites. And the trappers had no hopes of peace with them.

The main result of that scrape was Jim Bridger's terrific headache — and the two iron points in his back. He carried them for nearly three years. Then Jim ran into Doctor Marcus Whitman at rendezvous on Green River, in the summer of 1835, and induced the doctor to butcher out those pesky souvenirs. Jim said they tickled his old fleece a leetle too sharp. It was quite an operation, and struck admiration in the Indians who looked on. The points were of iron, made out of a frying-pan, and nearly three inches long. One of them had been bent into a hook by striking a bone and was wedged in cartilage, but the doctor finally got it out.

Loretto left Jim Bridger the first chance he got, and made tracks to Blackfoot country. There he hired out as interpreter at Fort McKenzie, one of the American Fur Company's posts, where he lived happily ever after with his handsome Blackfoot wife. Prince Maximilian saw him at Fort McKenzie in 1833.

On August 28 of that year, when six hundred Assiniboines and a hundred Crees combined to rub out the small band of Blackfeet and Gros Ventres camped about that fort, Loretto showed what stuff he was made of. With only a dozen companions he left the shelter of the fort, went boldly out upon the prairie, attacked that horde of howling savages, shot down the nephew of the Assiniboine chief, and actually prevented the enemy from carrying off the body!

Loretto was a free trapper. It took such fellows to qualify as mountain men.

XI. THE WINTER IT RAINED FIRE

NOT all the first-rate mountain men got their start under General Ashley. Theirs was a profession which attracted bold and hardy men from all quarters, from the Mexican border to the British Possessions. In fact, one of the chief centers of the fur trade was Bent's Old Fort on the Arkansas, deep in the Southwest. There, for many years, Kit Carson and his band of mountain men made headquarters, working for the Bent Brothers. Among Kit's band, known widely as the Carson Men, were many seasoned old-timers, all of them among the best in the Rockies — men like Oliver Wiggins, Tom Tobin, Rube Herring, Maxwell, Uncle Dick Wootton, Tim Goodale, Honus, Hatcher, Blackfoot Smith, Markhead, Hawkins, Bill Mitchell, Ike Chamberlain, and Old Bill Williams. Of these Solomon Silver was one of the most competent, and certainly one of the most picturesque.

In the booming days of the fur trade, the mountain men found it convenient to adopt the ways of the Indians, and everywhere in the accounts of those days, we read how closely they imitated their redskin friends — in dress, in manner, and, as time passed, often in their very ways of thinking. They wore their hair long, painted their faces as a protection from the weather, donned buckskin clothing and moccasins decorated with bright patterns of quillwork embroidery. They hunted, on occasion, with the bow and arrow, or brought down their buffalo with the lance. They habitually ate Injun vittles, slept in Injun lodges, smoked Injun pipes, danced Injun dances, married Injun women, and had Injun children galore. They liked nothing better than to be taken for an Injun, tried to fit the wild life as well as he did, and were delighted whenever they could better the instruction of their Injun brothers-in-law. The life they led demanded this close imitation of Injun ways, and naturally those who had lived most closely with the redskins found themselves with a great advantage over other men.

The trapper and trader had to adopt these Injun ways at first, in order to keep on good terms with the redskins. Later, such habits became second nature — especially to those who lived long and intimately with the tribesmen in their camps. Of these, Kit's friend Solomon Silver was one. For he had been for years a captive.

Sol Silver never knew his real name. Though perhaps not a Spaniard by blood, he was carried off from some town in Old Mexico (Saltillo, he believed) by raiding Comanches, who dashed into the lonely ranch one day, murdered his parents, ran off the stock, and then rode night and day back to the Staked Plains and the camps of their people. Sol became so tired on this long trip that he could never remember anything about it.

But when the Comanches halted at last and began to dance the war-dance around their small prisoner, poor little Sol was so frightened that he never could forget it after. He formed a strong dislike for those Indians that night, and never got over it. The Comanches, however, treated him as one of their own until he was about fourteen. Then his Comanche owner traded Sol to a drunken Kiowa, who gave four butcher-knives, two buffalo robes, and a plug of tobacco for him. Sol used to say the Kiowa must have been very drunk to give such a lot for a skinny, shock-haired brat like him.

Sol was swarthy, with stiff black hair, and some people thought that, since he was taken in Mexico, he must be a Spaniard. This annoyed Sol, who had made up his mind that his parents were *Americanos*. As a rule, Mexican captives preferred life in the Indian camps to peonage on some Mexican *hacienda*. The fact that Sol was always trying to escape seemed to him proof that he was not a Mexican. But, however that may be, Sol certainly did *not* like the Kiowas. When his master sobered up, he evidently regretted having paid so much for young Sol. He took it out of the youngster's hide with a bull-hide quirt.

The Kiowas were a small tribe, very warlike, and therefore always short of men, and they had to recruit where they could. As a result, their camps were filled with captives. Many of these were well content with their lot, and, when ransomed by the authorities, would slip away and return to the Kiowas. But the Kiowas never let them escape. Every Kiowa made it his business to keep an eye on the captives, no matter how long they had been in the camps. Of them all, Sol found the old women most watchful. He soon found that these old hags knew his every move. Day and night they watched him, and — as he put it — 'they *never* died!'

Then came the autumn of 1833, when the great meteor shower took place — the winter it rained fire.

One day Sol tried to slip away and hide in the brush when the tribe was on the march down the South Canadian River. But one of those old harpies saw him, and pointed him out to the boy's master, Old Lamey. Old Lamey rode into the brush and drove the lad back onto the prairie, lashing his bare back with a quirt, herding him along the trail afoot until the Indians made camp. Sol was scared, marked with several broad welts, and exhausted from the long run. But Old Lamey showed him no pity.

He spread-eagled the boy on the buffalo grass, staked his wrists down with two forked sticks driven into the ground, and whipped him within an inch of his life. When Sol had passed out, Old Lamey let him lie there. Next morning, when the cold dews had revived Sol, his master came out and let him up. 'Now, you young dog,' he said, 'I am going to turn you loose, so that you can take care of my horses. Go out and get them, water them, and take them out to grass. And remember this thing. Next time you try to run away, I will not whip you. Next time I am going to *kill* you. *Sabe?*

Sol staggered away, picked up the old piece of lodge-cloth which was his only garment, and went after the horses. Only one thought burned in his brain: *revenge!* Until that morning, he had thought only of escape. But now escape was second in his thoughts. All day long he schemed and planned to get even with his master; at night he dreamed of that.

Out on the cold hills, Sol watched the ponies, huddled over a small fire in a dimple on the hillside. In that herd were several fast horses, race-horses, buffalo ponies, war-horses. Sol had studied them, knew the best — those which were fast, those which were long-winded. He set his heart on a clean-limbed bay as the horse to carry him to freedom.

But Sol was never left alone, even when out with the horses. Always some older boy was with him, some young man. Always he was within sight of some Kiowa who could give the alarm. As a rule this was a big, scrofulous orphan, a bully, who delighted to challenge Sol to a wrestling match, get him down, and make him eat dirt. Day after day the bully tormented Sol, until spring turned the brown prairies green, and the sun shone warm on his naked back. Sol saw that he would have to get the best of that orphan, and trained himself as he saw the warriors train their best horses. He ran every day, exercised, slept long, and at night sneaked among the tents to steal drying meat from the racks to feed his growing strength. By early fall, he found he could hold his own with the lubberly orphan. But he was not ready to strike yet.

He had to have a weapon. He dared not steal one. Somebody would be sure to miss it and suspect him, even if no one saw him take it. He was surrounded by spies. Even if he had a knife, he could not carry it concealed in his scanty clothes. And as the camp was always moving, he could not keep it hidden anywhere. Wherever he went, the ugly orphan was with him. Sol used to dream of killing that ugly bully — with a lariat, with a stone, with a stick. But he never had a chance.

Then one day a jack-rabbit jumped up as the camp was moving along. A dozen Injun dogs took after it. Away they went through the tall grass of the bottoms, dragging their little travois behind them, losing their packs. The women screamed and pursued, but when the dogs were caught and tamed by blows and kicking, several packs were missing, and could not be found.

One of the women set fire to the grass in the bottom in the hope of finding her valuables. The grass burned fiercely, and spread towards the camp downstream. Then all the Kiowas were kept busy fighting fire. Sol worked with the others, beating the blaze with his old lodge-cloth blanket. And in the smoke and the confusion, he found a pack, and in it a bone-handled knife.

But Sol was not allowed to keep that knife. The orphan saw it on him, and Sol gave it to the fellow, as the price of silence. Then Sol's heart lay on the ground. But that night a grand idea came to him. He waited for a chance to use it. He had not long to wait.

One day the buffalo scouts brought word that the herds

were near. The heralds announced a hunt. All the men mounted their best buffalo ponies and set out to the southward. All the women began to make drying racks for the meat, or saddled their pack-horses and set out on the trail of the hunters. Sol and the orphan boy were left alone with the rest of Old Lamey's ponies to the north of the camp. Old Lamey was satisfied; he had seen the knife in the orphan boy's belt.

When the dust of the pack-train had vanished beyond the hills across the river, Sol began to egg on the orphan to tackle him. The bully, sure of his superior strength, readily accepted Sol's challenge. They clinched and rolled over on the buffalo grass. But this time Sol was in deadly earnest. He gave the orphan boy the tussle of his life.

The orphan was astonished at the strength Sol showed. He decided to teach the slim captive a lesson. He grabbed Sol's long hair, twisted his head round, stuck a thumb into Sol's left eye. But Sol, who knew all the dirty tricks of Injun wrasslin', suddenly rolled free, flung himself on top of his adversary, and got such a hold on the bully with his right hand as left the orphan without strength or even desire to resist longer. The ugly face relaxed, the eyes glazed, the bully lay helpless, groaning. Sol's moment had arrived.

Tightening his hold, Sol used his free hand to slip the knife from the young man's belt. He plunged the blade into the ugly, scarred throat, drew it swiftly sidewise. Then he leaped back, away from the pulsing blood that squirted over his knife hand. The orphan rolled gurgling on the bloody grass. He would never give another alarm. When he was quiet, Sol covered him with his own scrap of lodge-cloth.

Sol stuck the knife into his own belt, took the dead man's buffalo robe and lariat, and turned towards the grazing horses. It was almost time for the noonday watering; nobody would think it strange if he were seen driving the ponies to the river. Sol had his eye on Old Lamey's clean-limbed bay. But he knew that, if he were seen riding such a good horse, people would think it strange. And so he jumped upon the back of an old pack-horse, and, rounding up the herd, urged them gently towards the river.

There, hidden from the camp by brush and cottonwoods, he tossed the end of his rope across the back of the bay. The animal had been roped too often to move when it felt the rope, even though the noose was not around its neck. Sol caught it, contrived a rope bridle, jumped upon the bay, and rode downstream, away from the camp, out of sight in the brush. When he had gone a mile or two, he turned up a creek that ran in from the north, and whipped the bay into a lope. At the head of the creek, he came out upon the prairie, and raced away, hard as the horse could go. All that afternoon he pushed on, riding north and east, until he got among the blackjacks, out of the open prairie.

But Sol did not stop. All night he kept going, and by noon the next day saw the dark winding fringe of green timber which marked the course of the Arkansas River. In crossing that stream, the heaving bay stopped to drink.

Sol was worn out; he had not the strength to control the horse, which was frantic for water. The animal bucked him off, drank its fill, and staggered out upon the bank to die.

Sol, still fearful of the Kiowas, waded up the stream to cover his trail in the water, and after a mile or two struck out northeast again. Somewhere in that direction were the white settlements, men of his own blood. Towards the middle of the afternoon, the boy saw the white tilts of a train of wagons moving slowly along. He hurried forward, sure of a welcome.

To his surprise, he was greeted by a bullet, which went zinging past his ear. The wagon-train swung hastily into a corral formation, and men with rifles came swarming out of the corral to face him.

Sol, however, did not turn back. As he put it later, he was 'too scairt of the Kioways fur that.' He went ahead, holding up both hands above his head to show that he came in peace. He had not realized how much like an Injun he looked.

He came near the wagons, and found himself facing a score of rifles. But the wagon-master began to yell orders, and the men lowered their guns. Afterward, when Sol had learned some English, he understood what they said: 'Shucks, put up yore rifles. Caint ye see it's jest a boy?'

The wagon-master befriended Sol, and took him into the corral. There the men all gathered round, while Sol, gorging on salt sowbelly and corn pone for the first time in his life, tried to let them know by signs who he was and where he came from. The wagon-master gave the lad some pants and a hickory shirt. After that the men accepted him, since he looked 'purty nigh human agin.'

The wagon-train headed for Fort Gibson, and Sol liked the wagon-master so well that he would gladly have spent the rest of his days with the train. But after a time something happened to make him change his plans.

A party of Shaved Heads — Osages — met the train. They were all warriors, had no women with them, and were traveling on foot. Sol had heard that the Shaved Heads always went to war on foot. For this reason the Kiowas feared them, since footmen can easily keep hidden and cover their trail, and therefore can surprise their enemies with greater ease than horsemen. As the redskin proverb has it, it is better to go to war afoot and ride home than to ride to war and walk home.

To Sol, these big, fierce-looking men, with their roach of stiff hair waving above their shaved heads, looked more than a match for the Kiowas. It was a large war-party, too. Sol hoped they would go after the Kiowas and rub them out.

The Osages, always friends to the whites, visited the wagon-train and smoked with the wagon-master. Sol was there, looking on with the rest. And when the Osages learned that he had been a Kiowa captive and had killed a Kiowa, they proposed to buy him from the wagon-master. They thought he might be useful to them, since he hated the Kiowas and knew their camps and country. They said they would like to take him along on that warpath.

The wagon-master said he could not sell the boy, but that he could go if he wanted to. He was a free man. And so the Osage chief put it up to Sol. And Sol, who had enough Injun in him to wish to make his mark as a warrior, and was eager to get back at Old Lamey, jumped at the chance. That night he camped with the Shaved Heads on the war-trail. He could talk with them in the sign language. By the time they reached the Kiowa range, the Osages had accepted Sol as one of the war-party. They dubbed him Little Captive.

On the ancient war-trail from the Arkansas River to Texas and Old Mexico, just north of the Wichita Mountains, stands a detached butte known to the tribes as Rainy Mountain. Sol knew that the Kiowas would be camped somewhere near-by. He led the Osages to that place. The Osages hovered around, keeping to the north of the Washita River, killing their meat with arrows, to avoid alarming their enemies with the sound of guns.

The Osages did not feel numerous and strong enough to attack the whole Kiowa tribe. Every night the Kiowas were dancing, as they intended to send off a war-party against the Utes. Sol advised the Osages to wait until the Kiowa warriors had gone to war.

So they hung around, keeping out of sight. But one morning a wounded buffalo cow ran away from an Osage hunter, plunged into the brush along the river, and disappeared, carrying his arrow sticking between her ribs. The cow died later, and some Kiowa hunters found her. They knew from the markings on the arrow that it had been made by an Osage. Immediately they gave the alarm. The Kiowas feared the Osages, who were well armed with guns. They were frightened, postponed their warpath against the Utes, and threw up earthworks (still to be seen).

Seeing these preparations, the Osages knew they had been discovered, and decided to retire until the Kiowas recovered from their alarm. The Kiowas could not find a trace of them.

After waiting a few days, the Kiowas became impatient. The warriors wanted to be gone against the Utes. They started. Then the chiefs voted to scatter, each band going in a different direction. The big tribal camp broke up into three or four bands. The principal chief, A'date (Island-Man), went by way of Otter Creek past Saddle Mountain and on through Cut-Throat Gap to the headwaters of Otter Creek.[1]

All these camps, left almost without defenders, offered tempting victims to the Osages. At first they could not decide which camp to follow — not that it mattered much to the Shaved Heads. But Sol was determined to follow the camp of A'date, because he knew Old Lamey would be in it. Boy as he was, he asserted himself in council, and won over the Osage warriors to his plan. The argument which told most was that A'date was the head chief, and a victory over his camp would give the Osages more glory. Finally, Sol won out, and the Shaved Heads hit the trail of A'date.

Very early one morning, before it was light, the Osages

moved silently to the attack. Creeping through the rocks, they advanced on the sleeping camp. As the light strengthened, a Kiowa youth, out early after his horses, saw the shaved head of an Osage bobbing among the boulders. He turned and sprinted silently for camp. When he reached the chief's tipi, he found his old woman, who had just come out to scrape a hide she had pegged to the ground. Ducking through the lodge door, the breathless boy roused the chief, gasped out his message.

A'date rushed out of the tent, yelling to the people, '*Tsó bätsó! Tsó bätsó!* (To the rocks! To the rocks!') Instantly the people rushed from their lodges, streaming towards a small rocky butte just south of the camp.

When the Osages heard the chief yelling, they knew that the alarm had been given. They leaped from hiding, and ran forward after the fleeing Kiowas, screeching like devils. Sol was among the first to reach the open.

In that little cove among the hills all was confusion. Women dragged their children madly along. Old men and women hobbled on their sticks as fast as their shaking legs would carry them. Boys and girls raced for the butte. The Osages raced after them, gaining, shooting, stabbing.

The Kiowas had no thought but escape. They dropped everything, and ran. They abandoned their shields, the weapons, their medicines. It was a mad flight of panic-stricken women, children, and old men, and everyone caught was butchered on the spot.

Sol and the Osages had it all their own way. A'date

was wounded, but got away. His wife, Sematma (Apache Woman), was caught and held prisoner. Ansote, keeper of the sacred *taime* puppets, the palladium of the tribe, ran off and abandoned them. His wife stopped to untie the holy bundle from the tipi-pole, was caught and killed. One woman fled with a baby girl on her back and dragging an older girl by the hand; an Osage, pursuing, caught the older girl and was drawing his knife across her throat when the mother rushed to her aid and succeeded in beating him off, and rescued the child with only a slight gash upon her head. One brave man, carrying the cradle of his infant son by holding the top of it between his teeth, made a series of stands, keeping his enemies back with bow and arrows, then turning to run again. He saved the boy, Aya, who lived to a ripe old age.

Of all these enemies, the bravest man was a lone Pawnee, then visiting in the camp. He stood off the Osages single-handed, and fought so stubbornly that he was able to save a large number of women, who escaped to the rocks, and at last he got away himself, unhurt. The hatred between Pawnees and Osages was so bitter then as to make other tribal enmities seem trifling.

But Sol was not looking for women and children to butcher, not even the old women who had made his life such a burden. He was looking for Old Lamey, his former master. Quick enough he saw him. The big buck was legging it up the slope fast as he could go, naked to the gee-string, just as he had jumped out of bed, with his long hair floating out over his left shoulder. Sol sprinted after him, caught up with him, yelled in his ear: 'Turn and fight, dog. Do you want to be shot in the back?'

The Kiowa was so astonished to hear that familiar voice at his heels that he looked round, open-mouthed. At that moment Sol let his arrow fly. The shaft struck Old Lamey square in the open mouth, and cut the artery in his neck. He tugged at the arrow, utterly dismayed, and staggered on a few steps before he went down. Sol yelped in triumph, and struck him with his bow, counting the *coup*. Then Sol unsheathed his knife and scalped him. From his ears he tore out two large rings of *silver*. These he afterward wore in his own ears, and from them he took his name.

The fight, or rather flight, lasted but a few minutes. The Osages were soon in possession of the camp. They looted the tents and took, among other things, the sacred *taime* puppets, used to make the Kiowa Sun Dance. In Old Lamey's tent they found several hundred dollars in silver. Old Lamey had been in a raid the year before and had taken the coins from some white traders. Sol did not know the value of money then, but the Osages did. They let him have a pouchful to take back to Fort Gibson. Besides the chief's wife, they had two captives — a boy and a girl. Sol had himself stood in a captive's moccasins; he felt sorry for them. He advised the Osages not to kill them, but to hold them for ransom.

The Osages counted the dead. They had not lost a man. They found five dead Kiowa men, and a large number of women and children.

It was a complete victory. The Osages were elated at their easy success. They felt like making fun of their defeated enemies.

Now, the Osages are a Siouan people. In old times the sign for Sioux was a sweep of the open hand under the chin, meaning Beheaders. So that morning on Otter Creek, the Osages lived up to their ancestral customs. They cut off the heads of all their dead enemies. They did not scalp them, that was not their custom; Sol was the only man present who took a scalp that day. He naturally followed the custom of the Comanches and Kiowas who had brought him up.

In the camp the Osages found a number of brass buckets (one of which may be seen in the museum at Fort Sill today), and when they had cut off the heads, they put them into these buckets — one in each — and placed the buckets at intervals around the camp. Then, having set fire to the tents, they packed their loot on the captured ponies and started.

The frightened Kiowas hastened to join their relatives near the mouth of Elk Creek, and soon after the whole tribe reunited and joined the Comanches for safety. But the Osages did not pursue. They were well content with the success of their raid. They hit the trail to Fort Gibson.

Sol rode back triumphant, with a good horse under him, silver dollars in his pouch, a scalp in his belt, and the respect of all the Osages to cheer him on his way. He had had his baptism of fire, had gained the name of a warrior.

Best of all, he had had his revenge on the man who had so cruelly flogged him. He was happy.

On reaching the settlements, Sol soon left the Osages, and joined a party of mountain men heading for the Rockies. It was natural that he should become a mountain man, for the Kiowa name for white men was Hañpóko (Trappers). But few beginners can have had the training with which Sol started.

He could ride, and shoot, and pack a horse. He knew the wild country, and the habits of wild animals. Few of the mountain men started with his skill and knowledge of trailing, scouting, warfare, and hunting. And more than most he understood Injun ways, and how an Injun thought. To his last days, he was always a good deal like an Injun. He loved fine horses, gaudy clothes, company, and display. His squaw was always the best-dressed at rendezvous, his horse among the fastest. No wonder such men were successful in the Old West. They were bred for it. And though the training was rough and hard, it made men.

XII. BLACKFOOT TOPKNOTS

O F ALL the mountain men in the Southwest among whom Solomon Silver spent his active years, his best friend was 'Blackfoot' Smith. 'Blackfoot' started life with no more exciting a name than John: how he gained his other moniker is a story never yet published: Sol Silver is our authority.

Though Smith lived most of his days in the Southwest, he began his career as a mountain man in the Northwest, where he won his name. Like the Western Indians, the mountain man had an extensive range: at one time he might be in St. Louis, at another on the Pacific Coast; sometimes in Old Mexico, or again north of the line in the British Possessions. But in this, as in most other matters, the mountain man bettered the instruction of his Indian model. How he rambled!

The mountain men were fellows of all professions — or of none. John Smith began his active life as a tailor. But it appears the old proverb — that it takes nine tailors to make one man — did not hold good in his case, though the craft he had learned proved very useful to him on the frontier, where buckskins took the place of broadcloth, and an awl and sinew that of needle and thread. Like Kit Carson, Smith ran away from his employer. He joined a party out of St. Louis, bound for the Upper Missouri. As Garrard tells us, Smith was 'so enamoured of the desultory and exciting life that he chose rather to sit cross-legged, smoking the long Indian pipe, than to cross his legs on his master's board.' [1]

At the time Smith reached the Upper Missouri, the Rocky Mountain Fur Company was in its last season. For twelve years the Company, under the leadership of such partisans as Ashley and Henry, William Sublette, Thomas Fitzpatrick, Old Gabe Bridger, Fraeb, and Gervais, had explored, exploited, and fought over a vast area in and around the Rocky Mountains. They had harvested more than a thousand packs of beaver, worth half a million dollars or more.[2]

Ashley and Sublette had retired with comfortable fortunes for those days, but the rest of these men were still without the reward of their labors, hardships, and warlike adventures. And just when they were at last ready to make their fortunes, they found their rivals, the American Fur Company — armed with huge capital, political influence, and a large staff of able and energetic men — gaining ground every day against them. This rivalry naturally came to the attention of the redskins, for whose furs and trade the companies were bidding; the result may be imagined.

The Indians, though at first deeply contemptuous of

the whites (after Leavenworth's failure to crush the Arikara), had been taught, during those intervening years, to respect the mountain men. They l'arned 'em. That lesson had been repeated again and again, to the redskins' bitter loss. But now, in the rivalry of the fur companies, the Indians found a weakness in the white man's strength. The men of each company begged and wheedled and bribed the Indians; worse, they slandered and belittled their rivals.

The Indian, who considered trapping a low form of life for a warrior, anyhow, and who naturally despised anyone who humbly sought his favor, immediately formed the opinion that he had been mistaken in thinking the white men so important and superior.

Incited by the company with which he traded, he was likely to rob, kill, or terrorize members of the rival company — and in the long run, all whites whatever. By 1834, white men were safe only when close by some trading-fort. This state of affairs, brought about by the booshways for their own selfish profit, meant disaster for their unlucky employees, who had to harvest the fur. Hostility towards defenseless white men lasted down to the end of the Indian wars in the West. Ashley had made his fortune by exposing his men to great risks; the later companies did the same thing — with even more appalling results.

The first thing that struck John Smith, when he got to the Upper Missouri, was the high death-rate among mountain men. Chittenden tells us, in the passage cited, that in the years during which the Rocky Mountain Fur Company operated, they lost (1822–1829) seventy men, all of whom met violent deaths, and that in the remaining years (1829–1834) enough more were killed to bring the total up to a hundred.

John Smith was a born calculator, and as soon as he was on the ground, he began to calculate what his chances of surviving in that hard profession were. The result of his figuring was that, counting all the mountain men together — both free trappers and *engagés* of the various companies then in the field — there were not a thousand men in the Rockies. Of these, one died a violent death every ten or twelve days, as a matter of course.

As he sat drying his moccasins by the campfire that winter evening, John Smith gave these figures serious thought. All during the autumn he had been learning the trapper's lonely trade. With one companion, he had marched up the streams looking for sign of beaver. When his mentor pointed out a slide where the animals had been disporting themselves, or a dam, or a lodge, Smith would take a trap from the trap-sack, and, following the instructions of his comrade, wade out into the shallow stream. There he would use his butcher-knife to cut a bed for the trap, perhaps six inches under water. Having set the trap and placed it in the bed, Smith then waded to the middle of the pool or stream, as far from the trap as the length of its chain permitted. There he firmly planted the 'float' (a stout stick of dry wood) in the mud, so that no beaver could possibly drag it out. To make doubly sure, Smith always attached the top end of the float by a strip of rawhide or tanned leather to a second peg on the shore. He soon learned that if the beaver pulled up the float, or gnawed it in two, swam off with the trap, and so drowned itself in deep water, the trapper would have to dive until he could find it and bring it up. Mountain water was always cold. But traps cost money — and without them the trapper could not pay his way.

Over the trap, Smith was taught to set up a stick smeared with the beaver 'medicine,' which was believed to attract the animals to the trap. Smith's mentor kept the ingredients of that unholy mixture a profound secret. All that Smith knew was that it smelled *turrible*, and that once he got it on his fingers and wiped them on his buckskins, he was never free of the odor after.

Having set the trap securely, Smith then had to splash water over those parts of the bank where he and his comrade had stepped, to obliterate their scent. Then, wading downstream, he would eventually be allowed to scramble out, throw the trap-sack on his shoulder, and hit the trail to the next likely place. Smith hated cold water, all the more because he was subject to neuralgia.

This routine soon palled on John Smith, especially as his more experienced friends, finding him interested in the dangers of the profession, kept filling his green ears with dreadful tales of how the Injuns had murdered, mutilated, and robbed sundry men of their acquaintance. They laughed uproariously at such stories, as if being murdered were a kind of practical joke on the victim. Smith didn't see much fun in that kind of thing.

It was no fun either to sleep in wet moccasins, and have them dry on his feet and wake him by their pinching. Neither did he enjoy getting his buckskins wet around the bottom, and having them stretch into the shape of a sailor's nether garments. All this, however, he could have endured if he had not discovered that the trappers were playing a losing game. Only the booshways made money — the trappers were always in debt, always behind, always poor. Smith was a born trader, and had all the independence characteristic of Americans of that day. He had a mighty small heart for working all his life in order to make somebody else rich. That was why he had run off from the tailor's shop.

Smith began to look into the profits of the traders.

The average trapper was paid around three hundred dollars a year for his work — sometimes more, often less. These wages, however, had to be taken out in trade — or in credit on the company's books, when the summer rendezvous came round and the furs were brought to market. Even expert trappers sometimes received less than a thousand dollars in trade goods for the year's catch. A beaver plew (or *plus*, as the French Canadians called a prime beaver skin), the furry banknote of the mountains, weighed a pound to a pound and a half or so, and sold at from four to six dollars. To make a thousand dollars, at six dollars the plew, made it necessary for the trapper to catch, dress, and bring to rendezvous about one hundred and seventy beaver. These beaver had to be trapped in the spring and fall, when the fur was in good condition. Half the year the trapper had no use for his traps.

Yet his employers managed to keep him busy, hunting, exploring, on the trail.

Like most successful entrepreneurs, Smith was a curious compound of caution and daring. Before he ran away from the tailor's shop, he had learned all he could from the mountain men who visited St. Louis, and had bought his own outfit there. He knew what he had paid, and could compare the prices in the settlements with those paid in the mountains. The immediate conclusion was that what cost one dollar at St. Louis cost ten dollars on Green River. The traders and booshways made nine hundred per cent gross profit, and at least (here Smith could get no exact figures, naturally) six hundred per cent profit, net. Alcohol, especially, brought handsome returns, though its introduction into Indian country was forbidden by the Intercourse Laws. A gill of whiskey (so-called) cost as much at rendezvous as a gallon of the stuff would bring at St. Louis. Smith had heard hard things about the fur companies. At the end of this lesson in arithmetic, he was ready to believe them all.

But Smith was no reformer. All his days his thrifty father had drilled into his mind the importance of money, money, money. And though — or because — he was a runaway, his father's words rang in his ears, still. The lure of adventure had brought him into the mountains, and he had no intention of returning to the settlements. He was not afraid of Injuns, b'ars, or mountain winters.

He liked the open-air life, the mountain men, the excitement of danger and travel. He was a good shot, and could appreciate mountain scenery, too. But his early raisin' made it *impossible* for him to work for nothing. Smith made up his mind that he would combine the pleasures of life in the wilderness with those of being well-to-do. He determined to set up as a trader.

To do this, he had to have a stake.

His first rendezvous had showed him how impossible it would be to take his furs there and come away with anything in his possible-sack. Everybody blew everything at rendezvous. Smith liked his fun as much as anybody, and was afraid that, if he took his beaver in, he would lose it all, one way or another. Accordingly, he cached part of his furs, and took the others in. There he paid up his debt, and vainly tried to find someone to go down to the settlements with him to dispose of his cache.

Smith then decided that he would build himself a bullboat and float downriver alone, rather than sell his furs for one tenth of their value. Smith had his own peculiar brand of courage.

The thing which decided him not to travel with one of the fur brigades was what had happened to White Head Fitzpatrick the summer before.

After the rendezvous of June, 1833, the outfits of trappers had scattered. White Head left his partners on the Big Horn and put out for Tongue River, in the Crow country, where he wished to make his fall hunt. He rode looking for the Crow village, as he wanted to get the permission of those Indians to hunt in their country. But there, to his surprise and secret dismay, he found the Crows looking for *him!* Fitzpatrick sheered off.

The Crow chief kept on his trail, day after day, overtook him, and proposed that they both make a single camp together. But the chief seemed too effusive in his offers of friendship; White Head was uneasy. He refused to camp with the Crows, but camped only a few miles off. Then, to make sure that the Crow chief's feelings would not be hurt, White Head led a few men over to pay a friendly visit. Most of his men he left in camp, to guard his hundred head of horse beast, his beaver, and his trade goods.

The chief met him and shook him warmly by the hand. He led White Head into his lodge, gave him water to drink, meat to eat, and smoked with him. Fitzpatrick, in turn, did all he could to show that he trusted the Crows. When the mock love-feast was over, White Head and his men started back to their own camp.

Meanwhile, a horde of young Crow warriors had gone in a body to White Head's camp, and, by a surprise attack in overwhelming numbers, had run off all his horses and stolen his packs and traps — everything but the clothes his men had on. The white men had no chance; there was no fight. It was just a holdup — and completely successful.

The young bucks, on their way back to their own camp, met White Head Fitzpatrick and his small escort. The young Indians were full of high spirits after their easy victory, full of a spirit of practical fun. They surrounded White Head and his men, and made him give up his gun, his horse, his capote, his clothing, even his watch! He and his comrades hit the trail back to camp, wrathy as a bear with a broken nose.

The men in the camp were uneasy. They knew that White Head would be terribly angry when he got back and found all his stock and packs gone. They watched the trail with apprehensive eyes.

But when they saw White Head coming at the head of half a dozen men, all naked as picked chickens, the men in camp relaxed. The Crows had treated their booshway as bad as themselves. He was in the same boat as the rest of them. What could he say?

White Head said plenty — and the tune of it was that the American Fur Company had put the Injuns up to robbing him.

Next day White Head, wrapped in a blanket, held council with the Crow chief again. He blamed the chief for treachery, and demanded to know who had prompted the outrage. The Crow chief at first denied all knowledge of the business, blandly blamed his reckless young men, whom he could not control, and fiercely promised to have the property returned.

After a long time, the chief did return the horses, the rifles, a few traps, and a little — only a little — powder and ball. The rest of the stuff was lost, he said.

Fitzpatrick knew where he stood, then. That Crow chief was a yes-man. He had said yes to the American

Fur Company when they put him up to robbing Fitzpatrick; he had said yes to the young men who wanted to rob the whites; he had said yes to White Head when asked for the return of his property. White Head believed the chief would say yes again to the young men whenever they felt inclined to pillage his camp. White Head did not hang around long after that. He threw his outfit on the trail, and made tracks out of the country.

This event, among other similar happenings, convinced John Smith that it would be dangerous to travel with any of the outfits. He thought he could go it alone.

Smith's cache was on the headwaters of the Missouri, in the Blackfoot country. That far he rode with a party of free trappers, for until he reached his cache, he had nothing to lose but his hair and his rifle. But when he reached the creek where he had his cache, he slipped away from the others. He spoke Blackfoot well, being gifted with a talent for languages. He thought that, if he put his packs into a bullboat, and drifted down the river by night, leaving no visible trail, he might arrive safely at the settlements, and so get the full value of his furs.

Smith had made bullboats before. He knew how to cut limber willow shoots nearly as thick as his wrist; how to set the butts in the ground in a four-foot circle — as big as the round coracle was to be; how to bend them over and lash them into a rounded framework; how to weave and lash smaller branches across this sturdy frame into a basket.

That done, he skinned several buffalo, and, laying flesh-side against flesh-side, sewed the skins tightly together, making a sheet of hide large enough to cover his willow framework. Then he stretched this skin, flesh-side out, over the basket, and fastened it securely to the gunwale all around. He next built a small fire under the rawhide tub, to make the hides shrink and harden, all the time smearing melted buffalo tallow over the seams and surface of the hides. The smoking and the soaking in warm grease made the boat waterproof.

Finally, Smith had a leather tub big enough to float him and his packs, light enough to be carried on his back, and small enough to be easily concealed in any thicket or patch of tall grass near which he might drift on his lonely way down the muddy Missouri. A rough paddle gave him some control of the boat, enabling him to keep it in the moving current. And if it grounded on a bar, he had only to step out to lighten it sufficiently to shove off into deep water again. Smith believed he could navigate at the rate of a hundred miles a day downstream.

He had already decided what he would buy with his beaver when he got to Missouri again. The Indians, he knew, wanted Du Pont powder and Galena lead, Green River skinning-knives, vermilion, tobacco, gay handkerchiefs, pocket mirrors; their women liked fofurraw of all kinds. 'Fofurraw' (derived from the French-Canadian *fanfaron*) was the mountain man's word for everything that was showy, effeminate, or unnecessary. Blankets, rifles, red strouding, fine broadcloth — those might have to wait until Smith could increase his stake. But he was sure the bullboat would launch him upon a successful career.

It did — but not in the way Smith expected.

On the first night, the bullboat struck a snag in the darkness, turned turtle, and dropped him into water over his head. The boat drifted into shallower water before it sank, and Smith, who had taken the precaution of tying all his packs and bundles to the ribs of the framework, to avoid any listing, lost nothing from the boat. But he was chilled, and wet, and afraid to build a fire. He crawled into the bushes, trying to keep warm under a wet blanket. Before morning he had a raging toothache: the whole side of his face was racked with neuralgia.

The nearest doctor was some twenty-five hundred miles away.

Smith, however, needed no doctor. What he wanted was some pain-killer. That could only be had at some trading-post — if at all. When it grew light, he launched his bullboat, and, cowering in it to keep out of the chill wind, he floated along, his craft spinning and whirling in the eddies, or dancing along the ripples of the main current. Smith was too miserable to care whether any Injuns saw him or not. He sat nursing his sore jaw, staring miserably across the gunwale. He didn't even know where he was.

The current swung him around a bunch of small islands overgrown with willows and brush. And there, just below, on the open prairie, was a trading-post! Fort McKenzie!

Smith roused himself at that welcome sight. He got out his paddle, and, leaning over the side of his round boat, paddled first on his left and then on his right, in this way forcing the tub to move in the direction he was facing. Thus, like some clumsy turtle, he brought himself ashore. There was nobody about so early. No tipis stood on the flat around the fort. Hooray!

Smith pulled a few beaver from one of his packs, and hurried up the short slope to the level on which the fort stood. It had the usual block-houses and pickets. Smith pounded on the gate, and at last a yawning clerk came, peered out of the wicket, and stood open-mouthed with astonishment at sight of the lone stranger. Then, seeing the swollen jaw, the sleepy clerk grinned. Smith took a strong dislike to the fellow.

'Let me in,' Smith demanded. 'I got a turrible tooth-ache. I want something to kill the pain. *Quick!*' Poor Smith closed his eyes and groaned, as the twinge took him again.

By that time the clerk had wakened sufficiently to understand that Smith was not an *engagé* of the Company. His smile turned to a malicious grin. So the stranger was a free trapper, or a hireling of some other, rival outfit, was he? A poacher on the preserves of the American Fur Company? The clerk made no move to open the gate. He demanded to know who the stranger was, and showed plain disbelief when he heard the name John Smith. After that, there was an edge to his words.

'Open up,' Smith insisted.

'Too early for that,' the clerk objected. 'Nobody up.'

'Well, then,' Smith urged, 'trot out yore pain-killer. Hain't you got none?'

'Yes,' he said, nodding carelessly, 'but we keep it for our own men.'

'Wagh, I don't want much. Trot it out. I kin pay,' Smith insisted. 'You're a trader, ain't you?'

The clerk considered. 'The booshway won't like it. But I reckon a plew's a plew, whoever brings it in. I'll go and take a look. If we have enough and to spare, maybe I can let you have some — if you're willing to pay for it.'

'Run along, git it,' Smith urged, nursing his aching jaw.

The clerk departed, and, after what seemed hours to poor Smith, came back without haste, holding a big brown bottle in his hands. The bottle was well filled, and bore a label. 'Laudanum,' he declared, fingering the label. 'Lucky for you we had more than one bottle.'

'Hand it over,' Smith begged, reaching through the wicket. 'A gill of that will fix me up plenty.'

But the clerk kept out of Smith's reach. 'If that's all you want, I reckon you'll have to go without,' he said. 'I can't split the bottle with you. The booshway wouldn't like that. You'll have to take the hull bottle, or nothin'.'

'Wagh,' Smith objected. 'What do I want with all that pizen?' But seeing the clerk about to turn away, he made haste to call him back. 'Hold on thar. I'll take it. Hyar's the beaver.' Smith held up two plews — prime beaver — which he had brought with him from the boat.

The clerk eyed them without enthusiasm. 'This ain't

river-water in this bottle,' he declared, sourly. 'It cost plenty. We can't give it away.'

'Well,' Smith growled, 'if you aim to steal me blind, I got more beaver along.' He jerked his thumb over his shoulder towards the bullboat reposing on the beach. 'How many plew do you want for it? I can't stand here in the cold all day. My jaw's sore as a boil.'

The clerk perked up his ears at that. 'Huh? So you got more beaver in the boat? Don't you know we never trade with no man lessen he brings us *all* his furs? Trying to pull the wool over my eyes, war you?'

At that Smith exploded. 'Durn it,' he yelled, 'I'm takin' them furs to St. Looie.'

The clerk set the bottle down on the ground beside him — but where Smith could see it. Then he took hold of the wicket — to close it. 'Too bad,' he answered. 'If you don't want to trade here, get your pain-killer at St. Looie. I'm going back to bed.'

Smith was too quick for him. He shoved his shaggy head through the wicket.

'No, ye don't!' he yelled. 'I come here to trade, and I aim to do it. I got nigh on a pack of beaver in that bull-boat. I kin pay. I'll give what it's wuth. But you kin sculp me if you git all that beaver for one bottle of pain-killer.'

Smith ground his teeth with rage — then reeled from the pain in his jaw.

The clerk hesitated. 'Well, John Smith, all we want is *all* of your trade — or none. Fetch your beaver here.

When the bottle's paid for, you can trade in the rest of the fur for anything else that takes your fancy.'

Smith glared at the clerk — at the bottle — and the twinge took him again. He pulled his head out of the wicket, strode down to the river, shielding his aching jaw from the chill river-wind. He lugged all his furs to the gate.

'Thar,' said Smith, 'thar's the hull kit and kaboodle. But I won't give ye all that for a *barrel* of pain-killer. I'll die fust.'

The clerk began deliberately to finger the furs, mentioning prices for various things which Smith might want — prices which made Smith's blood boil. But the bottle was still inside the gate, out of his reach. And so Smith smothered his rage, and gave in — 'licked,' as he put it, 'by a sore tooth.' The way that clerk cheated him pretty nigh killed him, hurt him worse'n the tooth and the neuralgia together. And the thing that stuck in his craw perticler was the certainty that the clerk would pocket most of the extra profit himself.

Smith was aware of the outrageous prices paid at rendezvous — mountain prices: blanket, twenty dollars; tobacco, five dollars the plug; powder, four dollars the pound; hatchet, six dollars; sugar, three dollars a pint; and so on. But such prices were nothing to what the clerk made Smith pay that morning. For two cents Smith would have yanked out his pistol and shot the clerk dead. But, if he had, he could not have reached the bottle. Besides, his powder was wet. He received only about one seventh what the furs were worth — in trade. And even then not one drop of laudanum passed the wicket.

Only at the end of the swapping did the clerk loosen up a little, and let Smith have a gallon of firewater for five times its real value. Smith wondered why. He saw the fellow's eyes fixed on the hilltop behind him. But he did not bother to look round.

'Well, that's all, I reckon,' said the clerk cheerfully. 'Whar you headin'?'

'I war headin' downriver,' Smith growled. 'But now I reckon I'll have to make tracks to the mountains agin.'

'Keep your eye skinned, then,' said the clerk. He pursed his lips, like any Injun, pointing with them over Smith's shoulder. Smith turned and looked. A band of mounted warriors were riding over the hill towards the fort.

'Blackfeet!' Smith exclaimed.

The clerk nodded. 'Blackfeet don't like strangers stealing their fur,' he said. 'You'll be lucky if you get as far as the mountains. In the fort, we can protect you. But away from the fort there ain't much we can do. Maybe you'd better come inside and work for the Company.'

'The Company be damned!' Smith prayed fervently.

The clerk shrugged his shoulders carelessly. 'Have it your own way,' he said, and turned away.

Smith roared at him: 'Hold on thar. Give me my pain-killer.'

The clerk turned around again, as if he had forgotten. 'Yes,' he agreed, 'I reckon you want that, too. But there's one thing more: before I let you take it, you'll have to promise to fetch all your peltry here to trade. We trade only with our own men.'

Almost speechless at this demand, Smith could only get out a deep-throated 'Wagh!'

'Booshway's orders,' the clerk explained glibly. 'If you won't agree to that, of course I can't let you have the goods at the prices I made you. I'll have to keep the laudanum to make up the difference.'

Smith stared at the insolent young fellow for a long minute. Then he shoved the barrel of his waterlogged pistol through the wicket. 'Hand over that bottle, young un,' he commanded, 'and be quick about it. Fust thing you know, you'll find yourself a-clerkin' for the Old Black B'ar in hell.'

The clerk went white and shaky then; he could see the fury in Smith's eyes, and he knew the trappers. Trembling, he picked up the bottle.

'Don't drop it, mind ye,' Smith warned him. 'If ye do, I'll drop you, sartain.' Smith grabbed the slipping bottle with eager fingers, afraid the fool would let it go, spill the precious medicine — which had cost him a year's labor. He knew he could never get the clerk to bring him a second bottle.

'Now, you skunk,' Smith ordered, 'you kin shove my beaver back through yore leetle winder. I'm a-goin' to leave your fixin's on the prairie, where ye can step out and git 'em after I'm gone, happen the Injuns don't beat ye to it. Step lively.'

The frightened clerk stooped, picked up a dozen plews, and laid them on the small shelf under the wicket. Smith, with the bottle in one hand and the pistol in the other, reached for the furs. Quick as a wink, the clerk slapped the wicket to and ducked aside, where no lead could reach him.

Smith beat on the wicket. But he knew he was bested. The Blackfeet were coming close, too. Smith dosed himself with a swig of the laudanum, caught up as many of his scanty purchases as he could lug, and hurried back to his bullboat. The Blackfeet would stop at the fort. Like as not, the clerk would put those cussed Blackfeet on his trail. Smith wanted to be on his way around the bend before anything like that could happen.

Just below Fort McKenzie, the Missouri River flowed in a big bend. While Smith was spinning merrily on his way in the bouncing bullboat along the curving river, warmed by the rising sun, and lulled into drowsy comfort after his sleepless night by the pain-killer he had taken, the Blackfeet were riding at a lope overland, to head him off below the bend. Before he knew it, a shot sounded from the steep clay bank above him, a slug splashed water below his bullboat. He looked up, and saw the bank lined with Injuns — five of 'em. They signaled and called to him to come ashore.

Smith had no alternative. The current had swept him close under the bank. They could shoot him dead if he disobeyed. He had been so careless that he had not cleaned or reloaded his weapons; the powder in them was wet.

Cursing, he got out his paddle, and brought the leather tub to the narrow beach.

There the Blackfeet met him. They took his hands and dragged him from the boat, afterward helping themselves to all his property. Then they slit the bullboat with their knives and sent it drifting away, sinking as it went. They led Smith up the bank and out upon the prairie.

Up there the wind was chill and disagreeable. Herding Smith before them, the five warriors rode their ponies to a sheltered spot not far off, where they dismounted and built a fire to roast the meat they had found in the bullboat. Smith saw that they were going to eat first — and probably murder him after. Meanwhile, they had found the alcohol; it made Smith laugh to see them try to swallow the raw spirit. But hoping to get them all drunk, he showed them how to dilute it with water, so that they could get it down.

By that time his dose of laudanum had lost its power, and he took another dose from the bottle in his pocket. This aroused the curiosity of his captors; they tried to take the bottle from him. Smith would not let them have it. He would rather have lost his scalp than that bottle. He told them it was dangerous 'medicine.' But he offered to give each a little.

It came to him that the laudanum was the thing which would save his life. He gave each one a dose to knock him out.

When the drug took effect, one after another fell asleep. Smith relaxed. He had got the best of them. For he knew

they would not only sleep; they would have bad dreams.
And no Injun would go ahead with anything when his
dreams were bad. Injuns believed that their dreams contained their destiny. Smith felt safe; in time they would
wake up, but they would never take his trail.

Smith helped himself to their powder and lead and buffalo robes, cleaned and reloaded his guns, picked a fast
horse to ride, and filled his saddle-bags with meat. He
broke all the bows and arrows, threw them on the fire, and
tossed all the guns and knives into the creek. Then he
rounded up the ponies, and was ready to start. Sol Silver
used to rawhide Smith because he did not raise the Injun
hair. But at that time Smith had never killed a redskin;
it never occurred to him to scalp his helpless enemies.

However, just as he was ready to start, two more Blackfeet rode over the hill. Smith did not shoot, for he was
afraid they were only the leaders of a larger party. He let
them come up to the campfire. When they saw the burning bows and their friends lying around as if dead, one of
them drew a bead on Smith. But Smith had the first shot,
and dropped him. The second Injun tried to ride away,
but Smith shot his horse and the animal bucked the Blackfoot off on his head. Before he could throw off his daze,
Smith was on him. The Blackfoot was strong, and fought
like a tiger. Maybe he might have killed Smith — that
was Smith's belief. But in the tussle the Blackfoot happened to hurt Smith's sore jaw. This made Smith so mad
that it seemed he suddenly had the strength of two men.
He got the Injun down, stabbed him.

He was frightened then, and mad as a wet hen. His knees began to shake. Those Blackfeet had scared him nearly to death, had stolen his possibles, used up most of his precious pain-killer, tried to kill him.

Smith suddenly understood how the Injun-fighters felt. He scalped every one of those Blackfeet — seven of them — taking care to leave the white shells, the brass wire, and other trinkets tied to their hair.

Smith wrapped the scalps in a piece of buffalo hide and rode back to the fort. Leaving his captured ponies out of sight in the brush, he rode to the gate. When he banged on it, the clerk opened the wicket, expecting to see one of the Blackfeet. He held in his hand some trinkets, which Smith always claimed were intended to reward the Injuns for killing him. When the clerk saw Smith, he was frightened, and tried to shut the wicket. But Smith blocked that with the bundle of scalps.

'Wagh, what ye scairt of? You done told me to fetch you the next peltries I tuk, didn't ye? Well, hyar they air! Take a look, and tell me how ye like 'em!'

The clerk opened the package, and started back. Those fresh trophies, with their familiar hair-ornaments, told him plainly what had happened. He was terrified; and when he looked up he found himself staring into the muzzle of the trapper's long rifle.

'Now,' said Smith, 'I reckon ye kin see them thar bluffs acrost the river? Well, I aim to lay low over thar till sundown. That bluff is in easy rifle-shot of this yere gate. I got a durn good notion to kill ye now, only I reckon you ain't wuth the powder. Thar's one way — jest one way — you can save your pesky hide. You kin shet this yere leetle winder in the gate, and get back inside. And ye kin *keep* 'er shet. Happen I see it open, or anybody pokin' his nose out afore sundown, your booshway will have another scalp to hang alongside of these yere Blackfoot topknots I fotched ye. Savvy?'

The clerk, pale as a sheet, understood perfectly. He slapped the wicket shut, and Smith heard his feet on the gravel as he ran back behind the shelter of the inner gate. Smith rounded up his horses, swam them across the river, and, after firing a shot or two from the bluffs into the fort gate, struck out for Crow country, to the southeast. The laudanum so dulled his aches and pains that he was able to ride day and night as long as the horses could travel. On the Yellowstone he fell in with a party of trappers traveling with some friendly Sioux. Smith gave each of the Sioux a horse from his band — the animals were pretty well worn down by that time — and so made himself welcome in their camps. They dubbed him 'Blackfoot.'

Camping with the Sioux, he soon became known to the Cheyennes, their allies, and when some Arapaho ran off his horses, he followed the thieves south to the Arkansas River, where he lost the trail. Down there, Smith took a fancy to a Southern Cheyenne woman, and set up a lodge of his own, running buffalo with her relatives. His record among the Blackfeet, his shrewdness, his linguistic talents, combined with his ability as a trader, soon made him a big man among the Cheyennes. The Arapaho were old allies of the Cheyennes, often in their camps, and 'Blackfoot' Smith has the distinction of being one of the very, very few white men who have mastered their difficult language.

Garrard later knew him well. He says the New Mexicans often came in small parties to his Indian village, their mules packed with dried pumpkin, corn, and peppers, to trade for robes and meat; and Smith, who knew his power, exacted tribute, which was always paid. One time, however, on their refusing, Smith harangued the village, and, calling the young men together, they resolutely proceeded to the party of cowering Mexicans; emptying every sack on the ground, they called the women and children to help themselves, which summons was obeyed with alacrity.

'The poor *pelados* left for El valle de Taos, poorer, by far, than when they came; uttering thanks to Heaven for the retention of their scalps. This, and other aggravated cases, so intimidated the New Mexicans, and impressed them so deeply with a sense of Smith's supreme potency, that ever after his permission to trade was humbly craved, by a special deputation of the parties, accompanied by peace offerings of corn, pumpkin, and *pinole*.

'Once, as he was journeying by himself a day's ride from the village, Smith was met by forty or more corn traders, who, instead of putting speedily out of the way such a bane to their prospects, gravely asked him if they could proceed, and offered him *every third robe* (a large percentage) to accompany and protect them, which he did. For the

STOMIK-SOSAK, CHIEF OF THE BLOOD INDIANS, OF THE
BLACKFOOT CONFEDERACY

proceeds of his three days' protection, he received more than two hundred dollars. Indeed, he became so independent, and so regardless of justice, in his condescension towards the Mexicans that the Governor of New Mexico offered five hundred dollars for him, dead or alive; but, so afraid were they of the Cheyennes, his capture was never attempted.

'Smith was strange in some respects; his peculiar adaptation to surrounding circumstances, and perceptive faculties, enabled him to pick up a little knowledge of everything, and to show it off much to his own credit — an unaccountable composition of goodness and evil, cleverness and meanness, caution and recklessness.'

Smith's explanation of his success was this: 'When I trade with Injuns, I allus open my hand wide fust of all, make 'em presents galore. That makes 'em friendly, see. But one thing I've l'arned, sartain: once in every swap thar comes a time when you have got to be mean and ornery as any pizen varmint. That's all thar is to it.'

William Bent soon became aware of Smith's presence in his trading territory, and was quick to understand that such a man would be invaluable to Old Fort Bent. Bent hired Smith, and so at last 'Blackfoot' settled down in the profession he had hankered for from the first — that of trader, in which he stuck to the end of his days.

Perhaps he threw in with Bent, St. Vrain and Company partly because they were the biggest rivals of the American Fur Company, whose unscrupulous clerk had fleeced him so unmercifully. He must have got some satisfaction in knowing that he was helping to injure them, at any rate.

It was just as well that Smith quit the trade of trapping when he did. Two years later, the vogue of the silk hat had cut the price of beaver to one dollar the plew, and the extermination of fur-bearing animals over wide areas in the West made trapping not only unprofitable but twice as hard work. Moreover, the hostility of the Indians steadily increased everywhere, and as they became possessed of better arms they became more dangerous, if possible, than before. The cost of packing trade goods to rendezvous was as great as ever: mountain prices could not be brought down. And so those later fur fairs were sober meetings: traps could no longer provide beaver to be gambled away at rendezvous, or thrown away in drunken sprees. If no wiser, the trapper was certainly a sadder man.

It was not merely the fear of losing his hair which made 'Blackfoot' Smith make tracks away from the Blackfoot country; it was common sense.

The end of the fur trade was in sight.

XIII. PUEBLO REVOLT

THE end of the fur trade was not the end of the mountain men.

In truth, their greatest services to the nation were to follow, for they were then forced into other walks of life, most generally into the service of the public or the Government. Thus, they are memorable, not merely for their heroic character, their daring exploits, their severe hardships, their far-flung explorations in search of fur, but even more for their truly magnificent labors in behalf of the American people and the Government of the United States.

When the mountain men found their occupation gone, they also found their abilities much in demand as interpreters, Indian agents, and treaty-makers among the Indians; as guides to surveyors, colonists, railroad men, and military expeditions; as Army scouts; as pilots for wagontrains of movers; as leaders of great herds of cattle and flocks of sheep being driven to the Coast; as soldiers in the conquest of California and New Mexico — and Utah; and as patrols along the endless frontier trails.

Congenial work was also ready to their hands in the almost continual Indian wars; wars with Ute, Navajo, and Apache, in the mountains; wars with Kiowa, Comanche, Cheyenne, Arapaho, Blackfeet, and Sioux, on the Plains. In all these campaigns some mountain men figured; sometimes only one, or two together, sometimes a larger group.

These services, these wars, were not of their own seeking. Most of the trappers were ready to settle down when the beaver fur lost its value. And most of them, naturally, preferred to settle in the Southwest — in Santa Fe, at the Pueblo on the Arkansas River above Bent's Fort, and especially in Taos. Taos was the town they returned to, and Taos always made them welcome. Taos was the mountain capital of the fur trade, the permanent rendezvous of the trappers: they loved it.

It was small — of hardly five hundred people in those days — but its little plaza, surrounded by whitewashed, crumbling, flat-roofed, one-story adobe houses, with their small mica windows protected by iron bars or painted shutters, promised shelter and peace. The cottonwoods rustled soothingly above the hitch-racks in the plaza, the lazy burros wandered through the narrow, unpaved, winding lanes and alleys leading to some friendly doorway cut in the thick walls, opening upon a quiet, shadowy interior, or green patio, where the *acequia* rippled by. The beehive ovens in the yard and the smoke rising from chimneys made of broken pots smelled of hospitality, an open fire in a corner fireplace, where a tired trapper could warm his bones and burn his tobacco in comfort. Taos meant rest, peace, and comfort: it also meant talk, women, color, and the bustle and boisterous fun of the fandango and the American bar. There the mountain man found all that he needed: friends, credit, a new outfit, a market for his beaver.

What wonder that the mountain man, left to himself, inevitably turned his toes to Taos and its beautiful valley? Everything that he craved was there. There he wished to settle.

What wonder that the mountain men there fought their chief battle, gained their chief victory, at Taos, fighting as a separate force, in the final conquest of New Mexico — the crushing of the Pueblo revolt. In that campaign they fought, not merely for their own people, for their own flag, and to avenge their comrades: they fought for Taos, for their old home and headquarters. Taos was home to Kit Carson, Tom Boggs, Charles Bent, Lucien Maxwell, Ceran St. Vrain, Ewing Young, and many another veteran of the Injun fracas and the beaver stream. And if they had loved the valley and the town when it was in Mexican territory, they loved it even more after the Stars and Stripes floated from the flagstaff in the Taos plaza.

That happened after General Stephen Watts Kearny, at the head of the Army of the West, came marching into New Mexico.

The victory there, to tell the truth, was at first one rather of diplomacy than of arms. As in California, there were two conquests: the first, peaceful; the second, real and bloody. Indeed, the whole Mexican War was con-

ducted in an amateur spirit so far as the Army was concerned. Not that the soldiers were not brave, hardy, and
successful. But their commanders seem to have been so
highly charged with patriotism, idealism, and theory that
they seldom were aware of the actualities, whether of
international law or of fact. As usual in those days, the
Army made the mess, and the mountain men had to mop
it up. War was declared in May, 1846.

For a long time before, the Spanish and Mexican diplo-
mats had been aware of the probability of an American
invasion, and the manner in which Texas had won her
independence had only increased their fears. Many believed that American traders were in sympathy with the
Texans in their rebellion. In 1843, Texans had raided
Mora, and there had been other clashes. Every American
in New Mexico was regarded with suspicion by the authorities, and even at Bent's Old Fort beyond the frontier there
were spies in the pay of the Mexican Government. After
the Texan–Santa Fe Expedition, with its attendant atroci-
ties, had been given wide publicity in the States, feeling
there against Mexico was strong. The traders from the
States had always resented the high tariffs levied upon
their business by the authorities at Santa Fe and Taos.
Those authorities were in truth not always men of the
highest type, and the influence of money, of the clergy,
and of politics upon these officials seemed overstrong to
some of the men from the States. And though many of
the mountain men had originally left the States in order
to escape from American law and order, they were in favor

of the conquest, almost to a man. They were always ready for a fight. They knew that the annexation of Texas meant war with Mexico.

When Kearny had brought his fifteen hundred men as far as Bent's Fort, Governor Armijo called on the patriots of New Mexico to rally and defend the fatherland. But after James McGoffin had been sent forward in advance of the troops as an emissary of the President of the United States and the Government, and had conferred with the officials at Santa Fe, a change came over Armijo. Just what McGoffin said, or did, or offered, has never been revealed. But certain it is that, after making preparations to defend Apache Pass to the death, Armijo dismissed the levies he had called to the flag, and with his regular troops decamped without waiting to fire a shot. The Pass could easily have been defended, though of course Kearny could have reached Santa Fe by another route. Armijo had about two thousand men, many of them ill-armed and untrained. But, whatever his motives may have been, his flight without offering battle made many a patriotic New Mexican blush with shame. Even some who were inclined to welcome the Americans were thus embarrassed. As the Lieutenant-Governor declared, 'The Mexican Republic . . . was our mother. What child will not shed abundant tears at the tomb of his parents?'

Deserted by their Governor and his troops, the natives of New Mexico accepted the conquest with as much resignation as they could muster. To be sure, many of them had no love for Armijo or the Mexican Government, torn as it was by civil war. And when General Kearny arrived and read his proclamations, setting up a territorial government in New Mexico, and informing the inhabitants that he had transferred their allegiance from Old Mexico to the United States, they were nevertheless disturbed. Neither of these things was within the powers or the rights of the General, and it was not long until the President let it be known that Kearny had no such authority.

But Kearny, having organized his civil government and appointed a governor, took his troops and marched on towards California. Colonel Sterling W. ('Old Pap') Price was left in command of the garrison in Santa Fe. His handful of troops were scattered about the territory, wherever they could find forage for their horses.

As the autumn dragged on, New Mexican dissatisfaction increased. The troops sent to bring them the blessings of freedom and civilization were too often overbearing and insulting, the political volunteer officers lax and sometimes dissipated. The troops were seldom drilled, and had to be kept busy building Fort Marcy to keep them out of mischief. As a result, the natives lost their fear and their respect for the invaders, and the Pueblo Indians — at first friendly — became sullen and dissatisfied. Those malcontent under the new Government soon began to work upon the minds of the rest. Among them were officials whom Kearny had ousted, and others who disliked the new régime. A revolt was planned for Christmas Day.

This revolt was discovered: some of the leaders were arrested; others escaped. Then a second, more secret plot was formed. This time the center of rebellion was in the northern counties, where people began to arm and prepare for a general and simultaneous uprising. In this they were perfectly within their rights, since they had *not* sworn allegiance to the new Government. But Kearny and his men considered such action was *treason!*

Charles Bent was then the leading American citizen residing in New Mexico. He had made his home there for fourteen years, and was one of the ablest, wealthiest, and most public-spirited Americans in the mountains. Before that time he had been a fur trader in the Missouri Fur Company, out of St. Louis, was a graduate of West Point and an old Army man. He was now senior partner in the second biggest fur company in the West. He was also thoroughly adapted to New Mexico, and married to Maria Ignacio Jaramillo, a lady of excellent family, by whom he had several children. It was inevitable that he should be chosen as Governor of the new territory. No other mountain man was so well fitted for the post.

However, like every son of Adam, Charles Bent had his weakness — a weakness which left him naked to the cruel dangers rising secretly around him. To grasp these fully, we must put ourselves in the moccasins and behind the eyes of the mountain men. They, always filling up on buffalo, bear, or venison, had only contempt for men who would subsist on pork. Those *mangeurs de lard*, or pork-eaters, formed the lowest class of employees in the fur trade. They served as boatmen, camp-keepers, and laborers about the forts; they worked like slaves — and usually for less than their keep. The ration of the United States soldier was then also largely of pork. Farmers in those days commonly referred to a pig as 'Ned,' and because the soldiers lived on pork, the mountain men contemptuously called them 'Neds,' too.

These pork-eaters also habitually lived in forts — or, as the mountain men put it, 'slept inside.' They depended upon walls and towers to protect them, instead of relying upon their own wits and good right arms, as the mountain men had to do. Such fellows, such pork-eaters and Neds, the mountain men despised.

Charles Bent was no pork-eater; his table groaned with the best the country afforded. Nor was he a Ned. He had been bred in the mountains, understood them and the men who had been bred there, knew Injuns and buffalo as well as any of them. But education at West Point had made him tolerant of military men, and years of family life, peaceful trading, and security in the Mexican settlements had robbed him in great measure of the mountain man's ingrained vigilance, his lively distrust of Injuns, 'Spaniards,' Neds, and men from the settlements in general. There was a leetle too much fofurraw in the life of a comfortable trader like Charles Bent. He was not soft, but he was easy-going. He had slept inside too long.

Enemies were at work, setting a death-trap for him and his like.

This new plot, hatched by those who had escaped punishment for the first attempt, was so well hidden that the Governor believed everything was settling down for the best interests of all concerned. He issued a proclamation announcing the end of the first revolt, and described himself therein as 'the best friend' of the people of New Mexico. Then, without fear of danger from the neighbors he had known so long, he set out for Taos to visit his family, refusing a military escort. That was the fourteenth day of January, 1847. The Governor had only five days to live.

Many of the most influential citizens in the northern counties were engaged in stirring up the rebellion, and they worked with especial success upon the fears and lusts of the Indians of the Pueblo de Taos. These Indians were told that their property would be confiscated, their children taken away, their wives stolen, and that they themselves would all be branded on the cheek and enslaved. Their leaders were enraged, not merely against the Americans, but against all who had accepted office under the new Government. When Governor Bent arrived in Taos, his undefended person only incited the ringleaders the more.

On January 18, a friend who had caught echoes of the trouble brewing urged Bent to get away while there was yet time. But Bent could not believe that his fellow-townsmen intended to murder him. Taos was so small, and he had known them all so long. The warning went unheeded. He was happy with his family, after the long separation caused by his duties in Santa Fe. He stayed at home that evening, and went to bed early.

All that night the village was in an uproar. The rising sun would be the signal for revolt throughout the territory.

The plan was simple — the same plan which had worked so perfectly against the Spanish *padres* in the seventeenth century: a sudden, simultaneous uprising, and the immediate slaughter of every alien upon New Mexican soil. The plotters simply adopted this old scheme, originally devised by the Pueblo Indians. It had succeeded once before in Taos: why not again? All that night the plotters were at work. Most of the Indians from the Pueblo, two miles away, were in town, and the saloons and public rooms were jammed to the doors. Taos Lightning and wine flowed like water, while the demagogues harangued the excited people.

Pablo Montoya, who aspired to be known as 'the Santa Ana of the North,' and Tomasito Romero, an Indian leader from the Pueblo, soon roused their followers, both Mexican and Indian, to a frenzy of rage and murderous hatred. Very early in the morning, they led the howling mob down the street leading to the Governor's home. That house still stands.

The Governor and his family were suddenly roused by the noise of the mob crowding into the *placita*. Bent, hearing the noise, went to the door and tried to pacify the people. He could hardly believe, even then, those men would attack him. He had always dealt fairly with them: why should they turn upon him?

Mrs. Bent was quicker to sense the danger to her husband. She snatched up his pistols, thrust them into his hands. But Bent laid them aside. 'If I fight, they'll murder you too,' he said gravely. 'They'll kill me, anyway.'

While he parleyed at the door, the frightened family crowded together in an inner room, shaken with forebodings: Mrs. Bent, her sister Mrs. Kit Carson, Señora Boggs, and the children, most of them little girls. The youngest, Teresina, was only five. When Bent turned back to reassure his family, his little son Alfredo, just ten, came lugging out an old shotgun. He had been bred on the frontier, and showed no fear. Taking his stand beside his father, he said, 'Papa, let's fight them!'

But Bent would not fight. He knew the Indian character too well. If he resisted, they would not only murder him, but his whole family. He would not touch a weapon. Gently he took the shotgun from his son and laid it aside. What a noble gentleman he was!

Meanwhile, the women, despairing of help, began frantically to dig through the thick adobe walls. They had only a poker and an old iron spoon. Mrs. Carson and Mrs. Bent, aided by a peon woman, wielded these, and to such good effect that they made a hole into a room of the house next door. Then they pushed the children through the hole, one after another. Afterward the women went through. Bent waited until the last one had passed through.

Even then he lingered, fearing to anger the mob, and so bring about a massacre of those he loved. His wife kept calling to him to come through the hole, and save himself.

But Charles Bent knew well it was too late for that. Had he been alone, he might have tried it, or attempted to fight his way out, or have died there with the song of battle in his heart. But as it was, he had his loved ones to think of, his family to protect. He could not escape and leave them behind at the mercy of that drunken, blood-crazy mob. He could not escape and take them with him; that would only mean quick pursuit, quick capture, and a general massacre. He could not even fight for them, or defend his own life, lest he endanger theirs. Poor, great-hearted gentleman, he even hesitated to follow his wife through the hole in the wall, in the vain hope that the mob would murder him where he stood, and leave the women in peace beyond the wall. She pleaded with him, while he stood facing the breaking door, hiding the hole in the wall as best he could with his body.

By that time, the mob had broken down the door with axes, and firing through, wounded him in the chin and in the stomach. Then they rushed in, shot him again with arrows, and, yelling like fiends, scalped him alive.

Bent staggered to the hole the women had made and crawled through, one hand clasped upon his bleeding skull. But the mob had tasted blood now; he was not to escape so easily. Some followed him through the hole; others came over the roofs, leaped down into the yard, and forced the door to the room where the pleading women and sobbing children huddled about the dying man. Before their eyes the cruel killers shot Bent, again and again, until he fell dead.

Then the shout was raised to take the family away prisoners. But soon they decided to leave them there, posting a guard to see that no one should feed them or let them out. Tomasito stripped off the Governor's coat, put it on, and led his triumphant murderers away, brandishing Bent's scalp, which was soon after tacked to a board and carried through the streets.

All that day and the following night the frightened women and children huddled in that grim room, starving, grief-stricken, and without any covering but their night-gowns in that wintry weather. All that time the body of their father and their friend lay naked and mutilated in a pool of dark blood. Hour after hour of horror.

Meanwhile, the mob scouted through the town, looking for other victims. They killed Lee, the sheriff, on his own housetop, and the prefect, Cornelio Vigil, who tried to argue with them. The district attorney, J. W. Leal, was scalped alive and dragged naked through the streets, prodded forward with the points of lances. After hours of such torture, they left him lying in the street on the snow. He begged those who passed to put him out of his pain. At last some Mexican, more compassionate than the rest, ended his sufferings by a shot.

When the massacre began, the young son of Judge Beaubien, Narcisse, a youth just back from college, ran with his body-servant and took cover in the stable. There he and his friend hid in the manger under the straw. But as the mob came prowling that way, and were about to leave again, a woman — a servant of the family — ran up to the housetop and called them back. 'Kill the young ones,' she screeched, 'and they will never be men to trouble us!'

The mob rushed back, searched the stable, dragged the unfortunate young men from the manger, scalped them, and killed them both.

Mrs. Bent's brother Pablo was also murdered. Tomasito and Montoya ranged the village, searching every house, looking for every *Americano*, or friend of an *Americano*, to be found. Those found were quickly destroyed. Then they set off to rub out the mountain men at Turley's Mill. . . .

Drained of men by this new excitement, Taos stood almost empty. And so, very early in the morning, two Mexican friends of the Bents slipped into the unwatched house, and found the room where the shivering women and children were waiting with their great sorrow. They brought them food and clothing. Then, with the generous and courageous kindliness natural to Spanish-Americans, they quickly spirited the little party away to their own home. There they disguised Mrs. Bent and the other ladies as Indian squaws, with the characteristic white boots and hair-dress of the Taos women, and set them to work in the kitchen, grinding corn on metates. The children also went in masquerade, with faces stained dark as any Indian's.

Mrs. Carson — Josefa — lamented the absence of her husband, Kit. He was well known in Taos — known, and *feared!* His reputation was one to inspire fear and reason in the most bloodthirsty Pueblo. And he had great influence with the citizens of San Fernandez de Taos also. Together he and Bent might have stood off that mob, and saved the life of a gallant gentleman.

But Kit was with General Kearny. Bent had no defender.[1]

XIV. TAOS RECONQUERED

WHILE revolt raged in Taos, William Bent, the brother of the Governor and his partner in business, was quietly busy in the Indian trade. His headquarters were at Bent's Old Fort, sometimes called Fort William, on the north bank of the Arkansas River on the plains of Colorado, more than a hundred miles east of the mountains. As usual in winter, William Bent was encamped in his big buffalo-hide lodge, trading with his relatives by marriage, the Cheyenne Indians. They were then snugly camped in that grove of huge cottonwoods on the Arkansas, known as the Big Timber, some distance below the fort. Alongside Bent's family lodge was another in which were his clerks and employees: Fisher and Long Lade, traders; Pierre and another pork-eater, name unknown. There Lewis H. Garrard, a young man traveling with Bent's trader, 'Blackfoot' Smith, joined them. It was cold and snowy, towards the end of January.

Garrard has given us a vivid account of what followed when the mountain men there learned of the tragedy at Taos.[1]

On the morning of January 28, Smith and Garrard were in the log house, trading beads to an old squaw for a piece of meat. While she haggled, demanding an addition to Smith's already generous offer, she pursed her lips, after the Cheyenne manner, and pointed with them at an approaching object, saying, 'Blackfoot! Look yonder! There's a white man.'

Smith and Garrard looked where she pointed, and recognized an old *compañero* — Louis Simonds, recently employed by the Government troops as a hunter, and evidently fresh from the fort upriver. As he came close, he hailed Smith, 'How are ye, John?'

'What Louy, old coon, down hyar? How's times to Fort William! — but let's see, you's the one as run "meat" for them gover'ment fellers to Bent's ranch — eh?'

'Yes! An' this child was mighty nigh losin' his har, he was.'

'How?'

'Them durned Spaniards!'

'H——! Anybody "gone under" to Touse?'

'Yes! Guverner Charles.'

'Wa-agh! But them palous 'ill pay for their scalpin' yet, I'm thinkin'.'

'We went in the lodge, where the men, after recovering from the surprise of seeing an old *compañero*, were told the sad news of Governor Bent's death, and while Louy was stowing away huge pieces of buffalo, he was interrogated by the anxious traders.

'Louy, tell all 'bout the whole consarn; it's all over now,

an' can't be worse. I 'spect the niggurs got my woman
too,' said Fisher, who was a resident of Taos, the scene of
the massacre. 'Who else is under, 'sides Charles?'

'Well, you see the Pueblos was mity mad fur the 'Mericans to come in thar diggins an' take everything so easy
like; an' as Injin blood is bad an' sneakin', they swore to
count *coups* when they could. So when Charles was down
to Touse to see his woman, the palous charged afore sunrise. The portal was too strong fur 'em, an' they broke in
with axes, an' a Pueblo, cached behint a pile of 'dobies,
shot him with a Nor'west fusee twice, an' skulped him.'

'Scalped him — scalped Charles?' cried the men, partly
springing to their feet, and clutching their knives. 'Thar
be heap of wolfmeat afore long — sartain!'

'Yes, an' they took the trail for Santy Fee; but afore
they left, Steve Lee dropped in his tracks too. "Hell!"
says I, "the palou as threw that arrer is marked," an' so
he is — Wa-agh!'

'Was Narcisse Beaubien killed, Louy?' asked one.

'Who? — that young feller as kem with the wagons,
last fall, with St. Vrain?'

'Yes, the same.'

'Oh, he's gone beaver 'long with the rest. He was Mexican blood, an' so much the better fur them. They had a
big dance when his topknot was off. Well, you see,' com-
mencing once more, 'a band of the devils got to the Poinel
Ranch, over Taos Mountain, and back agin with the
biggest kind of cavyard. Maybe *coups* wasn't counted
that trip! The sojers — a lot of greenhorns and Dutchmen

— came to Purgatoire, this side of Raton. Frank De Lisle had the company's wagons, an' the boys thar. We cached along the trail fur the Arkansas — *well*, we did! Mulemeat went a-wolfin' that spree — Wagh!'

'Where is Drinker? He was at the ranch, I believe.'

'Out in the piñon, that morning, with his big Saint Loui' gun — a Jake Hawkins gun, she was, eh? He had bullets an inch long, with a sharp pint — be doggoned ef they wasn't some, eh? — We had to leave him, but I guess he'll come in safe.'

'Will they take Santy Fee, think ye, Louy?' inquired Fisher.

'Now that's more than this hoss kin tell. He hasn't made "medicine" yet; but I'm afraid the 'Mericans will "go under."'

When this bad news was relayed to William Bent, he came and called Louis outside. No one followed. All pitied William. He was the second of the four Bent brothers, and as Charles was older, and had always been the head of the firm, William loved and respected him as a father.

Everyone in camp was much depressed by the sad news. They were also worried as to their own safety. Now that Taos had been taken by the rebels, Santa Fe would be their next objective. And if Santa Fe were taken, the whole country from El Paso to Taos would be in revolt. Bent's Fort was an important post, on the line of communications of the Army of the West. William Bent had let the Army use it freely. Besides, it contained much

valuable property. The mountain men fully expected a
Mexican force to be sent against it.

When the Cheyennes learned of the murder of their old
friend, Woh'pi Ve'hiu (the Gray-haired White Man), they
were thunderstruck. No mountain man was more respected or beloved by that tribe of fierce fighters; they had
known him ever since, as a young man, in 1822, he had
gone up the Missouri into the Sioux country to start life
as an Indian trader, a member of the Missouri Fur Company at Fort Recovery (Cedar Fort). Now, Bent's Fort
was the trade-house of the southern bands of the tribe.
The old men stalked about the snowy camp, shouting the
news, muffled in their shaggy robes, from which their
frosty breath jetted with their spouts of indignation and
grief. Soon the chiefs were seen, gathering at the soldier-
lodge. There they consulted briefly, and then went in a
body to their friend, William. Gravely they offered him
the pipe, explaining that they wished to help him in this
moment of need and sorrow. 'Friend,' they said, 'we will
send our young men to Taos, and they shall scalp every
Mexican in the country.'

William Bent was touched by this proof of their loyal
friendship, and he well knew that, if they went, they
would make good their word. Nothing would have pleased
them more than to rub out the killers of their old friend
Charles.

But William Bent would not assume responsibility for
such a raid. He thanked the chiefs with tears in his eyes,
but answered, 'Friends, if it is necessary, the white soldiers at the fort will go and punish our enemies.'

The Cheyennes were disappointed, but accepted William's word as final. That night he talked with his men, and decided to hurry back to the fort next morning and see what could be done. Garrard volunteered to go with him. He tells us of that melancholy journey, and of an incident which well illustrates the character of the old-time mountain man.

'At the following dawn, Mr. Bent and I left for the fort, some forty miles distant, taking no baggage but the ropes strapped to the saddles.

'The morning was cold and cloudy, in consonance with our moody taciturnity. Keeping the south bank of the river for some miles, we attempted a ford. Our fractious mules gave much trouble, detaining us a vexatious half hour; we then broke the ice, and dragged and pushed in their unwilling feet by main strength.

'While breasting the strong wind, which keeps the trail nicely swept as with a broom, we saw, emerging from a patch of high marsh grass, skirting a belt of cottonwoods on the river's margin, a Mexican, mounted on a strong, iron-gray horse. He wore, in lieu of a hat, a handkerchief bound over his head, under the edges of which long jetty locks flitted to the breeze. His right hand grasped a short bow and a few arrows. He was passing at a gallop when Bent, with his cocked rifle, shouted in Spanish to stop. The man stated that he belonged to William Tharpe's company; but the skulk's restless eye, and his every motion, seemed to indicate more than he told. After a searching cross-examination, Bent told him to *vamos pronto!* (go quick), or he would send a ball through him, anyhow. I expected to see the Mexican pitch from his horse through the aid of a bullet. Bent turned to follow him, expressing a regret at not having taken a shot.

'By sundown we reached the fort, having traveled the entire day without ten minutes' halt, or scarcely a word of conversation. Fifty dirty, uncouth, green-looking Missourians, in command of Captain Jackson, hung about us as we left the saddles.

'There was much excitement in regard to the massacre, some expecting a Mexican army to appear on the hill across the river; others, strutting inside the high and secure fort walls, gasconaded and looked fierce enough to stare a mad "buffler" out of countenance, declaring themselves ready to wade up to their necks in Mexican blood. Everyone, however, had cause for fear, as the American force was known to be small and much weakened by being scattered in small herding parties throughout the province. The traders, and the rest, proposed to push right on to Taos, steal all the animals, "raise" all the attainable Mexican "hair," burn every ranch, and "charge" generally.

'A while before dusk, an express from the Arkansas Pueblo, seventy miles above, arrived with the news that the United States detachment of volunteers stationed there were awaiting orders from Jackson, the superior in command. But the Captain (Jackson) would not act without orders from Colonel Price, at Santa Fe, at that time likely a prisoner. So the idea of aid in that quarter was reluctantly abandoned.

'Louy Simonds on leaving the ranch had cut across the country, by that means preceding the wagons several days. The morning after our arrival, Frank De Lisle's wagons corralled in front of the fort. My old friends the Canadian teamsters shook my hand heartily — finer fellows were never soaked by the prairie storms.

'About ten o'clock, as I was standing at the far end of the court, a tall man stalked in the gate, looking wildly around. A long, browned rifle rested on his shoulder, with that exquisite *négligé* air — firm yet careless-appearing; his long, black, uncombed hair hung in strings from beneath his greasy wool hat, and a frowning moustache gave a Satanic cast to his features. On his feet were thick moccasins, and to judge from the cut, of his own fashioning. His pantaloons, of gray cassinet, were threadbare, and rudely patched with buckskin. Instead of a coat, a blanket was thrown over the shoulder and fastened, at the waist, by a black leather belt, in which was thrust a brass-studded leather sheath, sustaining a "Green River" of no small pretensions as to length; and which, had it the power of speech, might dwell with ecstatic pleasure on the praise of choice morsels of fleece served by its keen edge — perchance astonish with the recital of the number of "Yutes," whose "humpribs" have been savagely tickled with its searching point. His quick eye, wandering, alighted on me, followed by —

'"How are you?"

'"Why, Drinker!" exclaimed I, in the utmost surprise, and taking his outstretched hand, "I'm glad to see you —

Louy Simonds told us that the Spaniards had taken your 'hair.'"

'"Oh pshaw! Not yet, I can assure you."

'"Did you travel by yourself all the way?"

'"No, not quite. I went out hunting that morning, and became so interested in a beaver dam that it was night before the ranch was reached again. Our men were gone, but I cooked some of the 'goat' I had that day killed, and on Louy's old deerskins, lying about camp, I slept until morning. I then followed their trail on foot, towards the Vermaho. The second day I caught up to a train, but they being too slow, I pushed ahead by myself. I overtook the company's wagons yesterday, and have been alone the rest of the time."

'"That's a quick trip for a pedestrian. How long were you in coming? It's about one hundred and seventy miles."

'"Oh! a little over six days. My moccasins nearly gone the way of all flesh" replied he, looking at his feet. . . .'

At the fort, William Bent, finding that the troops would do nothing, made up his mind to act on his own hook. He called his men together in the graveled patio. There he stated his case, proposed an expedition to Taos, and did not forget to remind the men of the many dangers such a small party might face — from Mexican troops, from hostile Injuns (now probably incited to attack the Americanos wherever met), and from the bitter weather. He ended by saying that whoever went should go as a volunteer; he would not try to force any man to go against his will. 'You can go or stay,' he said.

Every man in the fort — except the soldiers — offered his services!

Garrard has given us a detailed account of the hardships, the dangers, and the inconveniences of this warlike march of a handful of mountain men against the victorious hordes in Taos.

It was in the afternoon of the next day that the party was started, consisting of twenty-three men. Bransford was in charge of the seventeen employees and the wagon; the other five were free. One was Lucien Maxwell, a hunter to Frémont's expedition in 1842, a resident of the valley of Taos, and a son-in-law to Judge Beaubien (Narcisse's father). Manuel Le Févre, Lajeunesse, and Tom Boggs claimed a local habitation in Taos. They, very fortunately for themselves, happened to be on the opposite side of the mountain at the time of the massacre.

They crossed the river into Nueva Mejico at the fort ford, and followed the Santa Fe Trail, which kept to the river-bank. Five were mounted; the rest were to get animals at the Purgatoire, ninety miles distant. The object of the expedition in which they were about to engage was to travel as far as they could towards Taos, kill and scalp every Mexican to be found, and collect all the animals belonging to the Company and the United States.

Where the route diverged from the river at right angles for Santa Fe, they camped. On the west, white chalk cliffs cropped out from the brow of the hills; the soap plant spread its green fan here and there, and dead-seeming sagebushes, harsh and stiff, were dispersed in irregular

patches. No sun appeared; the chilling winds blew fit-
fully over the bleak plain, indicating an approaching snow-
storm.

As the Canadians trudged along, chattering in French,
overflowing with boisterous mirth, they thought not of
the fatigue of walking. All were equipped with Nor'west
fusils; with them, every prominent object in the road was
un sacré Mexican. When any one of them raised his fusil
to fire, all stopped; some leaned forward on tiptoe; others
drew back and sighted with one eye; and others again,
with half-open mouths, in anxious expectation, would
wait until the report of the gun rang out. Then all would
start forward at a run to the target. If a good shot, a *sacré
bon* of approbation might be heard; if not, they looked
carefully around, then examined the bushes twenty and
thirty feet from the target, in tones of solicitous irony
condoling and praising the marksman with such exclama-
tions as '*Un beau garçon!*' '*Votre fusil très bon*, wagh!'
'One Mexican he go ondare too, *parceque* you put de ball
through *son tête. Pauvre* Mexican!'

The wagon contained one barrel of flour for provision,
but no meat. Wood was scarce; with chunks from old
camps around, they cooked. They sat by the coals, Garrard talking to his Canadian friends of their trip to Santa
Fe, they to him of Indians. Their short clay pipes were
again and again filled before retiring. Bransford and Garrard slept together. With blankets and robes in a depres-
sion in the ground to keep off the wind, they made a snug
bed.

Some little effort was required to throw off the clothing, when getting up, by reason of the accumulated snow. A warmer covering could not have been made, as it effectually excluded the chill winds sweeping the hill behind them. The men, with their feet, found the wood and rekindled the fire.

What a sight greeted their eyes on rising! The hills, themselves, and saddles, were covered with the white drapery; bitter cold winds penetrated their clothes, while far off to the northwest the twin mountains — Las Cumbres Españolas — glittered with snow. The mules were starving; for the scanty grass was hidden early in the night with the same frigid envelope which contributed not an atom to their personal comfort, and they stood trembling over their picket-pins, pricking their ears at any noise, without moving their heads.

From the impossibility of journeying with any degree of warmth, and the fact of the total absence of wood at the next two camps, and the probability of more snow, it was decided by the leaders that all should stay in camp — choosing the lesser of two evils. Succeeding an unpleasant day of freezing on one side of their bodies and scorching on the other, with their eyes red, blinking, and weeping by reason of pungent wood smoke, they rolled into their robes to get warm all over — a desideratum not attainable outside of them. They slept in the open air, the sky their canopy, as usual. Trouble and many inconveniences, both great and small, are invariably attendant on the exposed life they were leading; and though there were too many harsh ejaculations and expressive curses at the ill luck for true philosophers, yet, from the frequent occurrence of such mishaps, they had learned to endure them as pains inevitable.

Here they had nothing but bread and coffee, which in truth, was less nourishing and acceptable than meat alone.

They were again on the road, the mules no better for their stay. The pedestrians, comprising four fifths of the company, had a laborious time walking through the snow, which, towards the middle of the day, melted, and rendered the ground slippery; but being Canadians was a sufficient guaranty for their acting with the proper spirit. Unpleasant matters will sometime end; and, following a tedious day's tramp, they made camp on Rio Timpa, a stream three or four feet in width, which, in pools and ripples, coursed along, a tributary to the great Mississippi. The Timpa rises in New Mexico.

Leaving the wagon on the bank, the men descended to the margin of the rivulet, to be free from the wind. The greasewood, so called from the crackling, eager flame in burning, afforded the only fuel; for the creek has ever been sparsely wooded, and General Kearny's division, en route to Santa Fe, had used the little that was left. The abovementioned bush here grows to the height of four or five feet, starting from the ground in uniform wiry stems, which, by a quick, bending motion, can be broken. It makes a hot, sparkling, though short durating fire, and, to judge from the odor exhaled, contained a large proportion of resinous matter. The green bush burns as well as the dry, and is well designed to supply the traveler with fuel. The teamsters and soldiers on the Fort Leavenworth and Santa Fe Trail are so improvident that not many had passed until the timber standing disappeared.

Unfortunately for the men's coffee, the waters of the Timpa were so impregnated with salt as to be scarcely drinkable, though not so brackish as in the dry weather.

Soon they were off again on their way. The small hills were thickset with a heavy growth of greasewood and sage, whose leafless, dead-appearing stems, protruding through the snow, gave a desolate, barren cast to the scenery. On the left were high bluffs, their tops crowned with stunted pine and cedar. The black-tailed deer, said to browse there, incited Garrard to a trial for meat; and, after much toiling up and down indentations and around chasms, the summit was reached. Reining in the mule, with forefeet on the highest rock, he looked around.

Far off to the northwest was the well-known Pike's Peak, connected towards the south, by a low range, to the Wet Mountain, so famed for the game within its very shadow; and, still farther to the south, the White Mountain, out-topping all; and yet below it, the twin Wah-to-yah, one beyond the other, rising until the farthest floated as clouds, their white crests apparently touching the sky — the whole view including a stretch of one hundred and fifty miles. From his position to the nearest was ninety miles or more, yet such was the extreme purity of the atmosphere that any one peak seemed attainable by a few hours' ride.

As the men (shortly after) pointed out the different spurs, they expatiated more particularly on the Wet Mountain, with its lovely savannas; its cool springs and murmuring rills; its shady bowers of fragrant cedar and sheltered spots of grass; its grizzly bear and mountain sheep; its silky beaver and black-tailed deer, with wide-spreading antlers; its monster elk and fleet-footed antelope; its luscious plums and refreshing grapes; its juicy cherries, delightful currants, and other attractions making it the hunter's paradise. That was a country worth fighting for.

They obtained a view of the effulgent snow-piled Raton, at whose base the road runs. At noon in came the hunters, with two antelope, scaring, as they descended the precipitous hills back to camp, a band of black-tail; who, clattering down, with graceful motions, sped across the plain, ears and head erect. They were much larger than the common deer, and the skin was preferred for dressing.

The sight of meat, slung across the hunters' saddles, gave avidity to the men's decidedly carnivorous appetites, as they had been two days without meat. The repast finished, and washed down with strong coffee, the officiating butcher-knives were wiped across their buckskins, with that deliberate languid air which plainly proclaimed 'Enough.'

Tom Boggs wanted some bullets. In lieu of a ladle he cut a shallow place in a stick of wood — a hunter's expedient — where, laying in the lead and piling on coals, the lead soon melted.

The wind rose at dark on February 3, driving most of

the men down by the water's edge, where, sheltered by the high banks, they talked and smoked. The Canadians were above, chattering in their usual glib style, when a sound like distant thunder filled the air. Down they rushed, all talking at once. All knew that it could not be thunder at that time of year, and the conclusion at which all soon arrived was that a battle was taking place in Taos; although it is a long distance there by the road, and a lofty mountain intervenes, it is not more than thirty-five or forty miles in a direct line. It was a hazardous trip for them to venture so far into Mexican territory, with no knowledge of affairs at Santa Fe and elsewhere, except those of an alarming nature; and they knew too well the carelessness and paucity of the American soldiery. They felt the Mexicans to be an injured people, possessed of vindictive tempers, who would, with a prospect of success, and under the guidance of brave leaders, revolt and fight well.

All were apprehensive that a Mexican force had over-powered the Americans at the Purgatoire (a day's ride in advance), and was on its way to Bent's Fort. Their position was anything but enviable. Maxwell, Le Févre, Lajeunesse, and Tom Boggs were cast down with thought of their families, who might at that moment be subject to the lawlessness of the infuriated populace. It was a gloomy night to those who, in anxious wakefulness, passed the long, dark hours till morning.

On awaking, spirits revived with the appearance of a happy sun; and, being thawed enough to raise a laugh and smoke a pipe good-humoredly, they hitched up and rolled over the prairie in earnest haste.

Now, although at night all the extra clothing was required as protection from the piercing winds, yet, towards noon, the heat was quite uncomfortable, and they encamped, after a long and warm drive, through a barren waste, save for an occasional stalk of cactus and scattering plants of the pamilla, from under whose sickly green leaves loped awkwardly large gray hares. They stayed in camp, without water, for the oxen to rest; and while waiting with thirsty impatience in the shade of the wagon, they saw advancing from the direction of the Raton an object, which was immediately pronounced a grizzly bear.

At the startling announcement, every man rose quickly to his feet, gun in hand, to encounter the unwelcome visitor. But the bear proved to be a worn-down ox with 'U.S.' stamped, in seared letters, on the left foreshoulder. The beast, though not grizzly by nature, was grizzly with age and hard work; his sharp bones nearly protruding through the lifeless-looking skin. He was, no doubt, journeying the prairie trail, on home intent, to the land of fodder and tall grass — the Platte Purchase, in Missouri; and how the poor thing came that far without being hamstrung by rapacious wolves was a wonder. The men, with self-interest at heart, detained the homesick youth, and that afternoon drove him, with many a harsh 'sacré' and 'wo-ha-a,' along the same road he had just languidly traversed; this time, with his head bowed in submission to the galling yoke of servitude, no more to see the land of promise but in dreams, while chewing the cud of hunger and disappointment.

Towards evening they came to a cañon, or enclosed creek, with bluffs forty, fifty, and even eighty or more feet in height. A diminutive streamlet trickled along the uneven bottom; in places disappearing, to reappear after a dark passage under the flat stones, to the brackish Timpa, thereby constituting the headwaters of that insignificant stream.

A camp, known as the Hole in the Rock — so called from the pools of water in the dry channel — was their resting-place for the night; the huge, detached masses lying around, the thick groves of cedar, and the shelving ground formed a good stopping-place, but in that state of insecurity, somewhat undesirable. All fixed themselves according to fancy, built cheerful fires, drank plenty of the mean water, ate considerable of the slim stock of poor provision, and smoked frequently, conjuring up, in the wreaths of strong smoke as they ascended, shapes both blessed and *au contraire*.

The fires grew low; all were in bed but poor Maxwell and Lajeunesse, both too uneasy to sleep for thought of their homes, when all were startled by the bark of dogs and the almost simultaneous rush of Bransford's hound from the camp. The men sprang to their feet, and ran from the fire in every direction, and Garrard, following suit, cached himself behind a large stone, with ready rifle. Everyone was in the bushes, ready for the attack, in a moment from the time the dog barked, though not a

shout of warning was heard from any. They reconnoitered,
now with faces flat to the ground to listen for footsteps,
now dashing through the bushes. After a quarter of an
hour, all ventured to return. Guards were set and continued through the night. What a train of new thought does
an affair like this bring! The anxious state of suspense,
the strain of the eyes in the endeavor to penetrate the
Cimmerian darkness, the dodging behind rocks and trees,
and the stealthy crawl of the older Indian fighters combined to work up to a greater tensity the men's already
high-strung feelings.

The following morn, ere the mists were fairly dispersed,
they were again in their hard saddles, trotting down the
little hills and walking up the elevations in the same old
way. They came in sight of the groves of dead cottonwoods on the Purgatoire by noon, and, diverging to the
right of the trail, took a short cut for the camp of United
States teamsters, whom they expected to find in a bend
of the stream.

Bent's men made camp in a small grove of dead cottonwoods, sheltered in the rear by a gentle hill, and surrounded by long bottom grass. They were as far from the
teamsters as safety dictated, for the never-satisfied inquis-
itiveness of the Government men was unbearable. Some
soldiers of Captain Fischer's artillery company were here.
They, too, left the ranch, driving with them large droves
of horses and cattle belonging to the United States
and Bent, St. Vrain and Company. When Bent's men
claimed the company's animals, the soldiers murmured

and disputed much, in which the teamsters sided with them.

On the eleventh, a fall of snow covered the ground a few inches in depth. Towards night the party was increased by the arrival of Sublette, an old *compañero*, accompanied by Bill Garmon and Fred Smith. They had ventured from the States with the United States express, this inclement season of the year, bringing with them the news that General Wool had been ordered to join General Taylor, and that forty thousand men were enrolled for Mexico.

All now felt badly indeed — Doniphan's regiment was in Chihuahua, with no force to support it, and its certain defeat would give the Santa Feans additional courage. Nearly a month had passed since Governor Bent was murdered; several expresses had been sent from this side into New Mexico, but none had returned. Their position, more than a hundred miles in the Mexican territory, was unsafe.

But the mountain men, instead of holding back, were only inspired to greater speed by this bad news. All that day they spent catching mules from the *caballada*, in order to make a dash for the valley of Taos, though the snow on the mountains in itself was enough to daunt any ordinary men.

On the thirteenth of February, the younger portion of the company, mounted on mules, with a few pack-animals, left La Barge and two more in camp with the wagon, to follow on the receipt of orders from Bransford. They bade farewell to the Purgatoire encampment, and, leaping the narrow stream and spurring the rejuvenated mules, gained the old trail; when, after a series of hill and dale, they turned to the left and commenced the ascent of the Raton Pass!

The route was up a steep valley, enclosed on either side by abrupt hills covered with pine and masses of gray rock, the course now along the points of hills, now in the rough stony bed of the creek itself. The sparkling, flitting waters, leaping and foaming against the mules' feet, now gliding under large flat stones, and now reappearing, bounding impetuously down the uneven flinty bed, mingled itself with the pure stream La Purgatoire, hundreds of feet below. As they ascended, the scenery partook of a bolder, rougher cast.

Towards four o'clock the party, fatigued with the incessant climbing, spurring, and walking, came to a valley gently sloping to the summit of the pass on the west, and rising on the east immediately by a continued succession of acclivities and terraces to the bare cliff, which, overlooking the country for leagues around, is known as the Raton Peak — a familiar landmark to the trappers and traders.

The summit of the ridge was reached after an hour's toil, and, stopping a moment for the fatigued animals to blow, they rapidly descended. The immense precipices of bare rock and earth, the confusion in which nature seemed involved, caused all to remark the forbidding aspect on the Rio Canadiano side of the summit. At some steep hills, near the pass terminus, they picked their way over a road which, in verity, might be termed rough. Pine trees interfered with the free use of the whip; large rocks obtruded their rude fronts in the tortuous road: one 'wo-ha-a' too many, or a 'gee' too few, here, endangered the safety of the unwieldy teams and burdens. The débris of wagons, such as felloes, loose tires, and tongues snapped short off, showed unmistakable signs of mismanagement, and told plainly that 'Government' was a loser in the Raton Pass.

Once more on the plain, rapid travel gave place to the late tiresome mule-wriggling; and at noon the saddles were pulled off the warm and thirsty animals under a cottonwood, on the banks of El Rio Canadiano, at this point a glassy, snow-fed streamlet, fifteen feet in width.

On crossing the stream, Maxwell, who had heretofore stayed with the crowd, kept some distance in advance as scout. The others were strung carelessly along, when he, jerking his mule around quickly, spurred her in a gallop, and diverged from the route, at the same time motioning to them to ride *à la Comanche* — with their bodies so that nothing could be seen on the opposite side but part of the leg with which, and the heel of the same, they held on to the saddle cantle. There was no hill, but the gradual rise of the ground served to conceal any object approaching from the other side. They were quite excited, thundering along at full speed, able to sweep the ground with the free hand, with rifles ready to jerk up to the face, not knowing whether the run was from Mexicans, or a band of Utahs, or Apaches, or whether they were trying to surprise a party themselves. But too well versed were all in Indian warfare, through practice or hearsay, to question at such a time, or to utter any noise except, indeed, a Canadian's impatient *sacré diable* to his shying mule, or a smothered curse from a less conscientious American.

On making the rise, they espied a man unconscious of their proximity, going at half speed on one horse, and leading another; but so soon as he caught a glimpse of the foremost hat, away he lashed his animals in a full run. With wild yells, they straightened in the saddles, and, with the report of two or three fusils, in the hands of as many half-frantic Frenchmen, they charged after him, endeavoring to escape; but seeing that it would be of no use, he fired his gun in air in token of submission, and rode slowly towards Maxwell. It was Haw-he, an Indian, belonging to George Bent, now on his way to the fort. He brought them news.

Haw-he spoke American in broken sentences only. Said he: 'I see you come on de *caballos* (horses), and de *mulas* (mules) *poco tiempo* (swiftly) — me tink you *los Utes* (Indians), *carraho;* — me hair gone — me rubbed out (killed), but *quien sabe el caballo colorado esta bueno* (who knows but that my red horse here is good). Me be off *pronto* (at once); you fire de carabine, den I fire — me no want *nada* (nothing).' Maxwell knew from experience that no prairie traverser would permit a body of men to approach him for fear of undergoing the painful scalping operation. By surprising this man, he would be sure of him. Bransford, hastily writing a few words to our men at the Purgatoire to come on, sent Haw-he on his way.

Manuel Le Févre, Maxwell, and Tom Boggs left for Taos.

While William Bent's men were pushing through the snow to Taos, mountain men in other parts of New Mexico were not slow in organizing to revenge the death of the Governor. It was the old story all over again. Kearny, like Leavenworth, had been too ready to make peace without a substantial victory. Too well the mountain men knew that ye caint pacify Injuns, lessen ye lick 'em fust. Redskins, like small boys, have to fight before they can be friends.

News of the uprising in Taos reached Santa Fe on January 20. By that time the poorer people of the whole Taos Valley had joined the rebellious Pueblos, and were busy at pillage and murder. Other small communities all round joined with them, sending out manifestoes calling upon other towns to aid them. They organized themselves into an army of volunteers, elected leaders, and speedily armed themselves. Las Vegas and Tecolote remained loyal to the new Government, but all other towns in the north went over to the insurgents. They declared they would march on Santa Fe.

Meanwhile, eight mountain men at Turley's Mill, twelve miles from Taos, at Arroyo Hondo, were besieged. Turley was a distiller, manufacturer of the celebrated *agua aguardiente*, or fiery Taos Lightning. With him he had only eight men, but they were all well armed. When Otterby brought the news of the killing of Governor Bent, Turley could not believe he was in any danger, but finally agreed to close the gate to his yard. Soon after, a mob of five hundred Pueblos and Mexicans appeared, sent forward a white flag, and called upon Turley to surrender.

They boasted that they had killed every American at San Fernandez de Taos and at the Ranchos de Taos. They told Turley his life would be spared, but that all other Americanos in New Mexico were to be wiped out.

To all this, Turley replied, 'If you want my house, or my men, come and take them.'

Then the mob scattered, and took cover among the rocks and bushes which surrounded the house: both sides began to fire at every target which exposed itself. The mountain men in the fort had plenty of ammunition, and were all good shots: they kept their enemy under cover, and whenever a mark offered, shot to kill. They could see the dead and wounded being carried off all day. During the night the mountain men in the mill ran bullets, cut patches, and strengthened their defenses. The walls of adobe and logs were too strong to be broken down.

Some of the Pueblos had taken up a position in the stable, and wanted to get out again. But when they tried to duck across the space between the stable and the main building, the mountain men soon observed it. They dropped the first who tried to cross — a Pueblo chief; he fell dead in the middle of the narrow space. Three times a single Indian rushed out, trying to carry off the chief's body, and each time the mountain men killed the rash Indian. After that, three Indians ran out together, caught up the dead chief, and started back with him. Their bodies were immediately added to the heap. Seven Indians had now been rubbed out, and not a white man hurt.

Then the luck changed. All the Indians fired together, and two of the whites fell, mortally wounded. At noon the Indians attacked again. The mountain men now had little ammunition left, but they made every shot count. While they defended themselves, the Indians broke into the corral and slaughtered the cattle and sheep there, then managed to set fire to the mill.

Those mountain men fought the fire and the Indians alternately, but could not get rid of either. They saw that the mill would burn; they made up their minds to run, come sundown. Finally they rushed out, firing into the faces of their crowding enemies. Turley and Albert got away, and struck out over the mountains, each for himself. Turley was discovered, betrayed, and killed. Albert eluded the Indians, and, after days of starvation and hardship, crossed the mountains and reached the Greenhorn. Tom Tobin legged it safely to Santa Fe. The mill was looted and burned.

Colonel Sterling ('Old Pap') Price, then in command of the scanty garrison at Santa Fe, hastily ordered in outlying detachments, and on January 23 was on the road to Taos with a force of more than three hundred and fifty men. He had five companies of the Second Missouri Infantry, and a battalion of Captain Angney's infantry. With these rode a company of Santa Fe Volunteers, most of them men who had been warm personal friends of Governor Bent — both men from the States and natives like Nicolas Piño and

Manuel Chaves. These mountain men were mounted, naturally, and led by Bent's old friend and partner, Captain Ceran St. Vrain. St. Vrain was of aristocratic French-Flemish ancestry, and as good a man as the mountains had produced.

Next day, soon after noon, Price found fifteen hundred enemies waiting for him on the hills east of La Cañada de Santa Cruz, defending the road to the village. They fired on him from the houses below, as well. St. Vrain and his mountain men prevented the enemy from capturing the wagon-train in rear. Meanwhile, the artillery and infantry drove out the men in the houses, and then the attack was launched up the hill. The mountain men rode round to cut off retreat, and within a few minutes the Pueblos and their allies were on the run, leaving thirty-six dead and forty-five wounded behind them. Among the dead was one of the ringleaders of the uprising, Tafoya.

Price remained in the village that night, and cared for his six wounded. He had lost only two men.

On the twenty-eighth of January, Captain John Henry K. Burgwin and other officers brought fresh detachments to swell the Colonel's column as it advanced up the Rio Grande.

Price had now nearly five hundred men, but, owing to the difficulty of the road past Embudo, he sent his wagons another way, thus dividing his forces. The mountain men went round past Embudo with some troops, making a force of one hundred and eighty men. The enemy had taken position on the steep mountain slopes, well protected by

CAPTAIN CERAN ST. VRAIN

rocks and piñon and cedar trees. St. Vrain and his mountain men here found a fight to their own liking. They led
the way, rushed up the slopes, and, flanking the enemy on
both sides, quickly put them to flight, with a loss of one
killed and one badly wounded — a negro once slave to
Governor Bent. Both casualties were in St. Vrain's company. The enemy lost twenty killed, sixty wounded.

Plodding on through two feet of snow, breaking trail for
the wagons and horses, tired and frostbitten, the men
steadily advanced up the cañon and out of it, until they
could see, across the snow tufted with sagebrush, the
whitewashed walls of the Mexican village, San Fernandez
de Taos, on its hill, shining in the afternoon sun.

They marched into the town. No one opposed them.
Colonel Price was informed that the Pueblos and their
allies had taken refuge in the Indian village, Pueblo de
Taos, about two miles beyond. Having searched the Mexican village, and found the survivors of the massacre, the
mountain men joined the troops in advancing on the
Pueblo.

As they approached, they saw a low wall of adobes and
puncheons enclosing a rectangle, through which flowed a
lively little stream under a log bridge. On either side of the
stream stood an irregular, immense pile of adobes, seven
stories high, each story being smaller than the one below it.
The walls contained no windows, and the only doors were
holes in the roof, to be reached ordinarily by ladders, now
drawn up out of the way. The walls of these two great
communal Indian houses were pierced everywhere with

loopholes. The North House and the South House stood
on opposite sides of the stream. In the northwest angle of
the enclosure stood the great church built by the *padres*
long before, a massive structure of adobe, with walls of
great thickness, but with few windows, its heavy doors facing the south. Each of the three buildings made a strong
fort. The Pueblos were waiting, safely inside their massive
walls.

Immediately the artillery went into action from the
west side, and banged away without result, until sunset.
The thick mud walls absorbed the cannon balls without
cracking, or bounced them off like so many peas. The
twelve-pound howitzers proved useless. When night came
on, the Americans withdrew, glad to sleep under roofs by
comfortable fires for a change. The Pueblos, much encouraged, yelped and jeered as they departed. That night
there was time for rest.

Next morning, when Price and his men advanced against
the Indians, they found them in the great church. Maybe
the Indians, part Catholic as they were, believed those
holy precincts would protect them better than the walls of
an ordinary house. Maybe they preferred to stand together there, in one body. At any rate, there they were,
defying the Americans.

The American batteries opened fire once more — this
time from the north and west sides, and St. Vrain led his
mounted men around beyond the town, to cut off retreat.
But two hours of firing produced no apparent effect upon
the heavy walls of the church. The mountain men waited
impatiently.

At length Price sent his infantry forward. The men rushed forward from both sides of the angle, and though the Pueblo loopholes blazed fire, successfully reached the shelter of the low wall around the village, just west of the church. This wall was so close to the church that only a narrow passage was left between.

From this position, Captain Burgwin with a small detachment stormed the door of the church, trying to force it. Burgwin was mortally wounded; his men could not break in. After a futile attempt and some further loss, they retreated, carrying their brave leader to his friends.

A ladder was brought forward, and, scaling this, the Americans managed to set fire to the *vigas* which supported the roof. At the same time, a small detachment clambered over the outer wall and attacked the church wall with axes, hewing holes in the adobe. Through these holes they tossed lighted shells by hand, doing fearful execution within. All this was done during a furious hail of grapeshot from the six-pounder, covering their attack.

By mid-afternoon, the Americans were still outside the church. They ran the six-pounder up to within a few yards of the wall, and from that position pounded away at the sides of the breach made with axes, until it had been widened enough to admit a man. Then, for the first time, the Pueblos felt the force of superior arms. The mingled roar of the cannon, the bursting of shells in that confined space, the rattle of muskets, the yelling of the Americans, and the screams of the wounded made the old church an inferno. The Americans stormed the narrow breach.

Inside the room, half-seen through the smoke of burning rafters and bursting shells, crouched a Delaware Indian, Big Nigger, who hated the whites. His Taos wife crouched beside him, loading his weapons as he fired them. When the first dragoon jumped through the breach, Big Nigger fired point-blank, and dropped him stone-dead. Handing his rifle to his woman, Big Nigger snatched a pistol from his belt, and shot down the second American, to fall on top of the first. The third he wounded, and brought down; and the fourth he killed. By that time, the wounded man threatened him, and at the same instant Fitzgerald came storming through the breach. Big Nigger had to give ground, as others poured through the hole on the heels of Fitzgerald.

By that time, the Pueblos and Mexicans in the church knew that their fort was lost. More and more Americans swarmed into the church, firing at the dim figures in the smoke. The defenders broke open the big south doors, and rushed out across their plaza, across the stream, over the fields, heading for the mountains. But Big Nigger, scorning to run, retreated to the room behind the high altar. There the Americans found him cornered, and, after a stubborn fight, killed him. His body was riddled by thirty bullets. Big Nigger died like a true son of his tribe — the only tribe from which the mountain men accepted recruits on equal terms. His defiant death reminds one of how those other heroes perished in the Alamo.

By that time, most of the Pueblos and Mexicans in the church were wounded, killed, or captured. The others, to the number of several hundred, swarmed over the open meadows, legging it for the hills.

But there rode St. Vrain and his mountain men, ready to cut them off. They dashed among the running redskins, riding them down, shooting, stabbing, clubbing them down. It was a wild, running, open fight, across the cornfields, the snowy pastures, the *acequias* full of sluggish water which irrigated the Indian fields. It was a series of single combats, of hand-to-hand fights, a mixup where a man's personal qualities could show themselves, a man-to-man struggle where there was a chance to count a *coup*.

The mountain men were a different lot that day from the 'old women' whom Chief Fireheart had taunted at the siege of the Arikara villages twenty-four years before. Now they were seasoned fighters with all the Injun tricks at their fingers' ends, and more of their own to boot. For once, the military had given them a chance to fight in their own way, and without interference.

They made full use of the opportunity. On every hand could be seen a trapper swinging his rifle-barrel at some black head; firing with a pistol from the saddle, like a man running buffalo; on his feet in a grapple with some desperate savage armed with a Green River blade; or kneeling with leveled rifle to 'bring' a fugitive too swift-footed to be overtaken.

An Injun bested is an Injun twice licked. But, if cornered, no man is more dangerous. There were many single combats on that snowy battlefield. It was characteristic of the mountain men that the best men led, always. And so St. Vrain, their Captain, was that day as active as any nameless volunteer. When the fight was over, and all had been downed or had escaped to the hills, St. Vrain and his men rode about the field, mopping up the wounded, looking for those who might be playing possum.

St. Vrain saw a redskin lying, apparently dead. No wound showed, no blood. St. Vrain dismounted to see if the Injun was shamming: the Captain knew all the old Injun tricks. No sooner had he stooped above the body than the Injun jumped up, grappled with St. Vrain, and tried to stab him with a sharp iron-pointed arrow held in his hand. Both men were big and powerful, and the struggle was equal. They wrestled fiercely for some minutes.

Dick Wootton, seeing St. Vrain's danger, ran up to end the bout. But the redskin saw him coming, and managed to keep St. Vrain between himself and Wootton. Says Uncle Dick: 'The Indian was so active ... that I found it hard to strike a lick which would be sure to hit the right head. I managed after a little, however, to deal him a blow with my tomahawk ... and when he stretched out on the ground again, there was no doubt about his being a dead Indian.' [2]

The victorious Americans quartered themselves that night in the village. They had lost seven killed and forty-five wounded, of whom several died later. The loss of the Pueblos was one hundred and fifty killed, and an even larger number wounded or captured. Two of the leaders were taken: Montoya and Tomasito, the Indian chief. Next day Montoya was tried by drumhead court-martial and promptly hanged. Tomasito was held in prison.

Fitzgerald, the hero of the breach, whose brother had been murdered by Salazar (the cruel captor of the Texan–Sante Fe Expedition) thought even that military justice too slow. He had killed three men in the battle. But the day after, he walked into the prison to look at the prisoners, suddenly raised his pistol, and deliberately shot down the *alcalde*, Tomasito!

For this cold-blooded crime he was arrested, and confined in a house in the village, to await trial for murder. As Uncle Dick Wootton said, 'The Indian deserved to be killed, and would have been hanged anyhow, but we objected to the informal manner of his taking off.'[3]

It was cold, and Fitzgerald begged his guard to bring him wood for a fire. The guard, who probably sympathized with the prisoner in some measure, complied. Fitzgerald piled the piñon in the middle of the floor, climbed upon it, and broke a hole through the primitive roof of sticks, straw, and mud. He crept out upon the housetop. The sentinel below him, wrapped in his heavy cloak, walked his post patiently. But Fitzgerald, slipping from the roof when the guard's back was turned, swung himself down quietly, walked to a neighboring mess fire, and soon found friends who supplied him with a pistol and blankets. When day broke, he was far off in the mountains, bound for Bent's ranch on Rio Vermejo.

Meanwhile, the remnants of the Pueblo de Taos found themselves in a changed world, and moved about dejectedly. They might well be sad and frightened. Their *alcalde* was dead, their grain and cattle gone, their holy church in ruins, the flower of their nation dead or under sentence of death, and the rest refugees in the mountains. The day after the battle, the old men and women came bearing their *santos* and their crosses, humble suppliants, begging the *Americanos* for peace and mercy.

So much for the work of the mountain men in pacifying the Pueblos. They had done most of the work of extermination. William Bent's small party arrived only in time to take part in the trial and executions.

After that, the Americans speedily mopped up the surrounding areas, caught and punished the rioters, and made everyone realize once and for all that the new régime was a strong and lasting one. For two generations thereafter, the Pueblos de Taos made no trouble. The last of the mountain men was dead before the Taos Indians ventured another uprising.

By that time the conquest of the West had been completed.

XV. FREMONT MAKES TRACKS

FROM the beginning American statesmen of imagination had looked to the West, realizing that the real business of the nation was the conquest and development of that great region beyond the frontier. In 1840, the United States Senate contained a strong and energetic Western bloc, headed by Thomas H. Benton, of Missouri. They stood ready to fight, if need be, to hold the last mile of Oregon and the Louisiana Purchase. To do this, they knew that settlers must be moved into the unoccupied lands, and in great numbers. To insure that, they fought to pass appropriations which would pay for the exploration of the trails and passes, and advertise to the world the promise of the West. Their field-worker was John Charles Frémont, an officer in the Topographical Corps of the United States Army, and son-in-law of Senator Benton.

Frémont was young, energetic, enthusiastic, with a talented wife and a powerful bloc behind him. He amply fulfilled their demands, and before he was through not merely explored and advertised the West, but materially

enlarged the domain of the United States, by taking a leading part in the conquest of California. Few generals have
accomplished as much for their country as did this sub-
altern of the Topographical Corps.

His first expedition started in May, 1842, with the purpose of charting the best route to the South Pass, and so
lay out the trail to Oregon. Many a mountain man had
passed that way before, ever since Jim Bridger had discovered the South Pass, but the facts had never been made
a matter of official record; the American public knew little
about the region. Frémont was just the man to advertise
it. With Kit Carson to guide him, Frémont not only surveyed the route and reported on the country, but prepared
for another expedition by learning all he could from Jim
Bridger, Thomas Fitzpatrick, Ceran St. Vrain, Jim Beckwourth, and other mountain men of standing. He went to
South Pass, and returned in October, 1842, to write his
Report.

His second expedition was an extension of the first, with
the purpose of charting the country beyond the Rockies.
Again he set out — in May, 1843. This time White Head
Fitzpatrick was chief guide, and with him a number of
others served — Alexis Godey and Basil Lajeunesse among
others — who had gone with Frémont before. Kit Carson
joined the outfit on the way out, and soon supplanted
White Head as the leader. This time Frémont followed the
line of the Oregon Trail to Idaho, then headed northwest
to the Columbia, and downriver to the mouth. On the way
back, on Carson River, he changed his direction and

headed for California. Warned by the mountain men that he could not expect to get through the Sierras in winter, he stubbornly persisted, and managed to arrive at Sutter's Fort, in spite of snow and starvation. His way back led him by the Spanish Trail to Bent's Fort on the Arkansas River. By August, 1844, he was home again. This fearless expedition through unknown country and mountain snows earned him the name of the Pathfinder. Thereafter, he believed nothing could stop him. He was entertained in the White House, and his Report was printed at the expense of the United States.

The Western bloc in the Senate were now feeling their oats, passing resolutions for the annexation of Texas, and advocating the conquest of the Southwest. They managed to have Frémont sent on a third trip, early in 1845, with the object of exploring the Central Rockies, the Great Salt Lake, the Californian Sierras, and the passes through them to the Pacific Ocean. The expedition was actually, though not openly, a military reconnaissance. The Western bloc saw that a war with Mexico was inevitable. This time Kit Carson, Godey, and Dick Owens were the principal scouts. Old Bill Williams joined them for a while. Old Bill got to know Frémont, and Frémont became acquainted with Old Bill.

Frémont wasted little time on the Central Rockies. He hurried on to California, took part in the rebellion there, and in the conquest of the Coast. There he fell foul of General Stephen Watts Kearny, commander of the Army of the West, was relieved of his command, and sent back under arrest. In 1846, he was court-martialed in Washington. Army officers had no love for Frémont and his politician father-in-law. The verdict was 'guilty,' and Frémont resigned his commission.

From that time on, Frémont was an embittered man. Formerly he had been a lively, spirited youngster, ready for anything, inspired by his rapid rise, his great services to his country, the love of his brilliant wife, and the backing of important statesmen. But after that disgrace, he soured. All the less admirable traits in the man gained strength. Frémont was a different man.

Yet, even as a private citizen, Frémont was still the Pathfinder. If Uncle Sam would no longer finance his explorations, Frémont would carry them out on his own. With the backing of some Western friends, he set out once more, in October, 1848, to find a route for a transcontinental railroad. He had determined to go through the Rockies *in the winter* in order to prove that a railroad could run over the ranges the year round. He proposed to follow the thirty-eighth degree of latitude. He needed a guide.

The old-time mountain men were scattered. Now that the fur trade was a thing of the past, most of them had found other work, as ranchers, Army scouts, traders, gold-seekers, pilots for wagon-trains, Indian agents. Many, of course, had gone under fighting Injuns, or died early as a result of their wounds: Jedediah Smith, the Sublettes, John Colter, Hugh Glass, Fraeb, Vanderburgh. Fontenelle had committed suicide. A few remained at Bent's Fort, or

Taos, or at the Pueblo in Colorado. When Frémont reached Bent's Fort, he halted to secure a guide.

Thomas Fitzpatrick was Indian Agent for all the tribes from Platte to Arkansas. He had a good, permanent job, and was doing a useful work. Frémont could not win him away from all that to make a fool trip into the Rockies in the dead of winter. Already there was a foot of snow on the ground around the fort.

Kit Carson was not available. But Frémont was well content: he talked Uncle Dick Wootton into undertaking the trip. No man knew the mountains of that region better than Uncle Dick. But when Wootton had advanced far enough to see how thick the snows were on the Sangre de Cristo peaks, he threw up his job. Wootton saw that Frémont was biting off more than he cared to chew. He quit and turned homewards, saying simply, 'Thar's too much snow ahead for me.'

Frémont pushed on to 'the Pueblo' — a small settlement about seventy miles above Bent's Fort, on the Arkansas, composed chiefly of old trappers and hunters — a home for retired mountain men. It was fortified by an adobe wall twelve feet high, and sheltered about one hundred and fifty souls. Of these about sixty were men — Americans, Missouri-French, Canadians, Mexicans. They all had wives, some one, some two, apiece. These women were of 'various Indian tribes, as follows: Blackfoot, Assiniboine, Arikara, Sioux, Arapaho, Cheyenne, Pawnee, Snake, Sinpach (from west of the Great Lakes), Chinook (from the mouth of the Columbia), Mexicans, and Americans. The American women were Mormons; a party of Mormons wintered there and on their departure for California, left behind two families.'[1] These people had another settlement at Hard Scrabble, near the Wet Mountains, which they occupied in summer. They had a tolerable supply of cattle, horses, and mules, and raised corn, beans, and pumpkins and other garden truck. Some of them were engaged in smuggling liquor from New Mexico.

There, in the adobe houses, the Pathfinder found a number of old mountain men, and among them Old Bill Williams. Bill was then more than sixty years of age, already somewhat stooped with years, but 'with a fine profile, quick restless eyes, and with strong marks of humor about his mouth.'[2] Knowing Bill of old, Frémont demanded that Bill act as guide to the outfit. Bill had recently crossed the Sangre de Cristo Range.

Bill Williams was getting old; it was winter, and a winter that already promised to be one of the worst in years. Bill had settled down for the season with his old cronies, to nurse his shattered arm, broken in an Injun fight the previous summer. He was content there, and in no mood to traipse around the peaks, frostin' his old bones. All the mountain men declared that the cold was turrible that season, and the snow deeper than they had ever seen it so early. Even Old Bill, they implied, could never get through.

Whether this challenge, or Frémont's offers — tempting to a man so sadly out of pocket — or a restless desire to travel the mountain trails again, even in the snow, roused Old Bill, we cannot know. However, he sucked his old dudheen, and, taking it from his bearded lips, reckoned that mebbe they *could* manage to git through, though not without consid'able hard doin's. Old Bill had been in some pretty tight fixes in his day. He reckoned that, if he war headed for hell, he would shorely be given a constitution to stand it.

Old Bill led the outfit up the Arkansas. We have plentiful records to tell of the dreadful days that followed. Those who survived had much to say about that journey of death.

On Hard Scrabble Creek, at the foot of the Wet Mountains, the outfit halted to shell, sack, and pack the corn stored by the settlers there. Frémont had bought it. Then the pack-train moved on, even the saddle-horses carrying packs, while the men walked. Here an old French mountain man quit; he had too much sense to go on. '*C'est impossible,*' he declared. Others, too, began to express their misgivings. But Frémont moved on, and late in November started into the mountains. The whole country was covered with an unbroken blanket of white.

All the way in, the temperature remained below zero, and the snow fell day and night. There was no trail, only drifts which balled the horses' feet, hampered their movements, and forced the party to travel along the slopes above the drifted valleys, where the cold wind cut them to the bone, and the animals slipped, fell over the cliffs and were lost. There was no grass, and the horses had only the corn on their backs to eat. Going over Roubidoux Pass, the mercury was lost to sight in the thermometers. Old Bill showed Frémont the place where two men had frozen to death only the winter before. Beyond the Pass, Old Bill led them down into the San Luis Valley.

By that time, Bill had begun to realize what he had undertaken. He had never known such bitter weather there, never seen such deep snow. Frémont still held to his plan of following the thirty-eighth degree of latitude, which would carry him straight through the forty miles of mountains — the impassable La Garita Range.

Bill Williams had considered heading northwest to cross the Continental Divide by the Cochetopa Pass. But now he did not even believe they could get through that, and proposed a more southerly route, heading around the San Juan Mountains by going up the Chama River, past Abiquiu and the San Juan River. But Frémont, apparently hoping to force his way up the headwaters of the Rio Grande, covered his ears. He would not listen to Old Bill, declared he was no longer guide, and put Alexis Godey in charge. Frémont doubtless felt that, as the dauntless 'Pathfinder,' *he* could overcome all difficulties, and show West Point what a mistake his court-martial had been. That was the beginning of disaster.

They went on. The wind was cruel, the cold bitter, and on the open plain they had no fuel but sagebrush, which burned faster than they could gather it, and gave out little heat. It was nearly twenty degrees below zero. Already one or two of the men had been frosted. The snowstorms beat upon them, blinding them, preventing them from seeing that Frémont and Godey were headed into a valley from which there was no outlet.

All Old Bill's words were wasted on Frémont. He would neither go north to the Cochetopa Pass nor south to the San Juan. He pushed on into that blind valley, then deep with snow. Short cuts are always hazardous things in the mountains, and in such weather must prove suicidal.

Every mile the mountains grew steeper, the valley narrower, the snows deeper. To make matters worse, the drifts often concealed water, into which the men fell. A blizzard came up one day, and Old Bill lost consciousness. He slumped down upon his mule, and had to be revived when they got him to camp. By this time, the corn was gone, nearly all the men had frozen some portion of their bodies, and the horses were reduced to eating each other's tails. They, too, began to freeze. They could make only a mile a day, pounding out a trail with mauls. The weather grew colder, the drifts bottomless, only treetops showing above them. By the middle of December, they had to stop, dig into the snow, and crouch in holes around fires. All they talked of then was how to save themselves. The animals tried to run back out of the mountains.

At last, just before Christmas, they headed back, leaving their mules to die in the snow, thus abandoning their only available meat. The men packed out the instruments and baggage — including some twelve hundred dollars in coin! Coin — in those barren, snow-drowned wastes! At the end of a week, they had made about two miles.

Stubborn as Frémont was, even he began to understand then that they *must* have relief. He had been arbitrary and caustic enough in rejecting Old Bill's advice, but now — in the hour of desperate need — it was to Old Bill that he turned for help. Frémont must have known him for the ablest and most trustworthy man in the outfit.

It was fully one hundred and sixty miles to the nearest settlements. Frémont ordered Bill Williams, King, Creutzfeldt, and Breckinridge to go to Taos and bring back supplies — within sixteen days! He himself had been making less than a mile a day — he expected them to make twenty. They were given one blanket apiece, a handful of frozen mule-meat, a pound of sugar, and some candles. Three of them carried Hawkins rifles, one a shotgun. They had half a hundred bullets and some powder — in case they met Injuns. Not that it was likely any redskin would be fool enough to be in such country at that season!

Probably Old Bill had ideas of his own as to what Frémont should have done. Frémont could have cached his baggage, and led the men back in a body while they were still able to travel. There was no sense in proceeding — even a redskin could see that no railroad could pass the mountains on that trail. But Frémont must have been thinking of the I-told-you-so West-Pointers, and what they might say of his failure if he turned back; no other explanation can account for his stubborn persistence. He would not give in. Instead, he shifted his responsibility to the sixty-year-old back of Bill Williams. Old Bill was glad enough to get away from Frémont. He and his three companions put out.

Meanwhile, Frémont and his men started for the Rio

Grande, making a mile or two each day. Many of them bled constantly at the nose because of the altitude. Their food gave out, and they ate the rawhide bags they carried. Before they reached the river, the first victim of Frémont's folly lay down and froze to death. It was after New Year's when Frémont reached the river. Then Frémont took a few men and set out on the trail of Old Bill.

Bill Williams had left Frémont on Christmas Day. After three days' march, he reached the Rio Grande, with a tightened belt and no rations. Once the party killed a bird, another time they found a dead otter; most of the way they lived on such scraps of leather as they had along. Two weeks later, they were still a long way from the settlements. One of the four, King, played out then, told his comrades to go and leave him. 'I'm gone,' he said. 'Let me rest.'

There was nothing they could do for him. After a while, they staggered along and left him. Then they stopped to rest, and Creutzfeldt went back to see if he could get King on his feet. Old Bill, seeing a buzzard circling above the dying man, said it was no use, but Creutzfeldt went back. He found King already dead.

Soon after, Creutzfeldt himself gave out. Old Bill sat with him, so that he should not die alone. Breckinridge went on, saw a band of deer, shot one, and returned with venison.

Old Bill tore the raw meat with his bony hands, and wolfed it down. The smell of the flesh reached Creutzfeldt's nostrils, and he revived. The three of them remained there to rest and eat, so that they could go on again. Creutzfeldt was saved.

Thus it was that Frémont found them, 'the most miserable objects he had ever seen.' Yet Frémont went on and left them, heading down to Taos. It took Old Bill and his friends ten days to cover the forty-odd miles to Taos; they had to crawl much of the way, their feet were so badly frozen.

In Taos, Frémont stayed in the snug Kit Carson home, and sent Godey back to rescue the rest of his party. Apparently, Frémont passed the time in thinking up excuses for his failure. If so, he showed himself adept at both the old tricks: 'throw the bull, pass the buck.' An embittered, disappointed man, he laid the blame for his failure upon others, especially Old Bill Williams. Bill, he claimed, had misled him, betrayed him. Bill was incompetent, treacherous. Bill had failed to bring back supplies, as ordered. The story got out that Bill had even eaten the flesh of his dead comrade, King! But all this false propaganda was not published until Old Bill was safely dead and out of the way.

While Frémont sat by Kit Carson's comfortable fire, Godey went back into the frozen wastes to save what was left of his men. Those men whom Frémont had left to find their way in suffered more than either of the other parties. Their foolish leader let them break up into small groups. Some of them deserted their weaker companions. Half-frozen, snow-blind, and starving, they could never walk more than a few steps at a time. But, feeble and wretched as they were, they staggered desperately on, till they could go no farther. Finally they heard a shot fired — and realized that they were saved. But when Godey arrived, they were all so snow-blind they could not recognize him. Some of them actually took him for Frémont!

The expedition ended in disaster: eleven of the original thirty-two men had died in the snow. No wonder Frémont and his friends were put to it to find justification for such a tragedy. As time passed, more and more of the blame was laid at the door of Old Bill Williams!

Such talk could only deceive people in the East. Nobody in the mountains was taken in by it. William Bent (I have the word of his son George Bent for this) declared: 'Old Bill knew those mountains as well as any man living; if Frémont had followed his advice, not a man would have gone under. Old Bill made only one mistake — that was in not turning back alone when Frémont refused to listen to him. Old Bill was not treacherous; his trouble was too much loyalty.'

All the mountain men worth shucks heartily backed the opinion of William Bent. Uncle Dick Wootton (whom Frémont thought worthy to act as his guide — a first-class mountain man, who had spent his life in those mountains); Antoine Leroux, famous guide and scout; Tom Boggs, who had worked with Bent in the Southwest for a generation; Bob Hatcher, Bent's foreman at the fort, all exonerated Old Bill. Even Kit Carson, though under heavy obligations to Frémont, privately expressed resent-

ment at the accusations against Bill. Frémont — if he was
the author of these yarns — was discreet enough not to
publish them while he was still in Taos.

That was one reason why they gained circulation: nobody in the mountains took them seriously. And even
though Frémont did find King's body partly devoured,
that was the buzzard's work — not Old Bill's. Nobody
around Taos believed Bill Williams was a cannibal.
Even the Kern brothers, Easterners who were on that
fatal trip, and who had been Frémont's loyal defenders at
the time of his court-martial, could not swallow those
yarns.

The question arises: If Frémont believed Old Bill a
traitorous, irresponsible rascal, why did he send *him* back
to bring relief to the party?

Of course, it may be argued that, until Old Bill failed to
bring back the supplies within sixteen days, Frémont was
not convinced of his treachery. But, even so, if Frémont
believed Old Bill unreliable, how did it happen that *he* was
the man selected to return to the snowbound mountains
and recover the cache containing all Frémont's valuable
instruments, collections, records, and the twelve hundred
dollars in coin? Bill Williams was an old man, and hard up:
if he had been a scoundrel, as is claimed, how easy it would
have been for him to kill Kern, intimidate the Mexican
packers, and make off with all that booty!

No, the story won't wash. The whole rigmarole was
only intended to whitewash Frémont and camouflage his
failure. Most of the story was simply political propaganda

published much later by parties unknown — when Frémont was running for President.

Doctor Kern and Bill Williams rode out of Taos to recover the cache late in February, 1849. That was Old Bill's last trail.

XVI. OLD BILL WILLIAMS GOES UNDER

IN THOSE days the Ute Indians held a vast area of the Rocky Mountains. Their range included the western half of what is now Colorado, the east side of Utah, and even lapped over into New Mexico on the south. These warlike people lived by hunting and raiding their neighbors, and with their cousins the Snakes (Shoshones) were reckoned the best fighters in the Rockies. In the course of Old Bill Williams's endless wanderings, he had sojourned with many tribes. On the Plains, the Osages had been his favorites, and with them he had spent years. But in the mountains, Williams liked the Utes best of all the tribes. He had lived with them, and had their respect and liking. Old Bill had no reason to fear a trip into their country. That was where he and Doctor B. J. Kern were heading when they went after Frémont's cache.

As usual, the Utes were then at war with their neighbors, the Arapahos. The Arapahos had just given them a drubbing, and the Utes, feeling sore about their defeat, were taking it out upon anybody handy — which included the people in the settlements. For centuries all the tribes had habitually preyed upon the Mexican settlements. And now that New Mexico had become a part of the territories of the United States, they had difficulty in understanding that this made any difference. Mexicans were Mexicans to the Utes: they raided them, as they always had done. And so the United States troops were called out to teach the Utes a lesson.

At that time no treaty between the Utes and the United States had been made, and the Indians might plead that they had never been officially informed of their transfer from one government to another. Neither they nor the mountain men took much stock in such paper arrangements. But down at Taos, Major Beall, commanding the First Dragoons, decided he would give them a lesson.

It may be that Frémont, or Doctor Kern, feared that someone would beat them to the cache. At any rate, Old Bill's expedition was kept secret, and Major Beall never learned of their plans. Therefore, of course, they never knew of his. The misunderstanding was fatal.

Bill Williams, dean of the free trappers, had always come and gone at his own will, without consulting anyone. Apparently not even his old *compañeros* Lucien Maxwell, Antoine Leroux, or the Otterby boys knew what Bill was up to. For they led the troops up the Rio Grande after the Utes, and never dropped a hint of it to him. He and Kern went on their way, unaware of danger.

Lieutenant Whittlesey and a company of dragoons rode after them. It was nearly the middle of March.

The scouts soon discovered a Ute village on the river.

The troops, advancing through the deep snow, were met outside the camp by the chiefs, who wanted to know what was doing. The officer told them he wanted a fight; they agreed to oblige him immediately. The battle began at once.

It was a complete victory for the troops, who ran the Utes out of their camp, and then discovered another band of Utes coming in, unsuspicious of danger. Then the dragoons went for the second outfit, and sent them scuttling. Ten Injuns were rubbed out that day, and many others wounded. Three women and children were taken, and about twenty head of horses taken or killed. The fifty lodges in the camp were burned. The whites lost only two men. The Utes scattered, bent on wiping out the first whites who crossed their path. Then the troops, having roused all that hostility, went home and let nature take its course.

Several stories are told as to how Old Bill met his death at the hands of the Utes. The Utes themselves appear to have no tradition about this; probably they felt sorry, after their anger had abated, for having killed such an old man and old friend of their people. They had no wish to remember that deed. But other accounts remain to us.

Uncle Dick Wootton has told of Old Bill's pet superstition. 'One night when there were a dozen or more of us together in camp — that was when he was growing quite old — he told us, with as great an air of solemnity as though he had been preaching his own funeral, that when he ceased

UNCLE DICK WOOTTON

to be "Bill" Williams he was to become a buck elk, and
would make his home in the very neighborhood where we
were then encamped. He had pictured out, in his own
mind, what kind of a looking elk he would be, and described to us certain peculiarities he would have, which
would enable us to distinguish him from other elks, and
cautioned us not to shoot an elk of that description, should
we ever run across one after his death.' ¹ Old Bill also believed in dreams, like his friends the Indians, and had had
warnings in his visions that his time was not far off. But he
felt safe enough in Ute country.

The attack was made at night — or very early in the
morning (according to Uncle Dick — and Indian custom,
for that matter) — while Old Bill and Doctor Kern sat by
their campfire, after making all preparations to start back
to Taos next day. They felt no alarm when the Utes
turned up, and went on with their conversation. Then
'two of the Utes suddenly raised their rifles and fired.
One bullet struck Bill Williams in the forehead, and
another passed into the heart of the Doctor. The Mexicans
prepared to fly, but the Indians called to them and said
they were at war only with the whites, and did not intend
to harm them. The murderers, however, took possession
of the mules and packs, and ordered the Mexicans to remain where they were until morning.' ²

Old Bill's body was discovered soon after by a party of
mountain men. The party 'found themselves, one stormy
evening, in a wild and dismal cañon. . . . The rocky bed of
a dry mountain torrent, whose waters were now locked up

at their spring-heads by icy fetters, was the only road up
which they could make their difficult way; for the rugged
sides of the gorge rose precipitously from the creek,
scarcely affording a foothold to even the active bighorn,
which occasionally looked down upon the travelers from
the lofty summit. Logs of pine uprooted by the hurricanes
which sweep incessantly through the mountain defiles, and
tossed headlong from the surrounding ridges, continually
obstructed their way; and huge rocks and boulders, fallen
from the heights and blocking up the bed of the stream,
added to the difficulty, and threatened them every instant
with destruction.

'Towards sundown they reached a point where the
cañon opened out into a little shelving glade or prairie, a
few hundred yards in extent, the entrance to which was
almost hidden by thickets of dwarf pine and cedar. Here
they determined to encamp for the night, in a spot secure
from Indians, and, as they imagined, untrodden by the
foot of man.

'What, however, was their astonishment, on breaking
through the cedar-covered entrance, to perceive a solitary
horse standing motionless in the center of the prairie.
Drawing near, they found it to be an old grizzled mustang,
or Indian pony, with cropped ears and ragged tail (well
picked by hungry mules), standing doubled up with cold,
and at the very last gasp from extreme old age and weakness. Its bones were nearly through the stiffened skin, the
legs of the animal were gathered under it; whilst its forlorn-
looking head and stretched-out neck hung listlessly down-

wards, almost overbalancing its tottering body. The glazed and sunken eye — the protruding and froth-covered tongue — the heaving flank and quivering tail — declared its race was run; and the driving sleet and snow, the penetrating winter blast, scarce made impression upon its callous and wornout frame.

'One of the band of mountaineers was Marcelline, and a single look at the miserable beast was sufficient for him to recognize the once renowned Nez Percé steed of Old Bill Williams. That the owner himself was not far distant he felt certain; and, searching carefully around, the hunters presently came upon an old camp, before which lay, protruding from the snow, the blackened remains of pine logs. Before these, which had been the fire, and leaning with his back against a pine trunk, and his legs crossed under him, half covered with snow, reclined the figure of the old mountaineer, his snow-capped head bent over his breast. His well-known hunting-coat of fringed elkskin hung stiff and weather-stained about him; and his rifle, packs, and traps were strewed around.

'Awe-struck, the trappers approached the body, and found it frozen hard as stone, in which state it had probably lain there for many days or weeks. A jagged rent in the breast of his leather coat, and dark stains about it, showed he had received a wound before his death. . . .

'A friendly bullet cut short the few remaining hours of the trapper's faithful steed; and burying, as well as they were able, the body of the old mountaineer, the hunters next day left him in his lonely grave, in a spot so wild and rcmote that it is doubtful whether even hungry wolves would discover and disinter his attenuated corpse.' ³

So died Old Bill Williams, having seen, within one lifetime, the beginning and the end of the mountain men.

Those mountain men were only a few hundreds in number, hardly more than a thousand all told. Of these the free trappers were the cream, men whose careers illustrated perfectly the principle of the survival of the fittest. To be rated one of the best of these is as proud a title to manhood as the history of these States affords.

Fittingly, that old hero has been commemorated by the monuments that stand to him in the mountains where he passed his later years: Bill Williams Peak and the station of Williams, in Arizona; the Williams Fork of Grand River, and Williams Pass on the Sangre de Cristo Range, in Colorado. And if vindication for Old Bill is required, it should be noted that Bill Williams Peak was named for him by the brother of Doctor Kern, in 1851.

XVII. JIM BRIDGER'S PROWESS

OF ALL the mountain men, after Old Bill Williams died, Jim Bridger was most in demand as guide and scout. Of course, others served as guides as well as Bridger — Kit Carson, Uncle Dick Wootton, White Head Fitzpatrick, for example. But they were only part-time guides and scouts; most of their time was spent in other work. As the West changed, they changed with it. But Old Gabe (as Bridger was known to his comrades of the beaver trail) stuck to his last: he remained guide and scout to the end of his active days. And in this work he excelled them all.

No wonder. None of the mountain men living after the Mexican War had served a longer apprenticeship; none was better trained for such work.

Born in Virginia in 1804, Bridger first learned the blacksmith's trade. But he soon quit the settlements, as we have seen, and went up the Missouri in 1822 with Ashley. From that day he shared the dangers and explorations of the mountain men, and soon rose to become a leader among them. It was Bridger who, on a bet, went down Bear

River and so discovered the Great Salt Lake, and on the return trip visited the wonders of the Yellowstone Park. He was one of the party that first crossed the South Pass, and his later ramblings gave him a knowledge of Western topography unsurpassed in those days.

Jim's stories of Yellowstone were not believed, and — like John Colter — Old Gabe was rated a prodigious liar by unimaginative greenhorns. But he had his revenge on those doubters by enlarging upon his experiences, and telling whoppers which have become classics of the folklore of the frontier. Jim's yarns concerning geysers, glass mountains, and petrifactions he had seen set a pace which other Westerners have labored in vain to equal. Jim was a creative liar, something of an artist in his way. Some amends have been made to his memory by naming a small lake near the headwaters of the Yellowstone River, Bridger Lake.

Jim Bridger also had a comprehensive knowledge of the Injuns. He had fought them, traded with them, hunted with them, intermarried with them, until he knew their customs and understood their manner of thought. He knew the tribes on both sides of the Rockies from Mexico to the British Possessions. He could speak some of their languages, and was expert in the use of the sign talk universal on the Plains. He knew the country — no man better: he knew the Injuns as well as any. These skills made him an unequaled guide and scout, whether serving with the Army, or leading civilians through the wilderness. No wonder that with such talents and training he stuck to the beaver trail longer than most mountain men.

No doubt many of his early exploits have been lost to history for want of a recorder, but enough remain to account for his reputation, and for the respect in which he was held by the mountain men, and by the Injuns, who knew him as Casapy, the Blanket Chief. Some of these moving accidents have been narrated in my life of Kit Carson,[1] and elsewhere, and need not be repeated here.

In his later years, Old Gabe was much too skillful and wary to put his foot in a trap. He knew how to avoid the dangers which destroyed so many of his less capable fellows. Like most brave men who have risked their lives in youth, Bridger was careful not to throw his life away in manhood. He followed the old Army rule (better than some of the officers he worked with) that 'the object of war is victory' — not carnage. Old Gabe believed that competent explorers have no adventures. Therefore he is remembered for his invaluable services to others.

Some men became notorious on the frontier because of the number of persons they killed. It is Jim Bridger's proud distinction to be remembered rather for the number of persons he saved from death or disaster. He was the mountain man's trouble-shooter, always on hand when a rescue was required.

He saved Joe Meek, Kit Carson, and scores of others. Whenever other trappers, soldiers, or emigrants had been robbed, defeated, wounded, or burned out, Jim Bridger was the man they turned to. The disastrous Frapp Battle is an example.

When the Rocky Mountain Fur Company went under,

Bridger, Fitzpatrick, and Milton Sublette organized
another company. But, finding the competition of the
American Fur Company too strong, the new outfit dis-
solved. Bridger decided to settle down, build a trading-
post, and abandon the unprofitable beaver trail. He looked
round for a partner. It had to be a seasoned mountain
man — somebody who would settle in Snake country —
on that Green River which ran through Bridger's favorite
haunts.

Nearly every mountain man knew some tribe of Indians
to which he was attached. Some threw in with a tribe because of opportunities for trade, some because of the Injun
gals they married, others because of common hatred for
enemy redskins, or tested friendship for their companions
on the hunt. Thus, Blackfoot Smith and William Bent
preferred the Cheyennes; Gant and Fitzpatrick, the Arapahos; Loretto, the Blackfeet; Old Bill Williams and Sol
Silver, the Osages; Drips, the Otoes; Fontenelle, the
Omahas; Rose and Beckwourth, the Crows; Hatcher and
Kit Carson, the Utes; Meek, Fraeb, and Bridger, the
Snakes (Shoshones). Each man, as a rule, thought the
tribe he ran with superior to all the rest. And one thing
is to be noted: almost to a man, the trappers married
women of the tent-dwelling, buffalo-running tribes, since
a Pueblo house-bred woman was no mate for a wandering
mountain man. Old Gabe liked mountain Injuns.

Bridger expressed his approval of the Snakes in no uncertain terms, as Lowe has recorded:[2] 'These are the finest
Indians on earth. . . . It'll be a proud day for the Snakes if

any of these prairie tribes pitch into 'em, and they are not a bit afraid.... They'll never be caught napping, and they're prepared to travel anywhere. Awful brave fellows, these Snakes; got the nerve; honest, too; can take their word for anything; trust 'em anywhere; they live all about me, and I know all of them.'

Bridger found an old comrade and partisan of the beaver trail — Henry Fraeb, of St. Louis, a German trapper. Fraeb (or Frapp, as the mountain men called him) spoke only broken English. But he was brave, competent, and well seasoned — a fit partner for Old Gabe — if only he could have l'arned to open his ears when Old Gabe was offering his sage advice.

The two partners gathered a band of 'free' men, and went into the valley of Green River. There, on the Black Fork, they built their post, that summer of 1841. Bridger had charge of that work; Frapp went over to the Little Snake, a branch of the Yampa River. There, at the mouth of Battle Creek (in Routt County, Colorado, within a mile of the Wyoming line), Frapp's Battle took place.

Not much has been recorded about this hard-fought scrap, but it was one of which the mountain men never tired of telling — one of the fiercest fights in the mountains. Because of this, it has been commemorated no less than three times on the map, and Battle Mountain, Battle Creek, and Battle Lake all take their names from this stubborn conflict.³ So far, nothing has been printed about it from Indian sources.

Though in the country of the friendly Snakes, and west

of the Continental Divide, Bridger and Frapp soon discovered that they were not to be free from attack by the
Plains Indians. There were two causes which drove these
hostiles over the Divide: first, the growing scarcity of
buffalo on the Plains east of the range, which made it
necessary for them to seek their meat in Snake hunting
grounds; second, the smallpox plague of 1837–38, which
had swept away the flower of the tribes along the Missouri
River, and so left the Sioux and Cheyennes free to turn
their warlike strength against their other enemies to the
westward. As the white men began to cross the Plains in
ever-increasing numbers, the buffalo dwindled alarmingly
— with a constantly growing hostility to white men as the
inevitable result. In the long run, the Sioux and Cheyennes drove the Snakes and Crows back into the mountains. But from first to last they had a healthy respect for
these mountain Indians — more especially for the Snakes.
More than one old Sioux warrior has told me that the
Snakes were the bravest and best fighters of all their
enemies. Therefore, when the Plains Indians went west
to hunt on Snake preserves, they took care to go in large
numbers.

Frapp soon discovered that a camp of some five hundred
warriors — Sioux, Cheyenne, and Arapaho — were on the
Yampa River. He decided to trade for jerked meat with
them. Perhaps he thought this would keep them friendly;
at any rate, it would make it easy for him to get out of
their neighborhood in a hurry.

It happened that some emigrants (the Bartleson party)

had passed the fort, and the partners had purchased a supply of trade whiskey from them. This whiskey Frapp packed down to the village, and swapped it for as much meat as the Injuns would part with. Then, finding he needed still more, he left his camp, and took most of his men away with him to 'run meat' on his own hook. Of course, such a buffalo hunt led him a long way from his base camp.

This camp consisted of only a few whites, several more Snake Indian men, and the women and children of the hunters. These women were, of course, mostly Snake women, and the Snake men were their relatives. There were fewer than one hundred souls in those tipis. Frapp seems not to have taken the trouble to build a fort, or even a corral. He had only about twenty white men in his party.

When the Cheyennes and their friends recovered from their spree, they were not in a very good humor. They had parted with their jerked meat, which they had come so far to get and 'made' with so much trouble. They had no quarrel with the white men, but they had an age-old grudge against the white men's allies — the Snakes. More than all, they had a mean hangover. The Injun drunk was mean, but the Injun with a hangover was meaner. While the women went to work to jerk more meat, the young men began to talk war.

There could be only one end to that, for the horses in Frapp's camp formed a perfectly irresistible temptation. And after all, it was a Snake camp. The fact that it contained some white men was only incidental. At least, the young men thought it was only incidental *then*.

In their camp were more than a hundred lodges of Sioux (Hunkpapa, Sans Arc, Oglala), about half as many Cheyennes, and a lesser number of Arapahos. The Cheyennes and Sioux were keen for a raid, but the Arapahos were reluctant to attack the white men's camp. Perhaps they had been frightened, or some trader had bribed them to keep the peace. Maybe some of them thought the time unlucky — they were great believers in 'medicine.' They held out for peace. That, at least, is the Arapaho story.

As always in a mixed camp like that, there was much rivalry. The young men had been matching *coups*, dancing, and boasting, and martial spirit ran high. And under the taunts of their allies, the Arapahos got mad. They not only agreed to the raid, they insisted on leading it. They were going to charge first, and show those other warriors how good they were.

Accordingly, several hundred warriors rode to Frapp's undefended camp, charged it without warning, and swept off all the loose horses. There was no real resistance, and none of the attackers were killed. One white man was shot down, and two or three Snakes; the rest saved themselves, running and hiding in the brush. The young men were too busy capturing horses to bother much about women and children. They scattered all over the place, trying to catch the runaway animals, and the people in the camp made their getaway.

In this raid the Arapahos led the charge, as agreed,

with the result that they counted all the *coups*, and also caught most of the horses taken. After that, the Sioux and Cheyennes had no more to say about Arapahos lacking valor. All rode back to their own camp to dance and celebrate their victory.

As soon as they had gone, the victims of the raid sent word to Jim Bridger at the fort. He was the man to turn to whenever there was trouble afoot. Bridger heard their story and immediately sent a runner to his partner. Old Gabe urged him to clear out of such a dangerous neighborhood while he still had his hair. Old Gabe advised caching. 'Too many Injuns,' he said. 'No sense in stayin' thar.'

Frapp, however, was a stubborn old cuss; he covered his ears, and would not listen to Bridger's words of wisdom. Frapp had been all over the West — even to the Pacific Coast — only to return to his favorite hunting grounds — the land of the Snakes. He would not budge.

'Gott in Himmel!' he bellowed, between his yellow teeth. 'Ve vill see who dis country belongs to yet.'

Survivors of the first raid were not so eager for the fray as their booshway. And so, as soon as Frapp returned from his hunt, they started for the fort. Then the Snake scouts came running to Bridger with news that the Plains Indians were going to attack again. Frapp decided to send his women and children away to a safe place, where they could keep under cover and yet be within reach. He sent them to a mountain south of camp — Squaw Mountain.

While Frapp was 'making meat,' the Sioux and Cheyennes had been enduring the bragging and strutting of the Arapahos. At the end of about ten days they could stand it no longer. The warrior societies held elections, chose new officers (as the interpreter put it, they 'changed the detail of the suicide squad'), with the understanding that these new leaders would march at their head against the enemy next day. Then they consulted their medicine-man as to what luck they were likely to have. After making medicine, the prophet told them they must have a Clown for leader.

Among the Cheyennes, and some other tribes, there was a kind of men known as Clowns, or Contraries. A Contrary was a man who had dreamed of the Thunder — one of the great gods of those Indians. Such a dream obliged the dreamer to live alone, keep away from other people, wear old, ragged clothing, and be different from the run of redskins in all things. At times he had to paint himself white all over, wear weeds instead of feathers in his hair, and make himself ridiculous before the people. This was a kind of penance, and a hard one for Indians, who can endure anything but the laughter and mockery of their fellow-tribesmen. Of course, the wise men knew why he acted so, but the common people, being ignorant of the cause of his outlandish behavior, made him a laughing-stock.

A Contrary had to do everything backwards. When he meant 'yes' he said 'no,' and if anyone told him to do anything, he had to do exactly the opposite. Among the Sioux, such a man was known as *Heyoka*; among the Cheyennes, as *Hohnukhe*. He had a sacred weapon — a kind of cross between a bow and a spear — with two bowstrings, and a spear-head at one end.

The man who carried such a Thunder-Bow was regarded as a man to be feared and respected, and when the medicine-man told these Indians that they must choose a Clown for their leader, they were not dismayed. They knew such a man: his name was Snowshoe.

The chiefs went in a body to Snowshoe's tent, which was painted red all over. They went in and offered him the war-pipe, saying: 'We don't want you to lead us. Don't smoke this pipe.'

Then the Contrary smoked the pipe, and so pledged himself to go. They all said, '*Ah-ho*, thanks,' because he had done as they wished, and went away, leaving him alone.

Snowshoe was probably glad to act as leader, for it was only on the warpath that he had the privilege of associating freely with other men.

When the medicine-man heard that Snowshoe would act, he was pleased. 'Good,' he said, in effect. 'Now you can tell whether you are going to win or not. If the Contrary is killed, you will win; if he is unhurt, you are going to lose.'

The war-party set out, very early in the morning, heading for Frapp's camp. This time the Arapahos rode in the rear. They said to the others: 'Go ahead, friends. Last time we showed you how to fight. Now we are going to sit still and see what you can do.' Those Arapahos were very superior when they had a chance to be; for the Cheyennes had rubbed it into them often. Maybe they knew how well-armed Frapp's men were. At any rate, their words put the Sioux and Cheyennes on their mettle. There were between four and five hundred men in the war-party.

They caught Frapp near the mouth of Battle Creek. He was ready for them. With twenty-three white men, and an equal or greater number of Snakes — all well-armed — he thought he could stand them off. Bridger took care to arm his Snake friends well. When he led their delegation to the Treaty of Laramie, ten years later, every Snake had a good rifle provided by Bridger, while 'not one in a hundred of the Sioux had guns.' No wonder the Snakes were good fighters, with Old Gabe behind them!

Snowshoe charged first, on foot, far in the lead. As he advanced, he passed his Thunder-Bow behind his back from his left hand to his right. Then he ran forward to count the *coup*, making a noise like a burrowing owl — the Contrary war-cry. His comrades sat their horses in the rear, watching to see what might happen to him.

Seeing this lone warrior coming, the mountain men concentrated their fire on him. At the second or third shot, Snowshoe dropped his queer weapon, and fell on his face. He did not stir.

Ordinarily, the death of a leader had a very perceptible cooling effect upon the martial ardor of the warriors. But as the mountain men watched the long line of savages opposed to them, they were astonished. A moment before they had seen a long, motionless stripe of parti-colored horseflesh; above that a red stripe of naked Injun bodies;

atop of that the black band of their dark heads; above all bright spots of feathers, dancing scalplocks on lance-heads, puffs of white smoke from an occasional fusil.

But suddenly all this changed. The warriors yelped and whooped in triumph and joy, certain of victory. The whole mass came towards them like a tidal wave.

There was little time to act. The mountain men sprang behind their frightened horses, shooting over, or between, them at the advancing avalanche. But all their lead had no effect in stopping that charge; the Indians were too sure of victory. Saddles were emptied, but the warriors rushed on. Up they came — right up to the plunging mass of firing men and hobbled, rearing horses, which shrank away from them as their charge struck. Suddenly the air was full of stinging arrows, glinting like grasshoppers in the morning sun.

One or two of the Snakes were hit. On every side horses were rearing, kicking, plunging, jerking frantically at their ropes and bridles, rolling on the ground, while high over all the scream of some wounded horse chilled men's hearts. Animals studded with arrows staggered about, with hanging heads, coughing out their life-blood. At close range, the mountain men were at a dreadful disadvantage against bowmen. They had no revolvers in those days, and the redskins, used to killing running buffalo from the saddle, never needed to take aim at close range. Moreover, they fired too rapidly to miss often; it was well known on the frontier that a man hit with one arrow was sure to have two or three shafts in his body. At close range, the

rifle was useless against the short buffalo-bow. Had the
Cheyennes and Sioux dismounted, and fought hand to
hand just then, it might have been all over in three minutes.

But their charge was so swift, so headlong, that it defeated its own purpose, and suddenly split upon that
heaped confusion, as a mountain stream splits upon a
boulder. The Cheyennes and Sioux swept by on either
side, half-blotted out by the smoke and dust.

'Fort! Fort!' was the desperate cry. It was time. The
charge was coming back!

But not much remained to be done. The arrows had
already dropped a barrier of horseflesh around the excited
men. On every side the carcasses lay kicking, studded with
feathered shafts. Here and there a gap was filled by leading up some dying animal, and putting it out of its pain by
a quick slash across the throat with a trapper's skinning-
knife. And before the hostiles could turn, re-form, and
charge again, the Snakes and mountain men found themselves 'forted' behind those dead and dying animals. One
or two had found a convenient stump or a tree handy. The
men flung themselves down, leveled their rifles across the
horses, and picked their targets.

The second charge was no less determined than the first,
though some of the hostiles had begun to wonder whether
Snowshoe was really dead, after all. As they charged, they
swept by on either side once more, and while some circled
the fort, shooting down into it from their ponies' backs,
others leaned from their saddles, caught hold of Snowshoe's
arms, and snatched him away out of range.

There the warriors looked him over. He lay inert. They found him hit in three places; he gave no sign of life.

With new courage, the warriors jumped back upon their ponies, sure of victory. They charged again, while the Arapahos urged them on. The Cheyennes and Sioux were out to win, and a bitter struggle they made of it. Never had the mountain men seen such determination on the part of redskins — or such teamwork. But with every charge the barricade of dead animals about the defenders was widened and heaped higher, and between charges they were busy digging fox-holes and trenches with their skinning-knives. Those holes can still be seen there.

The fight went on all day, for the Cheyennes and the Sioux would not give up hope. Besides, there were the supercilious Arapahos, taunting them: 'Why don't you do something brave, and try to count a few *coups*, as we did?' So they charged, and as so few of them had guns, they had to ride right up to the trappers' fort to do any damage.

Says Jim Baker, 'It was the hardest fight I was ever in.' It continued until sundown, and during that time, as Baker tells us, 'the Indians made about forty charges on us, coming up to within ten or fifteen paces every time. Their object was to draw our fire, but old Frapp kept shouting, "Don't shoot till you're sure. One at a time!" And so some of us kept loaded all the time. We made breastworks of our horses and hid behind stumps. Old Frapp was killed, and he was the ugliest-looking dead man I ever saw, and I have seen a good many. His face was all covered with blood, and he had rotten teeth and a horrible grin. When he was killed, he never fell, but sat braced up against the stump, a sight to behold.' ⁴

When dusk came, the Cheyennes and Sioux quit fighting. They gathered up their wounded and as many dead bodies as they could recover, and prepared to hit the trail to their camp. They had lost heavily, and had many wounded. Yet they had not rubbed out those Snakes and white men.

The Arapahos threw this up to them. 'Well,' they said, 'we sure thought you would kill that little bunch of enemies. You tried hard; you shot lots of horses. But the men are there still!'

The Cheyennes were angry; they replied: 'Yes. It is the fault of that lying Sioux medicine-man with the double tongue. He fed us lies and sent us in there, and he has killed a lot of us.' Some of the Cheyennes tried to beat the medicine-man with their quirts.

Then the Sioux got round their prophet and protected him. He said: 'I am not afraid. I have not lied. Do you think, if I had lied, I would have charged along with you? My dream was straight and true.'

'Well,' others said, 'you may think so. But it has killed Snowshoe.'

So then they lifted Snowshoe up and laid him on his belly across his saddle, and tied his legs down on one side, and his neck on the other, so that they could pack him home to his relatives for burial. While they were making the thongs fast, Snowshoe opened his eyes. He came to. Maybe putting him across the saddle made the blood run to his head; at any rate, he came out of his faint, and said, 'Let me down.'

So they let him down. He had three wounds on him, and one of the slugs had hit him on the head and knocked him out. He had 'died' for a day. But now he came alive again.

That night, Snowshoe's strange adventure was the talk of the camp. Everybody came to see whether he was alive or dead, and he had plenty of visitors. But he did not mind; he liked it. His Thunder-Bow had been lost in the fight, and so now he was rid of it, and could live just like any other fellow. He had gained glory also. And maybe because of this, he did not die; he was still alive next morning.

Therefore, the warriors made no move to return and renew the battle. They could hear the Snakes firing guns and yelling to them to come back and fight again. But they never went back. They had no heart for another battle. Snowshoe was too hard to kill.

Those mountain men gathered the people from Squaw Mountain again, cached the jerked meat on the site of the battle, and made tracks for Fort Bridger. They had no horses to pack anything on. They had lost over a hundred head in the fight, and Basil Clement reports that, 'of the forty-five head of horses alive, there were only five not wounded.' [5] Frapp and three white men had been killed, and an uncertain number of Snakes. But the loss of the hostiles was much greater: twenty-seven, by Arapaho tradition.

As usual, Jim Bridger had to make good the losses and bind up the wounds of those who had neglected to follow his advice. When he had made everybody comfortable at Fort Bridger, he led a pack-train back to the scene of the fight and recovered the cached provisions. The Plains Injuns had hit the trail for their own country by that time. Bridger was unmolested.

Indian warriors generally recount the names and nature of the casualties in any fight with great particularity of bloody detail. But it is now too late to learn the names of the Indians who died in that fight, or to know how they were killed. The tradition among the Sioux is that their chief that day was Red Weasel. Two other leading men present were a Cheyenne named Bull-Rolls-Over, and a Sioux named Wooden Shoe. The name 'Wooden Shoe' does not indicate that the Sioux had come from Holland, but was merely a term applied by them to the hard-leather boots brought by white men from the settlements.[6]

After Frapp's death, Bridger carried on alone at his trading-post. When the great waves of migration to California came surging up the Oregon Trail, Bridger was ready to help them. He established a blacksmith shop, with a plentiful supply of iron, at his post, and there he was kept busy repairing the broken-down wagons of emigrants. By the time they had come that far, most of them were eager to sell for a song everything they had along — except the barest necessaries: wagons sold for less than a dollar, bacon and flour and other foodstuffs for a cent a pound; household goods and broken-down stock were given

away — if no one could be found to buy. Bridger bought
iron and supplies for nothing, and sold them again at
mountain prices; he was in a fair way to become rich, since
most of the movers had ready money, if nothing else. In
winter, Jim traded with the Injuns, or went trapping on
his own hook. But the great days were over, and once at
Fort Union, finding his spiritless men would not charge a
bunch of thieving Injuns, Old Gabe was so angry that he
fired them all, and lit out for his fort alone. There he remained much of the time, until he leased his post to the
United States in 1857.

Always his services were in demand as a guide. The
emigrants were, for the most part, green as grass, and utterly unable to foresee or to cope with the hardships, dangers, and many inconveniences of a transcontinental trek.
Their animals went lame, were galled and injured, stolen
by Injuns, strayed of themselves, or ran off with passing
buffalo. Their wagons shrunk and warped in the dry air of
the high plains and mountains, so that the wheels fell to
pieces. Rattlesnakes bit them; wolves gnawed their saddles
and ropes and harness to bits, terrific thunder, sand, and
hailstorms buffeted and tormented them. They bogged
down in the mud, trying to cross streams, or broke their
wagons among the rocks. Hot winds parched them, night
frosts nipped them. They got the itch from eating nothing
but salt pork and superfine flour, because they could not
hunt, or kill big-game animals when found, with small-cali-
ber long rifles intended for squirrels, deer, and turkeys.
They drank from shallow wells or prairie pools, and so got

fevers. Cholera plagued them; even peaceful Injuns levied tribute. In spring they found the grass eaten off at all the camping places; in fall they found it burned off, so that their horses starved. Even when they died, or were killed, they found no rest in the grave — for the wolves dug them up again!

It was Jim Bridger's job to lead such precious tenderfeet across the wilderness, and to show them how to avoid, or to make the best of, all these things. He did it — as far as one human being could.

It was Old Gabe whom Brigham Young consulted before choosing a route for his Young Mormons. And when Sir George Gore, a wealthy Irishman, came over to hunt big game in the Rockies in 1854 — with a retinue of forty men, one hundred and twelve horses, twelve yoke of oxen, fourteen hounds, six wagons, and twenty-one carts — it was Old Gabe whom he asked to guide him. Bridger had a most interesting winter on Tongue River with Sir George; the two became fast friends. Sir George was a late riser, but after hunting all afternoon would dine in state — and always had Old Gabe at his table. He liked to read Shakespeare, Sir Walter Scott, and Baron Munchausen to the old scout, to enjoy his comments. But he could never get Old Gabe to admit that the mendacious Baron could spin better yarns than himself.

The best brief account of how Bridger served the wagon-trains is probably that given by William S. Brackett in his *Bonneville and Bridger*, published by the Historical Society of Montana.[7] Bridger was guiding a party of federal judges and their families, with a military escort, in June, 1862. No Indians had been seen, and the greenhorns therefore supposed that none were about! Suddenly a terrified man came galloping after the Government train, yelling 'Indians!'

Twenty picked men, a sergeant, and Jim Bridger rode to the scene of the tragedy. A ride of five miles brought them to a corral of frightened emigrants. Beyond that, they found the victims:

'I was riding with Bridger over a long hill when we came upon the wagon that had been attacked, and the horribly mutilated bodies of two men. About a hundred yards from the wagon on the trail, we came first to the body of an old man. At the instant of attack he had probably jumped out and run toward the other far-off wagons. He was shot through the back and his head was fairly chopped to pieces, and the axe taken from the wagon lay beside him, covered with blood. His body was filled with arrows, and he was scalped and horribly mutilated....

'Bridger calmly dismounted, knelt on the ground, and closely examined the footprints around the body. Then he pulled three arrows from the old man's corpse and closely examined them. "Arapahos and Cheyennes," he said, as he followed the blood creases on the arrows with critical eyes.

'Leaving the first body, he went up to the wagon and found pieces of harness cut, with knives scattered about. The Indians had got the harness off the horses by cutting nearly every strap. At one side lay the body of a young

man who had been an invalid and was going to California
for his health. Firmly clutched in his bloody right hand
was a Colt's revolver with four chambers empty. The
Indians had vainly cut this hand many times trying to get
the pistol, but the grip of death held it firmly. Three
bullets had pierced his body, and he was also scalped and
mutilated. A dozen arrows bristled horribly upward from
his prostrate corpse. With fiendish malignity the savages
had cut off his ears, nose, and the fingers of his left hand,
and laid them on his body. Both eyes were obliterated,
and other dreadful brutalities had been enacted which are
simply unspeakable.

'As soon as Bridger saw the pistol, he walked around
the wagon in a circle, carefully examining the grass and
sagebrush. Suddenly he stooped and seized a piece of
sagebrush and broke it off. On it was a speck of blood.
Widening his search, he soon found more blood and came
back, saying, "The boy has peppered one of the scamps
anyway!" All around on the ground the Indians had
scattered rice, flour, coffee, and sugar in their hasty plun-
dering of the wagons. Of course they carried off both
horses. . . .

'Wrapping the poor mutilated bodies in blankets, we
laid them in the wagon they had often slept in during life.
They were afterward given decent burial by their friends
of the emigrant train. Under Bridger's guidance, our command then hunted for the trail of the Indians. Bridger
said they were about twenty in number, and were doubtless, by this time, far on the other side of the Sweetwater

on their scampering ponies, safe from capture or successful pursuit.' [8]

Bridger guided General Albert Sidney Johnston in the Mormon War of 1857–58, and so set the Latter Day Saints thirsting for his blood. Again, in the sixties, he acted as scout for General Connor on the disastrous expedition from Fort Laramie to Tongue River, when the Cheyennes under Roman Nose and the Sioux under Sitting Bull whipped the troops and drove them from the Indian country.[9] Too often the military men failed to appreciate Old Gabe's sagacity, and by disregarding his suggestions marched straight into defeat.

General Carrington, who took Bridger along with him to build and occupy Fort Phil Kearny, had a better understanding of Old Gabe's qualities. At that time Bridger had been forty-four years on the frontier. Old Sioux warriors, who took part in the slaughter of Colonel Fetterman's command near that post, are proud that they accomplished this feat in spite of the presence of the Blanket Chief. They did not think it much of a victory to lick the troops, but to lick troops for whom Bridger was scout is — in their opinion — something to crow about.

The Sioux, however, are too cocky about this disaster; it was no fault of Bridger's that Fetterman played the fool and walked into that trap. If those cocksure officers had listened to Jim, there would have been no disaster; General Carrington bears witness to this. Carrington valued Bridger's services so highly that when the department commander ordered him to discharge Bridger, Carrington declined to obey, and returned the order endorsed, 'Impossible of execution.'

Bridger's skill as trailer, scout, rifle shot, and horseman was outstanding. But the day was near at hand, and coming fast, when such talents would be useless in the West.

XVIII. COLONEL BENT BLOWS
UP THE FORT

WHEN General Kearny, leading the Army of the West, arrived before Bent's Old Fort on the Arkansas, William Bent received him with patriotic enthusiasm and gave him a royal welcome, fired the small brass cannon before the gate, and served him and his brother officers with mint-juleps, the only mint-juleps — with ice — between Missouri and the Coast. True mountain man, Colonel Bent — as he was thereafter called — knew how to open his hand when a feast was in order.

But that old brass cannon, which had stood guard before the gate for many years, welcoming chiefs and terrifying warriors with its roar, seemed to know that the old days were over. When it was fired in salute to General Kearny, it *burst!* That was a coincidence — and also a symbol, an omen. For when the Neds arrived, the time had come for the mountain men to go.

Bent's Old Fort, built in the late twenties, had been the last outpost of the States on the Mexican Border, the principal stopping-place between Missouri and Santa Fe, the headquarters of a firm which dominated all the tribes from

Mexico to the Black Hills. No other post — not even 'Red Coat' McKenzie's famed Fort Union at the mouth of the Yellowstone — was so well built; it was, according to the military men, 'the only fort' in the West.

There the Bents and St. Vrain had made a fortune. The trappers brought furs, the Indians buffalo robes and meat, the Mexicans silver and gold bullion, the Americans brought trade goods of every sort, horses and mules and cattle from the States. At times the whole of the Southern Cheyennes, Arapahos, all the Kiowas and Comanches, were encamped about the fort, or at the Big Timbers below. And though it contained men from every quarter of the continent, Bent maintained such order that no man ever lost his life within the walls.

Until the Mexican War, the trade of the fort steadily mounted in value: then it as suddenly declined.

For a generation its throng of *engagés* and their Indian families had strolled on the adobe roofs overlooking its broad patio, with the hide-press in the middle. Every traveler, hunter, soldier, explorer, trapper, and Indian who passed that way — whether bound up and down the Rockies or to and from the settlements — found a welcome at the Big Lodge on Arkansas. There they saw the Injun women 'tripping around its battlements in their glittering moccasins and long deerskin wrappers; their children, with most perfect' — and generally naked — 'forms, and the carnation of the Saxon cheek struggling through the shading of the Indian, and chattering now Indian, and now Spanish or English; the grave owners and their clerks and traders, seated in the shade, smoking the long native pipe, passing it from one to another, drawing the precious smoke into the lungs by short hysterical sucks till filled, and then ejecting it through the nostrils; or, it may be, seated around their rude table, spread with coffee or tea, jerked buffalo meat, and bread made of the unbolted wheaten meal from Taos; or, after eating, lying comfortably upon their pallets of straw and Spanish blankets, and dreaming to the sweet notes of a flute; the old trappers withered with exposure to the elements, the half-tamed Indian and half-civilized Mexican servants seated upon the ground around a large tin pan of dry meat and a tankard of water, their only rations, relating adventures about the shores of Hudson Bay, on the rivers Columbia and MacKenzie, in the Great Prairie wilderness, and among the snowy heights of the mountains...' [1] There the mountain men had come, as to a home, for both the fort and the men were shaped by a life that was swiftly passing away. They had, in one short generation, explored half a continent, cleared its streams of beaver, tamed the redskins, and opened a thousand trails for less courageous feet. They had lived with gusto, and often enough died fighting. And they were truly American figures — men of all breeds and conditions — of old American Colonial stock, French, Irish, Scotch, Welsh, English, German, Dutch, Spanish, Mexican, Injun, Negro, Kanaka, and mixed — but all with similar notions, the same habits and code. No more cosmopolitan group has existed in American territory — and none more homogeneous.

They had shared the Injun feast, the night alarm, the slow plodding of pack-train or caravan of rocking Conestoga wagons. They knew the patience of the still-hunt, the fun of tolling antelope, the speed and thunder and confusion of running buffalo. They had all shared in the tedious trading with their hard-bargaining redskin patrons. The trap-line, the snug, taper tipi, the lone campfire in the snow, while the wolves howled from the windy hills — they knew them all, as they knew their saddles and rifles and Green River knives.

But now, though some might close their eyes against the hateful fact, those days were ended. William Bent needed no prophet to tell him that. A pioneer in all things, he knew that his day was over.

The Neds had come, burst his cannon, cut down his timber, burned off his grass, and brought a swarm of emigrants on their trail. Already it had been years since buffalo had been seen within a day's ride of Old Fort Bent. The game was going. In 1849, cholera swept the Plains, and destroyed half the Indians Bent traded with: the rest were headed for reservations within a few seasons. The Neds and emigrants brought disease, famine, war, and despair to the tribesmen and those who lived by serving them. And if anything more had been needed to make William Bent conscious of disaster, the murder of his brother Charles sufficed.

When Kearny came through, Bent acted as a scout for his advancing column, and the Old Fort had been put at the disposal of the United States as a commissary and hospital. Uncle Sam was buying forts wherever he could find them in the Indian country in those days. One after another they were abandoned, destroyed, or sold by their owners of the fur companies. Colonel Bent naturally supposed that his own fort — rated by military experts as the best on the frontier — would command a fair price from the Government.

But the negotiations dragged on; his price was held to be too high. And at last, disgusted, and decisive as always, Colonel Bent one day ordered his wagons hooked up, loaded whatever he cared to cart away upon them, and sent the wagons downriver, telling the men to make camp for the night on Wild Horse Creek, five miles below. Then, having made sure the vicinity of the fort was cleared of men and animals, he turned back and entered the big gate. He would not leave his old home to be occupied by hostile Injuns, nor abandon it to have it taken over by Neds who would not pay his price. He had made up his mind to destroy it.

As he walked across the echoing patio for the last time, and passed through those empty rooms, littered here and there with abandoned objects not worth taking away, William Bent must have had other feelings than anger in his heart. There his children had grown up, there his family, his brothers, had lived and worked beside him. It had been the only permanent home he owned. More than that, it had been his castle — his stronghold in the wilderness — and the model of other frontier posts on half a continent. There he had dominated all men. There he had made his fortune. And outside in the graveyard, guarded from the wolves by growing cactus, his flesh and blood lay buried.

But all that was in the past now.

Colonel Bent smashed in the heads of the powder kegs in the fort's bastions. Then he set fire to the building. Afterward he went out, closed the gate, and locked it. He mounted, and rode away.

When the flames reached the powder, the Old Fort became a heap of rubbish. Days later, travelers found the smoking ruins, and imagined that Indians had destroyed it. They little knew William Bent, or the breed he ran with.

Those mountain men have left America an ideal of manhood to cherish, a memory to be proud of. Here ends their story.

THE END

NOTES

CHAPTER IV.

1. Hiram M. Chittenden: *History of the American Fur Trade,* vol. II, p. 606. New York, 1902.

CHAPTER V.

1. See Reuben Gold Thwaites (editor): *Early Western Travels,* vol. XXIII, p. 45. Cleveland, Ohio, 1906.

CHAPTER VII.

1. Colonel Frank Triplett: *Conquering the Wilderness,* pp. 429 ff. New York, 1883.
2. George F. Ruxton: *Life in the Far West,* pp. 123 ff. New York, 1849.
3. *Ibid.*
4. *Ibid.*

CHAPTER VIII.

1. LeRoy R. Hafen and W. J. Ghent: *Broken Hand: The Life Story of Thomas Fitzpatrick,* p. 96. Old West Publishing Company, Denver, Colorado, 1931.

CHAPTER X.

1. Washington Irving, in *Adventures of Captain Bonneville* (Chap. XI), states that she 'threw herself upon her brother's neck; who clasped his long-lost sister to his heart,' etc. However, Irving must have been misinformed, or romancing: among the Gros Ventres a brother never even addressed his sister directly, nor she him. Such conduct would have been considered scandalous. One likes to think that Loretto, brave as he was, had married into a better family than Irving's story would indicate. — S. V.
2. Irving, *op. cit.*

Chapter XI.

1. For a detailed account of all these movements see *Carbine and Lance: The History of Old Fort Sill.* By Captain W. S. Nye, U.S.A. University of Oklahoma Press, 1937. Other details presented here have come from Miss Alice L. Marriott, and from Mooney's *Calendar History of the Kiowa Indians* (see Bibliography).

Chapter XII.

1. L. H. Garrard: *Wah-To-Yah and the Taos Trail,* chap. iv ff. Cincinnati, Ohio, 1850.
2. These figures are given in *The American Fur Trade of the Far West.* By H. M. Chittenden. New York, 1902.

Chapter XIII.

1. The best contemporary accounts of this tragedy are to be found in the words of Teresina Bent, an eye-witness, quoted in *The Leading Facts of New Mexican History,* by R. E. Twitchell, Cedar Rapids, Iowa, 1912, vol. ii, pp. 233 ff.; in L. H. Garrard, *Wah-To-Yah and the Taos Trail,* chap. xv; and in George F. Ruxton, *Travels in Mexico,* pp. 227 ff.

Chapter XIV.

1. L. H. Garrard: *Wah-To-Yah and the Taos Trail,* chap. ix ff. Cincinnati, Ohio, 1850.
2. Howard Louis Conard: '*Uncle Dick' Wootton,* pp. 183 ff. Chicago, 1890.
3. *Ibid.,* p. 185.

Chapter XV.

1. Appendix to *Report of the Commissioner of Indian Affairs,* Executive Document 1, 1847.
2. See 'How Bill Williams was Killed,' in *Arizona Miner,* August 20, 1870.

CHAPTER XVI.

1. Howard Louis Conard: *'Uncle Dick' Wootton*, p. 202. Chicago, 1890.

2. From the notebook of Dr. H. R. Wirtz. See *Old Bill Williams, Mountain Man*, pp. 178–79. By A. H. Favour. University of North Carolina Press, 1936.

3. See the final chapter of *Life in the Far West*. By George Frederick Ruxton. New York, 1849.

CHAPTER XVII.

1. Stanley Vestal: *Kit Carson, the Happy Warrior of the Old West: A Biography*, chaps. VIII, XII, *et passim*. Boston, 1928.

2. Percival Green Lowe: *Five Years a Dragoon*. Kansas City, Missouri, 1906.

3. An excellent digest of the source material on this little-known fight will be found in an article, by LeRoy R. Hafen, in *The Colorado Magazine*, vol. VII, no. 3 (May, 1930), pp. 97–101.

4. See Denver *Tribune-Republican*, July 10, 1886.

5. *South Dakota Historical Collections*, vol. XI, p. 291.

6. Considerable discrepancy exists in the various authorities as to the number of casualties (on both sides) in this hard-fought scrap, as may be seen from the following table:

AUTHORITY	INDIAN DEAD	FRAPP'S DEAD
Rufus Sage	15–20	Frapp and 4 men
Jim Baker	'About 100 dead Indians'	'Three of our party'
Stansbury	40	Frapp and 7 or 8 men
Basil Clement	...	'Ten of our men'
Arapaho tradition	27	...

Of these authorities, I much prefer Stansbury, because he got his information direct from Jim Bridger, at a time when he was camped within two miles of the battlefield. It must be remembered that Basil Clement and Jim Baker were both young men at that time, new to Injun-fighting and the mountains. Jim Baker was evidently fond of round numbers, and used them for the Indian loss, as he could have no knowledge of the exact figure, owing to the fact that the Indians carried off their dead and wounded whenever it was humanly possible.

It must be remembered that the term 'forty' was used by the mountain men, as by many Americans of similar background still, for any considerable number. Thus, Stansbury's (Bridger's) statement that 'forty' Indians were killed simply means an unusual number — plenty. Jim Baker's statement that the Indians made 'forty' charges (in twelve hours — one every eighteen minutes) is also not to be taken literally, but merely to indicate that they charged repeatedly and often.

With regard to the losses of whites and Snakes, the difficulty probably arises from the fact that some informants referred only to the whites, others to the combined force of Snakes and whites. Thus, Jim Baker tells us that there were twenty-three men in the party, and states that he can give the names of every one. As he could hardly be expected to know the names of all the Snakes, he was probably referring to the twenty-three whites. Basil Clement's statement that there were forty-seven men in the party is thus no contradiction of Jim Baker's words, if we suppose Clement meant to include Snakes as well as whites.

The fact is that the white men generally greatly overestimated Indian losses, owing partly to the confusing nature of the Indian way of fighting, the smoke and dust, and the overwhelming numbers engaged. But since the Indian fought as an individual, and believed that victory was the object of war — and by that he meant a personal, individual victory — he was not at all eager to sacrifice his own life in order to enable his comrades to harvest the hair and the horses. Therefore, a loss of two or three per cent was usually as high as he cared to go. See 'Comparative Casualties as Between U.S. Troops and Indians During the Sioux Campaigns, 1865–1876,' in *New Sources of Indian History*,

p. 132, by Stanley Vestal, University of Oklahoma Press, Norman, Oklahoma, 1934. Of course, on this occasion the Indians were unusually determined. Still, I prefer the Arapaho estimate as to the Indian loss.

7. Historical Society of Montana, *Contributions,* vol. III, 1900, pp. 396–97.

8. On that occasion, Old Gabe had arrived too late. His surmise, however, was correct. Though a detachment was sent on the trail of the killers, and kept to it for five or six days, the Indians were never overtaken.

9. For this campaign see George Bird Grinnell, *The Fighting Cheyennes;* Grace Raymond Hebard and E. A. Brininstool, *The Bozeman Trail;* Stanley Vestal, *Sitting Bull.*

CHAPTER XVIII.

1. T. J. Farnham, *Travels in the Great Western Prairies.* New York, 1843.

ACKNOWLEDGMENTS AND
BIBLIOGRAPHY

ACKNOWLEDGMENTS

IN ADDITION to the authorities cited in the text and listed
in the Bibliography below, and to the sources indicated in
those which I have consulted, I have looked into files of old
newspapers printed in Missouri, New Mexico, and elsewhere,
and into the Historical Collections of the States concerned.

The original contributions made here have been derived from
two chief sources: (1) the researches of my stepfather, James
Robert Campbell, made a generation ago, after he became
acquainted with Plains Indians and certain mountain men in
the course of his work for Hubert Howe Bancroft; (2) my own
gleanings among the tribesmen. For these also I am indebted in
great part to my stepfather, since it happened that our home in
my youth was in Western Oklahoma, among the very tribes and
bands whom he had known before I was born.

My own immediate debts for information are: (1) To George
Bent, son of Colonel William Bent and his Cheyenne wife, Owl
Woman. George Bent was probably the best-informed historian
of Indian blood on the Plains; his knowledge of the Cheyennes
and Arapahos, and certain neighboring or allied tribes, was un-
excelled, while his father's standing insured to him the friendship
of most of the prominent white men in the West. (2) My information with regard to the Sioux comes from Moses Old Bull,
the Hunkpapa historian, and in less degree from other Sioux
informants now living.

James Robert Campbell found his best information among
the Arapahos in old days, as they proved far more friendly and

accommodating than the Cheyennes, Kiowas, and Comanches when questioned about their wars with the whites. He obtained from leading men of this tribe the stories concerning the Frapp Battle, the Battle of Pierre's Hole, and the death of Henry Vanderburgh, which appear in this book. In those days, when Indian customs and ways of thought were not well understood, Indian testimony was little regarded, and my stepfather, having turned to other fields, made no attempt to publish these facts.

His second source of information lay in conversations with such old-timers as Prowers (after whom Prowers, Colorado, was named) and Solomon Silver. Silver supplemented Arapaho data somewhat, but his chief contributions (as regards this book) were the stories of his own experiences among the Kiowas, and his accounts of Blackfoot Smith's adventures on the Upper Missouri (Chapters XI and XII herein). My stepfather found Silver a good story-teller, but somewhat histrionic, and therefore hesitated to vouch for the tales as absolute history. However, Sol's stories check with all facts known to me, and even though he may have touched them up a little (as Bridger, Meek, and Beckwourth are believed to have done in narrating their own adventures), they seem interesting and authentic enough to be included here. To me, at least, anything pertaining to the mountain men is full of interest — even their yarns. These stories of Silver's may have lost something of their original charm, as I received them by word-of-mouth, and in order to include certain pertinent facts gathered from other sources, have had to retell them here.

BIBLIOGRAPHY

James Bridger, Trapper, Frontiersman, Scout and Guide: An Historical Narrative. By Cecil Alter. Salt Lake City, Utah, 1925.

Mike Fink, King of Mississippi Keelboatmen. By Walter Blair and Franklin J. Meine. New York, 1933.

The Story of Jedediah Smith, Who Blazed the Overland Trail to California. By Noel J. Breed. Sacramento, California, 1926.

The American Fur Trade of the Far West. By Hiram Martin Chittenden. New York, 1902. 3 vols.

'Uncle Dick' Wootton, the Pioneer Frontiersman of the Rocky Mountain Region, etc. By Howard Louis Conard. Chicago, 1890.

The Ashley-Smith Explorations and the Discovery of a Central Route to the Pacific, 1822–1829, with the Original Journals. Edited by Harrison Clifford Dale. Cleveland, 1918.

The Indian Sign Language, with Brief Explanatory Notes. By W. P. Clark, Philadelphia, 1885.

Biographical Sketch of James Bridger: Mountaineer, Trapper, and Guide. By Major-General Grenville M. Dodge. Kansas City, Missouri, 1904.

Old Bill Williams, Mountain Man. By Alpheus H. Favour. Chapel Hill, North Carolina, 1936.

Wah-To-Yah and the Taos Trail. By Lewis H. Garrard. Philadelphia, 1850.

The Fighting Cheyennes. By George Bird Grinnell. New York, 1915.

The Cheyenne Indians, Their History and Ways of Life. By George Bird Grinnell. New Haven, Connecticut, 1923. 2 vols.

Broken Hand: The Life Story of Thomas Fitzpatrick, Chief of the Mountain Men. By LeRoy R. Hafen and W. J. Ghent. Denver, Colorado, 1931.

The Bozeman Trail. By Grace Raymond Hebard and E. A. Brininstool. Cleveland, 1922. 2 vols.

The Adventures of Captain Bonneville, U.S.A., in the Rocky Mountains and the Far West. By Washington Irving. London and Philadelphia, 1837.

Astoria. By Washington Irving. Philadelphia, 1836. 2 vols.

Five Years a Dragoon. By Percival Green Lowe. Kansas City, Missouri, 1906.

Life in the Far West. By George Frederick Ruxton. New York, 1849.

Early Western Travels, 1748–1846. Edited by Reuben Gold Thwaites. Cleveland, Ohio, 1906.

Kit Carson Days, 1809–1868. By Edwin L. Sabin. New York, 1935. 2 vols.

The Travels of Jedediah Smith. By Maurice S. Sullivan. Santa Ana, California, 1934.

The Leading Facts of New Mexican History. By Ralph Emerson Twitchell. Cedar Rapids, Iowa, 1911–17. 5 vols.

Kit Carson, the Happy Warrior of the Old West. By Stanley Vestal. Boston, 1928.

New Sources of Indian History. University of Oklahoma Press. By Stanley Vestal. Norman, Oklahoma, 1934.

The River of the West. By Mrs. Frances (Fuller) Victor. Hartford, Connecticut, 1870.

Lone Elk, the Life Story of Bill Williams. By Chauncey Pratt Williams. Denver, Colorado, 1935. 2 parts.

Conquering the Wilderness. By Colonel Frank Triplett. New York, 1883.

Calendar History of the Kiowa Indians. By James Mooney. In Seventeenth Annual Report of the Bureau of American Ethnology, Washington, D.C., 1900–01.

Carbine and Lance: The History of Old Fort Sill. By Captain W. S. Nye, U.S.A. University of Oklahoma Press, Norman, Oklahoma, 1937.

Bent's Old Fort and Its Builders. By George Bird Grinnell. Kansas State Historical Society Collections. Vol. XV.

Fraeb's Last Fight and How Battle Creek Got Its Name. By LeRoy R. Hafen. Colorado Magazine, published by State Historical Society of Colorado. Vol. VII. No. 3, May, 1930.

Exploration and Survey of the Valley of the Great Salt Lake of Utah, etc. By Howard Stansbury. Senate Executive Document No. 3, Special Session, March, 1851. Washington, 1853